The Lionheart & the Third Crusade

The Lionheart & the Third Crusade

Accounts of the Third Crusade—1189-92

ILLUSTRATED

The Crusade of Richard I

and

The 3rd Crusade

Thomas Andrew Archer

LEONAUR

The Lionheart & the Third Crusade
Accounts of the Third Crusade—1189-92
The Crusade of Richard I
and
The 3rd Crusade
by Thomas Andrew Archer

ILLUSTRATED

FIRST EDITION

Leonaur is an imprint of Oakpast Ltd

Copyright in this form © 2022 Oakpast Ltd

ISBN: 978-1-915234-44-5 (hardcover)
ISBN: 978-1-915234-45-2 (softcover)

http://www.leonaur.com

Publisher's Notes

Contents

Preface

As a subject for historical study the Third Crusade possesses certain advantages that are wanting to most other periods of the Middle Ages. It is one of the few events for which we have a really ample volume of contemporary evidence—evidence not representing one creed or party only, but Christian and Mohammedan, Frenchman, Englishman and Franco-Syrian alike. Here, at least, if nowhere else in twelfth century literature, we can listen, almost as if we were on the scene ourselves, to the babble and rumour and prejudice of rival nations and rival religions. We can see not only what the Saracens thought of King Richard but also how he was regarded by the Frenchmen, the Teutons and the Syrian Franks who reluctantly followed his lead.

We may temper the indignant rebukes of the Anglo-Norman chronicler on Philip-Augustus' return by the loyal, if somewhat feeble, excuses of this king's own biographer; and while, reading our native historians, we sympathise with Richard's troubles and misfortunes, or pity Guy de Lusignan for the loss of his kingdom, we may learn from writers of another nation how much the English king's pride and, it may be, his suspected treachery had to do with the failure of the expedition; and how Guy, though a brave soldier and a chivalrous knight, in other kingly qualities was no match for his Italian rival. It is thus that the various writers may be used to confirm, to modify or to supplement each other's narratives.

Though almost all the chroniclers cited in the following pages were contemporary with the events they describe, and though many of them were in the Holy Land during the times of which they wrote, they are not all of equal credit. Bohâdin and the author of the *Itinerarium* must be regarded as having the highest authority; but not everything that even the latter author tells us can be accepted as historic truth. Richard de Templo, if he be the writer of the *Itinerarium*, could hardly have had any other foundation than his fancy or current rumour for the details he gives as regards the quarrel of the Mamelooks and Curds on their way to seize Richard when asleep outside Jaffa; or again for the reproaches Saladin hurls against them when he hears of their failure. Other passages of a similar kind will doubtless strike the reader here and there throughout the work even in pages taken from the gravest writers.

Probably they are all or nearly all based upon historic truth, but are clothed with the garb of romance. To have entirely omitted them would have been to omit some of the most picturesque glimpses we get of the stir and movement of the Crusading camp; for in the Third Crusade, such passages, to some extent, correspond to the Corbahan incidents of the First Crusade, and like these, were doubtless soon the theme for more than one minstrel's song And yet in the heavy Latin of the chronicler such episodes have a somewhat incongruous effect; they read like a child's romance told in the imperfectly-mastered phraseology of a grown man.

But the Norman-French, in which they doubtless passed from mouth to mouth before they were translated into a learned tongue, must have lent them a charm they have now lost; and the few extracts given from Ernoul may help us to feel the glow and colour with which a contemporary writer, using his native language for his own people, could invest the story of his own days and of events in which he himself had taken a part.

In the notes I have striven to illustrate the narrative mainly from other writers of the crusading times. All the distances have been measured, with what accuracy I could, on the Palestine Exploration Survey's Ordnance Map. These distances, it is hoped, will help to render the military movements clear.

In conclusion, I have to express my thanks to several friends who have helped me in various parts of this book: to Mr. Oman of All Souls College, and to Mr. R. Lane Poole, both of whom have kindly found time to read and correct the notes on which I asked their advice. To Mr. J. H. Round I owe a few words of special thanks for the ready kindness with which he has, at all times, allowed me to draw upon the large stores of mediaeval learning of which is the master. It is to him that, among much else, I am indebted for the Pipe Roll Extract and the note on Henry of Cornhill.

The Crusade of Richard I.

The conquest of Jerusalem in 1099 was a success due rather to the weakness of the Mohammedans than the strength of their adversaries. The Mohammedan world in the East was divided into two sections, of which the nominal heads were the Sunnite *Caliph* of Bagdad—the "Papa Turcorum" of our Western chroniclers—and the Fatimite *Caliph* of Egypt at Babylon, *i.e.*, Cairo. Neither of these *caliphs*, however, possessed any real power; for all authority was exercised in the latter case by *vizirs*, in the former by the successive heads of the Seljukian Turks who since the days of Togrul Beg (1037-1063) had wrested all effectual authority from the hands of their nominal lords.

In the latter half of the eleventh century the cities of Syria, which had long been reckoned part of the Egyptian *Caliphate* at Cairo, fell into the hands of the Turks, who seemed to have taken upon themselves the duty of supplying a military guard for the feeble native inhabitants. Malek Shah, the last of the great Seljukian *Sultans* died in 1092 and, among the dissensions to which his death gave rise, the Egyptian *caliph* succeeded in regaining Jerusalem (1098) and several of the other towns along the coast.

Thus, the early Crusaders had to contend against a divided Islam, and their success was easy. Thirty years later Zengi, the Atabeg of Mosul, began to concentrate the power of the orthodox Mohammedans, and, towards the end of 1144, the tide of Christian success was turned by the capture of Edessa. Zengi's son Nuradin continued his father's work and, before his death in 1174 his lieutenant Saladin was ruling Egypt.

Saladin soon dispossessed his old master's son, and before 1187 was lord of all the country from the Mediterranean Sea and the Nile to the Euphrates, and even the Tigris. The great Battle of Hittin laid the kingdom of Jerusalem at his feet (July 4, 1187). Within three months of this date the Holy City had fallen and hardly a castle or a town, through the length and breadth of the land held out against him.

There was, however, one city in the kingdom of Jerusalem, properly so called, that Saladin could not conquer. Conrad of Montferrat who, sailing from Constantinople, had reached Acre only to find it in the hands of Mohammedans, managed to throw himself into Tyre just in time to prevent its surrender. Here he maintained himself, and is said to have refused to admit King Guy, who had been taken prisoner at the Battle of Hittin (July 4, 1187), when released in May, 1188 Guy then, collecting what forces he could, sat down before Acre towards the end of August, 1189.

Meanwhile all Europe had been stirred to its depths by the news of the fall of the Holy City. Henry II., Philip Augustus, and the Emperor Frederick I. all took the Cross. Constant bickerings prevented the first two kings from starting at once, but the emperor set out from Ratisbon about Easter, 1189. Richard I. had taken the Cross as Count of Poitou in 1187; but neither he nor Philip actually began their journey till the summer of 1190.

SEAL OF RICHARD I.

A CHARACTER OF KING RICHARD

Itinerarium

Richard I. was born Sept. 8, 1157, at Oxford. About August, 1187, he was made Duke of Aquitaine. He took the cross in Nov. 1187, and died Tuesday, April 6, 1199.

The Lord of the ages had given him (Richard) such generosity of soul and endued him with such virtues that he seemed rather to belong to earlier times than these... His was the valour of Hector, the

10

magnanimity of Achilles; he was no whit inferior to Alexander, or less than Roland in manhood. Of a truth he easily surpassed the more praiseworthy characters of our time in many ways.

His right hand, like that of a second Titus, scattered riches, and—a thing that is, as a rule, but very rarely found in so famous a knight—the tongue of a Nestor and the prudence of a Ulysses (as they well might) rightly rendered him better than other men in all kinds of business, whether eloquence or action was required. His military science did not slacken his inclination for vigorous action; nor did his readiness for action ever throw a doubt upon his military prudence.

If anyone chances to think him open to the charge of rashness, the answer is simple: for, in this respect, a mind that does not know how to acknowledge itself beaten, a mind impatient of injury, urged on by its inborn high-spirit to claim its lawful rights, may well claim excuse. Success made him all the better suited for accomplishing exploits, since fortune helps the brave. And though fortune wreaks her spleen on whomsoever she pleases, yet was not he to be drowned for all her adverse waves.

He was lofty in stature, of a shapely build, with hair half-way between red and yellow. His limbs were straight and flexible, his arms somewhat long and, for this very reason, better fitted than those of most folk to draw or wield the sword. Moreover, he had long legs, matching the character of his whole frame. His features showed the ruler, while his manners and his bearing added not a little to his general presence. Not only could he claim the loftiest position and praise in virtue of his noble birth, but also by reason of his virtues. But why should I extol so great a man with laboured praise?

Honour enough his merit brings,
He needs no alien praise,
In whose train, Glory, like a king's,
Follows through all his days.

He far surpassed other men in the courtesy of his manners and the vastness of his strength; memorable was he for his warlike deeds and power, while his splendid achievements would throw a shade over the greatest praise, we could give them. Surely, he might have been reckoned happy (I speak as a man) had not rivals envied his glorious deeds—rivals whose sole cause of hatred was his princely disposition; for of a truth there is no surer way of annoying the envious than by observing virtue.

C. JUNE, 1190.—RICHARD'S ORDINANCES OF CHINON.

Roger of Howden.

Meanwhile the King of England set out for Gascony, and besieging William de Chisi's castle took it. William himself the lord of that castle he hanged, because he had robbed the pilgrims to St. James (of Compostella) and other folk passing through his land. Then came the King of England to Chinon, in Anjou, where he appointed Girard Archbishop of Auch, Bernard Bishop of Bayonne, Robert de Sablun, Richard de Camville, and William de Forzo of Oleron, leaders and constables of his whole fleet that was about to set sail for the land of Syria.

★★★★★★★★

Compostella in Galicia claimed to possess the body of St. James, and was the most famous place of pilgrimage in West Europe during the Middle Ages.

Gerard de Barta, Archbishop of Auch from 1170 to 1192, died in the Third Crusade.

Bernard de Lescarre or de la Carre, Bishop of Bayonne from 1185 *A.D.* The date of his death is uncertain.

Robert de Sablun or Sabloil, like Richard de Camville, was one of the sureties to the treaty with Tancred, Nov. 1190. A namesake of his was Grand Master of the Templars about this time.

Richard de Camville, one of Henry II.'s statesmen. Died at the siege of Acre, June or July, 1191.

William de Forz married Hawisia, daughter and heiress of William "*le Gros*" Earl of Albemarle, died in 1195.

★★★★★★★★

And he gave them his charter as follows:

Richard, by the grace of God King of England, Duke of Normandy and Aquitaine, and Count of Anjou, to all his men who are about to journey to Jerusalem by sea—Health. Know that with the common counsel of approved men we have had the following regulations drawn up. Whoever on board ship shall slay another is himself to be cast into the sea lashed to the dead man; if he have slain him ashore he is to be buried in the same way. If anyone be proved by worthy witnesses to have drawn a knife for the purpose of striking another, or to have wounded another so as to draw blood, let him lose his fist; but if he strike another with his hand and draw no blood, let him be dipped three times in the sea. If anyone cast any reproach or bad word against another, or invoke God's malison on him, let him for every offence pay an ounce of silver. Let a convicted thief be shorn like a prize-fighter; after which let boiling pitch be poured on his head and a feather pillow be shaken over it so as to make him a laughing-stock. Then let him be put ashore at the first land where the ships touch. Witness myself at Chinon.

Moreover, the same king in another writ enjoined all his men, who were going to sea, to yield obedience to the words and ordinances of the aforesaid *justitiars* of his fleet. Then the king went to Tours, where he received the pilgrim's staff and wallet from the hand of William Archbishop of Tours. And when the king leant on the staff it broke.

★★★★★★★★

According to the Gallia Christiana this should be Bartholomew, Archbishop of Tours from 1174-1206. The ceremony of presenting the intending pilgrim with the wallet (*pera or sporta*) as the sign of his having commenced his journey was performed for Philip Augustus at St. Denys, by his uncle William, Archbishop of Rheims. Rigord gives a full account of the ceremony, telling how the king lay prostrate on the marble pavement before the shrine St. of Denys, and then, rising in tears, took down from over the relics two banners, blazoned with crosses wrought in gold, to carry with him in his wars against the enemies of Christ. The sign of a completed pilgrimage was a branch of palm, generally plucked after the pilgrim had bathed in the Jordan. According to Rigord, Richard and Philip reached Vezelai Wednesday, 4th July, 1190. Roger of Howden makes it June 29.

★★★★★★★★

ACCOUNT OF THE PURCHASE OF THE SHIPS WHICH WENT TO JERUSALEM AND OF WAGES PAID TO THE UNDERWRITTEN PILOTS AND SAILORS OF THE SAME FOR THE VOYAGE.

Extract from Pipe Roll of 2 Richard I.

Henry of Cornhill renders account of £2,250 which he had received from the Treasury by view of Peter of St. Mary church, clerk of the chancellor, John of Waltham, clerk of the treasurer, and Simon d'Avranches, of which sum £1,300 were in white silver and £950 in pence. And £2,500 which he received from William Puintell, constable of the Tower of London. And of £100 which he received from Richard, Archdeacon of Canterbury, and Robert, archdeacon of Gloucester out of the moneys of Aaron the Jew. And of 100 *marks* which he received from Alfwin Finke and Ralph of St. Helen the moneychanger of London. And of £40 which he received from the sale of the equipment of William de Stuteville's ships. And of 100 *marks* which he promised the king for the county of Kent.

Sum £5,023 6s. 8d. In the Treasury nothing. And for 33 ships of the Cinque Ports, two parts of which were bought for the king's use for the transport of his garrison with him to Jerusalem.

★★★★★★★★

Henry de Cornhill was the son and heir of Gervase de Cornhill, a city magnate, who was sheriff of London and afterwards of Kent and Surrey. Henry succeeded his father about 1183, and like him was in constant official employment. He was sheriff of London at the close of Henry II's reign and again in the crisis of 1191, and had charge of the Mint in 3 Richard I. Both he and his father appear to have lent money to the nobility and to have acquired landed possessions. See Note A on coinage.

★★★★★★★★

The price of which parts of the aforesaid ships is noted in the roll delivered into the Treasury by the said Henry £1,126 13s. 9½d. by the king's writ and by view of Peter of St. Mary church, clerk of the Chancellor, John of Waltham, clerk of the treasurer, and Simon d'Avranches who were assigned for this purpose. And in a whole year's pay of 790 captains and sailors, each captain of whom was reckoned at the rate of two sailors, £2,400 58s. 4d. by the same writ and view as aforesaid. And for 3 ships of Hampton and 3 ships of Shoreham, two parts of which were in like manner bought for the king's use by the hand of the aforesaid Henry, £257 15s. 8d. by the same writ and view as aforesaid. And in a whole year's pay of 174 captains and sailors, each captain being reckoned at the rate of two sailors, of which number 42 sailors belonged to William de Braiosa's ship which he gave to the king, £529 5s., by the same writ and view as aforesaid.

And for the whole ship which belonged to Walter the boatswain's son £56 13s. 4d. by the same writ and view as aforesaid. And in a whole year's pay of 61 sailors belonging to the king's "*Esneccae*," the captain being counted as two, £185 10s. 10d. by the same writ and view as aforesaid. And in repairs of the said "*Esneccae*" £10 by the king's writ and by view of Alan Trenchemer.

★★★★★★★★

Esneccae "smacks" were specially used for carrying the English king and his treasure between England and Normandy. In the *Itinerarium* they appear as ships of burden carrying horses. According to Jal they were round-shaped vessels.—See Note B.

★★★★★★★★

And in pay of 50 sailors, captain counted as two, of William de Stuteville's two ships £152 1s. 8d. by the king's writ and view as aforesaid. And in repairs of the said ships £10 by the same writ and view as aforesaid. And for repurchase of the ship which the king gave to the brethren of the Hospital, which was bought for 100 *marks*, £9 by the same writ and view as aforesaid. And in pay of one sailor additional in Eustace de Burnes' ship 60s. 10d. by the same writ. And for the coinage of £1,300 in white silver paid to the aforesaid sailors £32 10s. by the same writ and view as aforesaid. And for carriage of the aforesaid treasury and for chests, pouches, wax and other small matters for the same and in rations for the clerks and servants in charge of it on two occasions, £12 2s. 0½d. by the King's writ. And to Warin and Ermeric de Camberli and their partners £100 for the purchase of arms for the defence of the castles in England by the King's writ. And to William Puintell, Constable of the Tower of London £60 for works there by the same writ. And in default of pouches for the said receipt, £8 16s. 10d. by testimony of the aforesaid.

And he is quit.

AUG. 16, 1190.—K. RICHARD EMBARKS AT MARSEILLES FOR THE CRUSADE.

Itinerarium. Ric. II.

Thus, when the king with his followers quitted Tours, all the inhabitants of the land were moved by the din of so great a multitude. . . . . . It was in the first year after his coronation that the King of England started on his pilgrimage from Tours. From Tours he went to Laizi; thence to Mont Richard, to Selles, to La Chapelle d'Anguillon, Donzi, and lastly to Vézelai. When the two kings met here according to their agreement, the host accompanying each was reckoned innumerable. . . . . . .and here they made a bargain to divide equally all that they should acquire by war; and also that whichever of them should get to Messina first should wait patiently for the arrival of the other.

★★★★★★★★

This agreement is mentioned by various other chroniclers; according to one account, the main cause of the dispute between the two kings in Syria was that Philip claimed half of Tancred's treasure, and Richard retaliated by demanding half of the Count of Flanders'.

★★★★★★★★

. . . From Vézelai, stage by stage, the army came to Lyons on the Rhone, where it remained some days, owing to the difficulty of crossing so rapid and deep a river. After reaching the other side the kings fixed their tents in the open plain; but part of the army lodged in the town, part in the suburbs, and part in the green fields near. Afterwards the King of England, in his courtesy, accompanied the King of France and his men a space on their way to Genoa. For the King of France had already engaged the services of the Genoese to carry him across.

★★★★★★★★

The Italian trading cities were among the first to profit by the Crusading movement. In 1101 Baldwin I. promised the Genoese a street
in every town they should help him to take. So too, when Tyre was
captured in 1124, a third part of the city was assigned to the Venetians.

★★★★★★★★

Now whilst the crowd of pilgrims from every region was pressing down upon the narrow bridge across the Rhone, a part of it fell
through from the weight of those who were on it. More than a hundred men tumbled into the water, which here flows so swiftly that
scarcely anyone who had fallen in could, in ordinary circumstances,
have got out alive. But those who had fallen in, calling out with a loud
voice and humbly begging for aid, despite their weariness, managed
to struggle out unharmed, save two only, who were drowned, indeed,
according to the flesh. Yet do their souls live in Christ; for it was while
engaged in His service that they were cut off.

Then King Richard, pitying the plight of those who were still
desirous of getting across, had boats lashed together so as to make a
temporary bridge; thus they crossed over, though somewhat sullenly
and with difficulty. Then the king and his army tarried here for three
days; after which part of the host set out for Marseilles, part for Venice,
Genoa, Barletta, or Brindisi. Several also set out for Messina, the haven
at which the two kings had agreed to meet. After three days the king
departed, and on the same day was the bridge broken up. , ... At
Marseilles we tarried three weeks.

★★★★★★★★

We being the author of the *Itinerarium* and his comrades. Richard
himself reached Marseilles July 31, and left Aug. 7. He did not reach
Messina till Sept. 23rd, whereas Philip had arrived there Sept. 16th.

★★★★★★★★

Then on the day after the *Assumption* of the Blessed Mary (Aug.
16), the first year after King Richard's coronation, we put to sea and
crossed between two islands that lay to our right and left, Sardinia and
Corsica.

THE FIRST ENGLISH FLEET REACHES ACRE.—12 OCT. 1190.

Howden iii.

Meanwhile Baldwin Archbishop of Canterbury, Hubert Bishop of
Salisbury, and Ranulf de Glanville who had come with the King of
England to Marseilles, went on board ship there. And the Lord gave

them a prosperous voyage and thought them in a short time without hindrance over the great deep to the siege at Acre (Oct. 12, 1190).

★★★★★★★★

Baldwin, Prior of the Cistercian house at Ford in Devonshire, was consecrated Bishop of Worcester in August, 1180. He was elected Archbishop of Canterbury 16 Dec, 1184. He was a vigorous preacher of the Crusade after the fall of Jerusalem in 1187. It was his eloquence that moved Giraldus Cambrensis to take the cross. Baldwin died at the siege of Acre, 19 Nov., 1190. He left Hubert Walter as his executor.

Hubert Walter, Dean of York, was appointed Bishop of Salisbury 15 Sept., 1189. On Saturday, 29 May, 1193, he was elected archbishop by the monks of Canterbury. He helped to raise Richard I.'s ransom during his *justiciarship* (Sept. 1193-1198). He was chancellor during the early years of John's reign, and died July 1205. Baldwin's party seems to have left Marseilles c. Sept. 1.

Ranulf de Glanville was the famous *justiciar* of Henry II. He died at the siege of Acre, seemingly before Oct. 18th, 1190.

★★★★★★★★

But John Bishop of Norwich, going to the Pope, and getting leave to return home, put off his cross and went back to his own county. When this was made known to the king, his lord, he took of him a thousand *marks* redemption money at the hands of the Templars and Hospitallers.

★★★★★★★★

That is to say Richard borrowed the money from the two military orders, giving them a lien on the bishop. The Templars and Hospitallers, especially the former, acted as bankers for the great sovereigns of Europe. They furnished both Louis VII. and Louis IX. with money in the Crusades of 1148 and 1250. It was in their treasure houses at Jerusalem that Henry II., during the latter years of his life, was accumulating the fund for his contemplated Crusade. From the time of Philip Augustus, the treasure of the French kings was kept at the Temple in Paris; as was that of Hubert de Burgh, the English *justiciar*, in the year of his fall in 1232.

★★★★★★★★

LETTER FROM ARCHBISHOP BALDWIN'S CHAPLAIN TO HIS CONVENT AT CANTERBURY (DATED SUNDAY, 21 OCT., 1101).

Epp. Cantuar.

(The previous letter from Baldwin shews that he and the fleet reached Tyre safely on Sunday, Sept. 16, 1190, and after waiting there nearly a month on account of the general sickness reached Acre on

Friday, 12 Oct., with the news that the kings of England and France would come soon.)

I know that you are anxiously awaiting trustworthy intelligence as to the condition of the lord (archbishop) of Canterbury and our army. . . . When we had tarried some time for the kings (at Tyre), and they did not come, we proceeded to our army at Acre. There we found our army (I say it with grief and groaning) given up to shameful practices, and yielding to ease and lust rather than encouraging virtue. The Lord is not in the camp; there is none that doeth good. The chiefs envy one another and strive for privilege. The lesser folk are in want and find no one to help them. In the camp there is neither chastity, sobriety, faith, nor charity—a state of things which, I call God to witness, I would not have believed had I not seen it.

The Turks are besieging us, and daily do they challenge us and persist in attacking us; while our knights lie skulking within their tents and, though they had promised themselves a speedy victory, in cowardly and lazy fashion, like conquered men, let the enemy affront them with impunity. Saladin's strength is increasing daily; whereas our army daily grows smaller. On the feast of St. James (July 25) more than 4,000 of our choicest foot soldiers were slain by the Turks; and on the same day many of our chiefs perished. The Queen of Jerusalem. . . . the Earl of Ferrers, the Earl of Clare's brother, ... Ranulf de Glanville, and innumerable others are dead. The bearer of these letters leaves us on the Sunday after the feast of St. Luke the Evangelist (*i.e.*, 21 Oct., 1190); but the kings have not yet arrived, nor is Acre taken. Once more, farewell.

THE MAIN ENGLISH FLEET THAT WENT ROUND BY SEA, AND ITS FORTUNES. APR. 1.–SEPT. 14.

Howden, iii.

But the King of England's (main) fleet, commanded by the Archbishop of Auch, the Bishop of Bayonne, Robert de Sablun, Richard de Camville, and William de Forz of Oléron, started on its voyage to Jerusalem from the different harbours of England, Normandy, Brittany, and Poitou immediately after Easter, (March 25, 1190). Of this fleet a certain part met in Dartmouth harbour, where it tarried some days. Then these ships, ten in number, set sail towards Lisbon, passing by a certain promontory called Godestert, (now Start Point). And when they had coasted Brittany, having St. Matthew of Finisterre, or of *Finis Posternae*, on their left and the great sea by which men go to

Ireland on their right, they (sailed along) leaving all Poitou, Gascony, and Biscay on the left.

They had already crossed the seas of Brittany and Poitou and come to that of Spain, when on the day of the Lord's Ascension, (*i.e.*, May 3, 1190) about the third hour, a fierce and terrible tempest swept down upon them; in a moment, in the twinkling of an eye, the ships were parted one from the other. While the tempest yet raged, and all were calling upon the Lord in their distress, the blessed Thomas the martyr, Archbishop of Canterbury, appeared thrice very clearly to three persons who were in a vessel of London. On board this vessel were William Fitz Osbert and Geoffrey the goldsmith, citizens of London. To these three St. Thomas spake as follows:

> Be not afraid. I, Thomas Archbishop of Canterbury, the blessed martyr Edmund, and the blessed confessor Nicholas have been appointed by the Lord guardians of this fleet of the King of England. If the men of this fleet keep themselves from evil deeds and do penance for their past offences the Lord will grant them a prosperous voyage and direct their steps in His paths.

After repeating these words three times the blessed Thomas faded from their sight; the tempest subsided at once, and there was a great calm on the sea. Now this London ship, where St. Thomas appeared, having already passed the harbour of Lisbon and Cape St. Vincent, had drawn close to the city of Silvia, (Silves in Algarve, south of Portugal), which at that time was the furthest outpost of all the Christian possessions in those parts. Here the Christian faith was still young, seeing that the place had only been snatched from the hands of the Pagans and made Christian the preceding year, as we have shewn above.

Now those who were in this ship, not knowing where they were, sent out a boat to shore and found that the land belonged to Christians, but that they could not safely pass on any further without a large escort. Accordingly, they approached the city, and when their arrival was known the Bishop of Silvia with his clergy and people received them gladly, giving God thanks for their coming; for there were in the ship a hundred young warriors well-armed.

(At this time the Emperor of Morocco was attacking Portugal and the men of Silvia broke up the English ship and retained its passengers, promising them pay and recompense in the name of their king. The other ships gradually came up and so heartened Sancho I. of Portugal that he refused the favourable terms proposed by his Moorish enemy. The English were very unruly, and Robert de

Sablul had to put in force the ordinances given above. On Wednesday, 24th July, the fleet left Lisbon and fell in with William de Fors and his 30 ships, thus making up the total to 106 "great ships laden with men, victuals, and arms."

(After this they crept round the coast of Spain and came to the Straits of Africa (i.e., of Gibraltar) through which they passed on Thursday, August 1st.

("Here begins the Mediterranean Sea, which is so called because it has only one entrance and one exit, of which the one is called the Straits of Africa, the other the Straits of St. George near Constantinople. And it is a noteworthy thing that from the Straits of Africa as far as Ascalon, as you sail, all the land on your right belongs to the Pagans."

(Creeping northwards up the coast of Spain by Tarragona and Barcelona, they at last reached Marseilles (Wednesday, 22 August, 1190).

("And it is to be noted that from Marseilles to Acre it is only a sail of fifteen days and nights if the wind is favourable. But then you must go over the great sea so that, after losing sight of the mountains of Marseilles, if you hold a straight course, you will see no land to right or left, till you reach the land of Syria. And if by chance you do see any land on the right it will belong to heathen folk; but on the left it will belong to Christians."

(The fleet reached Messina on Friday, Sept. 14.)

KING RICHARD'S COASTING VOYAGE FROM MARSEILLES TO MESSINA.—AUG. 7– SEPT. 22.

(Richard I. had left Marseilles on August 7 and made his way slowly round the coast of Genoa, where he had an interview with Philip Augustus, 13 Aug.; Pisa, Aug. 20; Naples, 28 Aug. Here he stayed till Sept. 8, on which day he rode to Salerno, where he remained till Sept. 13. On Sept. 21 he reached Mileto).

On Sept. 22 the King of England left Mileto, having only one knight in his train. And as he was passing through a small town, he turned aside to a certain house whence he heard the sound of a falcon. This house he entered and took the bird; but the rustics, who were unwilling to let it go, came running up from every side and attacked him with stones and staves. One of them even drew his knife upon the king. Upon this the king smote him with the side of his sword and broke it. The other assailants he overcame with stones, and thus with great difficulty he reached the priory of La Bagnara, where, however, he made no delay, but crossed the great river which is called "*le Far de Meschines,*" (*i.e.* the Straits of Messina; Le Far gets its name from the Pharos or stone beacon tower here mentioned.) And that night he lay at a stone tower which is situated at the entrance of the Far, in Sicily. Now this River of the Far divides Calabria from Sicily, and at its entrance, near La Bagnara, is that famous sea-peril called Scylla, while at its exit is another called Carybdis.

RICHARD'S FLEET, AND HIS LANDING IN SICILY (SEPT. 23).

Rich. of Devizes.

The ships that King Richard found ready at the sea-coast numbered one hundred together with 14 *busses*, vessels of vast size, wonderful speed, and great strength. They were arranged and set in order as follows. The first ship had three rudders, thirteen anchors, 30 oars, two sails, and triple ropes of every kind; moreover, it had everything that a ship can want in pairs—saving only the mast and boat. It had one very skilful captain, and fourteen chosen mariners were under his orders, (*i.e.*, there were fourteen captains, one for each *buss*, all under the command of a head captain.) The ship was laden with forty horses of price, all well trained for war, and with all kinds of arms for as many riders, for forty footmen, and fifteen sailors. Moreover it had a full year's food for all these men and horses. All the ships were laden in the same way; but each *buss* took double cargo and gear. The king's treasure, which was exceedingly great and of inestimable value, was divided amongst the ships and the *busses* so that if one part was endangered the rest might be saved.

When everything was thus arranged, the king with a small following, and the chief men of the army with their attendants, put off from the shore, preceding the fleet in galleys. Each day they touched at some sea-coast town and, taking up the larger ships and *busses* of that sea as they went along, reached Messina without disaster. . . . . On the morrow after his arrival (23 Sept.) the King of England had gallows, erected outside his camp to hang thieves and robbers on. Nor did the judges spare age and sex, but there was the same law to stranger and native. The King of France winked at the wrongs his men inflicted and received; but the King of England, deeming it no matter of what country the criminals were and considering every man as his own, left no wrong unavenged. For this reason, the *Griffons* (Latin crusaders' name for the Greeks) called the one king The Lamb and the other The Lion.

****

Philip Augustus was born 22 Aug., 1165, and so was eight years younger than Richard. He was crowned King of France in the lifetime of his father, Louis VII. (Nov. 1, 1179) at the age of fourteen. Louis died Thursday, 18 Sept., 1180. Philip took the cross along with Henry II. shortly after the fall of Jerusalem, 21st Jan., 1188, between Gisors and Trie, on which occasion it was decided that the English Crusaders should wear white crosses, the French red, and the Flemings green. Philip died 14 July, 1223. His will, dated Sept., 1222, leaves large sums of money for the defence of the Holy Land.

★★★★★★★★

RICHARD'S DEMANDS ON TANCRED. ENGLISH "LONG-TAILS."—
C. 25 SEPT.-OCT. 4.

Rich, of Devizes

The King of England sent his envoys to the King of Sicily demanding his sister Joan, formerly Queen of Sicily, and her dower, together with the golden chair and the whole legacy that King William had left to King Henry his father, to wit a golden table twelve feet long, a silk tent, a hundred fine galleys fitted out for two years, 60,000 *silinae* (a mule or ass's burden) of corn, 60,000 of barley, 60,000 of wine, 24 golden cups, and 24 golden plates.

★★★★★★★★

William II., King of Sicily, having died (Nov. 16, 1189) without leaving any children, the throne should have gone to his Aunt Constance, the posthumous daughter of King Roger, who died in 1154. In 1185 she had married Henry, afterwards Henry VI., the eldest son of Frederic Barbarossa, to whom, as well as to his wife, the Sicilian nobles swore fealty before William's death. When William II. died Henry and Constance were both away from Sicily, and the crown was seized by Tancred, an illegitimate son of King Roger.

★★★★★★★★

The King of Sicily, thinking little of the King of England's threats and less of his demands, sent back his (Richard's) sister with just her bed gear; but at the same time, because of her queenly rank, he sent 1,000,000 *terrins* (small gold coins weighing 20 grains) towards her expenses. On the third day after this (Sept. 30) the King of England crossed the great river of Far, which parts Calabria from Sicily, and, entering Calabria in arms, took that most strongly fortified town called La Bagnara and turned out the Griffons. Here, when he had fortified the place with a band of knights, he set his sister. . . .

Before King Richard's arrival in Sicily the Griffons, who were mightier than all the great men of that region, though they always hated the Ultramontanes, were now hotter against them than ever owing to what had lately happened. So, keeping peace with all those who owned the King of France for lord they sought to take vengeance for all their wrongs from the King of England and his "tailed men." ("*Caudati*" or "tailed men," was a term of reproach specially used against the English.) For the Greeks and the Sicilians used to call all those who followed this king "English" and "tailed."

The English were then by an edict cut off from all trade in the land, and were slain by forties or fifties day and night wherever they were found. . . .Roused by these rumours of wrong done him, that wrathful lion the King of England raged terribly, conceiving anger worthy of so great a soul. His wrath frightened his nearest friends, his court is in alarm, the chiefs of his army sit around his throne each in his own rank, and it would have been very easy to read in the president's features what he was thinking of, had anyone dared to lift his eyes and look him in the face.

(The king then asks his soldiers how they imagine they will ever overpower the Turks and Arabs and restore "the kingdom of Israel" if they shew their cowardice before effeminate Griffons. Thus, conquered on the very borders of their own land, are they to go further so that the sluggishness of the English may be a proverb to the world's end? They must avenge themselves here or old women and children will mock at them over sea. But no one need follow him unless of his own accord.)

The king had scarcely made a good ending of his speech when all the men of valour trembled, being troubled that their lord seemed to distrust his own troops. They promise to obey whatever he may order and are ready to make a way through mountains and brazen walls. Let him move his eyebrow; and the whole of Sicily shall be his if he order it, conquered by their toil, aye, if he wish it, the whole (host) will go even to the Columns of Hercules in blood.

When the clamour ceased, quieted by the seriousness of the king, he said:

What I hear pleases me and in thus preparing to throw off your shame you strengthen my heart. And because delay is always hurtful to those who are ready, we must have none in order that our action may be sudden. I must first take Messina; and the Griffons must pay a ransom or be sold. . . . Each man shall have the booty he gets; only the strictest peace must be preserved with My Lord the King of the French who is resting in the city and all his men

Sept. 23-Oct. 2.—K. Richard comes to Messina and frees his sister, Q,. Joan.

Roger of Howden, iii.

On Sept. 23 came Richard, King of England, to Messina with many *busses* and other great ships and galleys; in such pomp he came with the sound of trumpets and horns that terror fell upon those who were in the city. But the King of France and all the great men of the city of Messina, and the clergy and people, stood on the shore marvelling because of all they saw and what they had heard concerning the King of England and his power.

When the King of England had come ashore, he at once had an interview with Philip, King of France. And after that interview the King of France at once went on board his own vessels as though he were desirous of setting out for the land of Jerusalem; but directly he left the harbour the wind shifted and blew against him, upon which he returned unwillingly and sadly to Messina.

But the King of England entered the house of Reginald de Muhec in the vineyards outside the city, where a lodging was being prepared him. On Sept. 24 and 25 the King of England came to the lodgings of the King of France to converse with him there, and the King of France visited the King of England. Meanwhile Richard, King of England, sent his envoys to Tancred, King of Sicily, and set free his sister Joan, formerly queen of Sicily.

On Sept. 28 the King of England went out to meet Joan his sister, who on that day was sent in galleys from Palermo to Messina by King Tancred. On Sept. 29, to wit, on St. Michael's day, came the King of France to the lodging of the King of England's sister, whom he saw, and rejoiced.

On Sept. 30 the King of England crossed the river of Far and took a most strongly fortified place called La Bagnara. Here on Oct. 1st, he brought his sister Joan and, leaving her there with many knights and sergeants, returned to Messina. On Oct. 2nd he took the monastery of the Griffons, a strongly fortified place in the middle of the Far, and here he stored the provisions that had come from England and other lands; and, after driving out the monks and their attendants, he set there his own knights and guards. Now when the citizens of Messina saw what the king had done, they began to conjecture that he would seize the whole island if he could; and for this reason it became an easy matter to stir them up against him.

1190, OCT. 3, 4.—K. RICHARD TAKES MESSINA, LOMBARD TREACHERY; FRENCH PERFIDY.

Itinerarium, Ric.

Now it chanced on a certain day that one of our men was bargaining with a woman over some fresh-baked bread she had exposed for sale. And, as they were talking together and he was disputing over the price, the woman suddenly flew into a passion because he offered her less for the loaf than she wanted. And she began to call him names, and could scarcely refrain from smiting him with her fists or tearing out his hair. And lo! suddenly there gathered together a crowd of citizens who had heard the woman's wrangling. These seized the pilgrim, beat him pitifully, tore out his hair, and, when they had trod him under foot, left him almost lifeless. But King Richard, as soon as the uproar arose, came forth and begged for peace and friendship, declaring that he had come on a peaceful mission and merely to fulfil his pilgrimage; nor did he cease from his efforts till everyone had departed without anger to his own home.

And yet, thanks to the industry of that old enemy of the human race, the contention was renewed on the morrow in a more deadly way. Meanwhile the two kings had been conversing with the justices of Sicily and the chief men of the city as regards the common peace and safety. And lo! there rose up a shout of men crying out that the natives were already slaying the King of England's followers. As the king paid no attention to this—chiefly because the Lombards (Italian merchants) declared it was not true—there came up a second messenger with news that the natives had set upon the pilgrims. (Probably in this passage the word stands for the Italian-speaking population generally.) The Lombards, though they had themselves just come from the contest, were dissuading the king from believing this information, when there hurriedly appeared a third messenger running up in haste and declaring that peace was not to be thought of while their very lives were in danger.

Then the king leaving the conference at once went out on horseback to appease the quarrel. Now there were two false and cunning Lombards at whose prompting the city crowd had been stirred up against the pilgrims. Their names were Jordan del Pin and Margaritus.

★★★★★★★★

Jordan del Pin and Margaritus are called wardens of Messina in Roger of Howden's account of Philip Augustus' reception at Messina. Margaritus is styled "Admiral," and is found acting along the coast of

Syria with a fleet in 1188. When Tancred made terms with Richard in Nov., 1190, they fled from Messina by night. After Tancred's death Margaritus aided the Emperor Henry VI. to conquer the kingdom, and was made Duke of Durazzo (1194). Three years later, however, the emperor had him mutilated. One of his servants slew him at Rome in 1200 while getting ready an expedition for making Philip Augustus Emperor of Constantinople. His energy in 1188 helped to save the remnants of the Christian possessions in the East; and so noted a sailor was he that his contemporaries called him "the King of the Sea" and "a second Neptune."

★★★★★★★★

When King Richard arrived on the spot, where the two parties were already contending with fists and cudgels as well as with words, the Lombards attacked him with scandalous reproaches, though he was eager to separate the combatants. At last, getting angry at their jeers, he put on his arms and driving them into the city besieged them suddenly. . . . Then came the Lombards to the King of France, making submission to him and praying him humbly for aid. Upon this the King of France took up arms (as a man who knew the real truth told us) and was ready to aid the Lombards rather than the men of the King of England.

And this though he was bound by an oath to lend the latter faithful assistance. The gates of the city were barred, watchmen were set on the walls, and there rose a great din from those attacking and defending. . . . The French acted with the Lombards, and together made as it were one people; but the besiegers were not aware that their allies had become their adversaries.

At the beginning (of the siege) certain Lombards had sallied out before the city gates were closed, to attack the dwelling of Hugh Brown and were assaulting it desperately when the King of England, hearing the news, came up quickly.

★★★★★★★★

This is Hugh IX. (le Brun) of Lusignan, the elder brother of Geoffrey and Guy de Lusignan. He married Matilda, daughter and heiress of the Count of La Marche, after her father's death. He had been taken prisoner by Nuradin in 1163 at the disastrous Battle of Harenc, near Antioch. About the year 1206 he is said to have started for the Holy Land once more, but, being taken prisoner, purchased his release and retired into a monastery, where he died in extreme old age. His son, Hugh X., married John's divorced wife, Isabella of Angouleme, and so was the father of the Poitevin favourites of Henry III.

On learning his approach, the Lombards immediately took to flight, and in a moment were scattered like sheep before the wolves. As they fled the king followed close on their heels to a certain postern gate in the wall, for which they made without daring to look behind them or to offer any resistance, though it is said that the king had not even twenty of his men when he first set upon them. At the postern entrance he laid low several of them, disabling them from fighting with pilgrims any more.

. . . . As the enemies' darts and stones were flying thickly we lost three knights of special repute, to wit, Peter Torepreie, Matthew de Saulcy, and Ralph de Roverei. . . . The number of citizens and others defending the walls was reckoned at more than 50,000. There might you see our galleys attempting to besiege the city from the harbour near the palace. But the King of France kept them out of the main harbour, and hence it came to pass that some of them who were already within and would not depart perished by arrows. . . . But why say more? King Richard got possession of Messina in one attack quicker than any priest could chant matins. Aye and many more of the citizens would have perished had not the king in his compassion ordered their lives to be spared.

Who can reckon the amount of money lost by the citizens? Whatever precious thing was found, whether gold or silver, became the possession of the conquerors. Moreover, fire reduced the galleys (of the citizens) to dust. This was done to guard against their taking to flight and offering fresh resistance elsewhere.

1190, OCT. 4 —RICHARD'S MODERATION AFTER HE HAD TAKEN MESSINA.

Roger of Howden, iii.

The King of England's men (after taking the city) set up the banners of their king along the circuit of the fortifications. At this the King of France was very indignant, and demanded that the King of England's banners should be taken down and his set up. To this the King of England would not assent; but to satisfy the King of France, he had his own standards hauled down, and gave over the city to the Hospitallers and Templars to keep till King Tancred should fulfil all his demands. (In the same way in 1161, when Louis VII. and Henry II. were disputing over Gisors and Neafle, they were entrusted to the guardianship of the Templars.)

1190, OCT. 6.—THE LADY JOAN'S DOWRY.

Benedict Petr., ii.

On the third day after the capture of Messina the chiefs of the city and province gave the King of England hostages for the preservation of the peace; saying they would deliver this city and the Lordship of the whole province freely into the king's hands unless that Lord Tancred, King of Sicily, should quickly make peace and do what was required of him. For the king was demanding from King Tancred Mount St. Angelus, together with the whole county and appurtenances thereof, on behalf of his sister Joan, to whom her husband William King of Sicily had given it in dower

To him Tancred, King of Sicily, replied in these words:

I gave your sister Joan 1,000,000 *terrins*, in lieu of her claim, before she left me. As for the rest of your demands I will act in accordance with the custom of this realm.

So it came to pass that by the advice of his men the King of Sicily gave the King of England 20,000 ounces of gold in quittance of his sister Joan's dower; and another 20,000 ounces of gold in quittance of all the other claims set up in regard of the bequest of the dead King William, and to secure a marriage between Arthur, Duke of Brittany, (Richard's) nephew, and one of King Tancred's daughters. (Arthur of Brittany, son of Geoffrey third son of Henry II., was born March 29, 1187. The rumours of the time make him to have been murdered by his uncle King John in 1203. This betrothal in the text came to nothing.)

1190, OCT. 8.—THE KINGS' OATHS.

Howden, iii.

On Oct. 8 the King of France and the King of England in the presence of their counts, barons, the clergy and the people swore on the relics of the saints to keep good faith to one another both as regards their own persons and the two armies during that pilgrimage. The counts and barons also swore that they would keep the same oath firmly. Then, with the goodwill and advice of the whole army of pilgrims the two kings decreed that all pilgrims who should die on the way might dispose of their personal equipment and that of their horses as they wished. So, too, as regards the half of their property, always providing that they remitted nothing home. The clerks of the chapels were to dispose of things pertaining to the chapel and of all their books at their discretion. The other half was to be delivered into the hands of Walter Archbishop of Rouen, of Manasser Bishop of Langres (1179-1192), the masters of the Temple and the Hospital, Hugh Duke of Burgundy, (son of Eudes II. Duke of Burgundy), Drogo de Merlou, Robert de Sablun, Andrew de Chaveni, and Gilbert de Wascuil.

★★★★★★★★

Walter de Coutances was made Bishop of Lincoln in 1183, whence he was next year transferred to Rouen. In 1192 Richard sent him home to England with sealed instructions which resulted in the fall of Longchamp. He seems to have died in 1207 *A D.*

★★★★★★★★

These were to spend the money thus acquired for the aid of the Holy Land as they saw necessary. And both the kings swore personally to keep this order leally and firmly during the whole journey on this side of the sea as well as the other. It was to hold good for the pilgrims of each kingdom both as regards those already arrived and others yet to come.

OCT. 8, 1190.—REGULATIONS FOR ENGLISH AND FRENCH CRUSADERS.

Moreover let no one in the whole army play at any game for a stake—saving only knights and clerks, who, however, are not to lose more than 20 *solidi* in the 24 hours. And if any knights or clerks lose more than this sum in the natural day, they shall for every offence give 100 *solidi* to the archbishop (of Rouen) and his fellow-treasurers to be added to the aforesaid fund. The kings, however, may play at their good pleasure; and in the royal lodgings the kings' servants may play for twenty *solidi* if the king so choose.

Also, by leave of the archbishops, bishops, counts, and barons and in their presence, servants may play for twenty *solidi*. If any sergeants, mariners, or other servants are found playing by themselves the sergeants shall be beaten naked through the army for three days unless they will pay a fine at the discretion of the aforesaid (trustees); so too with the other serving men. But, if the seamen gamble, they are in seaman's fashion to be ducked in the sea at early morn once every day, unless they too purchase exemption.

If, after starting on the journey, any pilgrim has borrowed from another man he shall pay the debt; but so long as he is on the pilgrimage, he shall not be liable for a debt contracted before starting.

If any hired mariner, hired servant, or anyone else, saving only clerks and knights, shall desert his lord on the pilgrimage no one shall take him in except with his lord's consent. . . . All transgressors of these statutes are subject to excommunication, and shall be punished in accordance with the aforesaid rules at the will of the aforesaid trustees.

Moreover, the kings have decreed that no merchant of any kind may buy bread or flour in the army to sell it again, unless indeed some stranger has brought the flour and the seller has made it into bread. . . . . . . .But it is utterly forbidden to buy any light bread, neither may it be bought in or within the banlieue of the town, (to prevent the waste of grain in making fine cake bread.) If anyone buys corn to make bread with, his profit shall only be one *terrin* in every quarter and the bran. Other merchants, no matter of what calling, shall only make a profit of one penny in ten.

No one may sound the king's money on which his stamp appears unless it be cracked within the circle. No one is to buy any lifeless carcass for the purpose of selling it again, nor any live animal, unless he have killed it in the army. No one is to raise the price of his wine after he has once had it cried. No one is to make bread for sale except at a penny cost. And let all merchants take note that the whole *Far* (probably the whole strait of Messina with the islands near) is within the banlieue of the town, and that one English penny shall be given in all mercantile transactions for four Anjou pennies. And it is to be understood that all the aforesaid decrees are promulgated with the consent and good-will of the kings of France, of England, and of Sicily.

Oct.-Dec, 1190.—Richard's penitence and interview with Abbot Joachim.

Howden, iii.

In the same year Richard King of England, inspired by the Divine grace, called to mind the foulness of his past life, and after contrition of heart gathered the bishops and archbishops who were with him at Messina together in Reginald de Moyac's chapel Then, falling naked at their feet he did not blush to confess the foulness of his life to God in their presence. For the thorns of his evil lusts had grown higher than his head, and there was no hand to root them up.

Yet did God the father of mercies, who willeth not the death of a sinner but that he may be converted and live, turn on him once more the eyes of His mercy, giving him a penitent heart and calling him to repentance. For he in his own person received penance from the aforesaid bishops; and from that hour once more became a man

30

fearing God, shunning ill and doing good. Happy he who so falls only to rise up stronger. Happy he who after repentance has not slipt back into sin.

In the same year Richard King of England, hearing by common fame and the report of many, how that there was in Calabria a certain monk named Joachim, a Cistercian and Abbot of Corazzo, sent for him and willingly heard the words of his prophecy, his wisdom and his teaching. (Abbot Joachim is said to have been born in 1130 or 1145, and to have died in 1201 or 1207. In his younger days he visited the Holy Land, and later was made Abbot of Fiore.) For this Joachim had the spirit of prophecy and used to foretell what was going to happen. Moreover, he was a man learned in the Divine Scriptures and used to set forth the meaning of S. John's visions—those visions which S. John narrates in the Apocalypse and wrote with his own hand. In hearing his words, the King of England and his followers took much pleasure.

(*Then follows an account of the abbot's explanation of the seven kings of Revelation, of whom five had already fallen including Mahomet. Saladin was the sixth, but he would soon lose Jerusalem.*)

Then the King of England asked him: "When will this be?"

And to him Joachim made answer: "When seven years have passed from the day on which Jerusalem was taken."

Then said the king: "Wherefore then have we come here so soon?"

To which Joachim replied: "Thy coming was an urgent necessity because the Lord will give thee the victory over his enemies and will exalt thy name above all the princes of the earth."

KING RICHARD'S CHRISTMAS FEAST.

Fr. *The Song of Ambrose. Pertz.*

The day of Nativity (I tell you truth) did King Richard cry that all should come and hold the feast with him. And he brought the King of France to feast with him; such trouble did he take. At Matte-griffun was the feast in the hall that the King of England had reared by his power, in despite of them of the land. I was eating in the hall, but never did I see there a dirty cloth, nor a cup or spoon of wood. And there I saw vessels so richly edged with *ovre trifoire* (open work patterns) and over-wrought with figures and with precious stones, that they were right pleasant to behold. And I saw there such a fine service that each one had what pleased him. Nor ever did I see—so I think—any one give such rich gifts as King Richard gave on this occasion. For he left to the King of France and his folk vessels of gold and silver.

Howden, iii.

On the same day after breakfast the Pisans and the Genoese made a seditious attack upon the oarsmen of the King of England. Now the noise came to the king's ears where he sat at meat in his castle Mattegrifrun.

****

The Castle of Matte-griffun—a wooden structure—had been built by Richard close to the walls of Messina It was intended, as its name "Kill-Greek" or "Check-Greek" implies, to overawe the Griffons. Before leaving the island Richard destroyed this fortress in accordance with his promise to Tancred.

****

And there were banqueting with him Reginald Bishop of Chartres (grandson of Theobald, Count of Blois), Hugh Duke of Burgundy . . . . . . many other of the King of France's household. Then, after removing the table, all these men rose, armed themselves, and followed the king for the purpose of putting an end to this quarrel. Yet, for all this, they could not do so; but when night came on the disputants were parted one from the other. And, on the morrow, when the people was gathered together in the church of St. John of the Hospital, to hear the divine service there, a certain Pisan drew his knife and wounded one of the king's oarsmen in the church; upon which the Pisans and the galley-men fell to again and many were slain on either side. Then came the King of France and the King of England, with an armed following, and made peace between the two parties.

1191, FEB.-MAR.—THE THREE KINGS IN SICILY. RICHARD'S BETROTHED WIFE COMES OUT TO SICILY.

Howden, iii.

In February on Saturday the day of the Purification of Blessed Ever-virgin (Feb. 2), after breakfast Richard King of England and many of his suite and that of the King of France met, as they were wont to do, outside the city of Messina, bent on diversions of various kinds. As they went home through the middle of the city, they fell in with a certain rustic coming from a neighbouring hamlet. Now his ass was laden with reeds that people call canes. Of these reeds the King of England and those with him each took one, using them to tilt against each other.

And it chanced that the King of England and William des Barres, a very noble knight belonging to the King of France's suite, charged one another, shattering their reeds to pieces. (William des Barres, one of Philip's greatest warriors. He was taken prisoner by Richard in 1188, but breaking parole escaped. He afterward saved Philip Augustus' life at the Battle of Bovines; 27 July, 1214).

By this blow the head-piece of the King of England was broken; whereon the king, being wroth, set upon William so furiously as to make him and his horse stagger. And as the king was attempting to throw William to the ground, his own saddle was upset; and the king came down quicker than he liked. Then a fresh horse, stronger than the other, was brought up. This the king mounted and made another attack on William des Barres, striving to bring him down, but without success. For William stuck fast to his horse's neck despite the king's threats. Now when Robert de Breteuil, son of Robert Earl of Leicester (grandson of Robert II., Earl of Leicester), whom the king had on the preceding day girt, (*belting the earl* was the ceremony of investiture for a man of that rank), with the sword of his father's earldom, began to lay hands on William des Barres so as to aid his lord the king, Richard cried out: "Hold off and leave us alone."

And after these two had striven together for a long while both with words and deeds the king said to his antagonist, "Get thee hence and take care thou appear not before me anymore, for from this moment I shall ever be an enemy to thee and thine." So, William des Barres departed from the king's face confused and grieving at the royal indignation. But he went off to his lord the King of France demanding his aid and counsel as regards this which had fallen out. And on the morrow the King of France came to the King of England on behalf of William des Barres, asking for peace and mercy in humble style; yet would not the King of England hear him.

Next day the Bishop of Chartres, the Duke of Burgundy, the Count of Nevers, (Peter de Courtenay II., son of Peter de Courtenay I., and so grandson of Louis VI. and first cousin of Philip Augustus), and many other French nobles cast themselves with the humblest prayers at his knees, begging peace and mercy for William des Barres; neither would the king hear them.

Accordingly on the third day William left Messina because the King of France would no longer keep him in his service against the will of the King of England. But sometime after, when the time for crossing over drew near, the King of France with all his archbishops, bishops, counts, barons, and the chiefs of the whole army came once more to the King of England, and casting themselves at his feet begged peace and mercy for William des Barres, shewing what loss and inconvenience the absence of so valiant a knight would cause. At last, after much difficulty, they got the King of England to consent to the peaceable return of the said William, Richard undertaking to do him no ill or harm, and not to proceed against him so long as they were both busied in the service of God.

Then the King of England gave many ships to the King of France and his men; after which he distributed his treasures lavishly to the whole company of knights and to the sergeants of the whole army, till many said that none of his predecessors had given away in a year so much as he gave away in that month. And of a surety we may believe that by this generosity he "won the favour of the Thunderer," since it has been written "God loveth a cheerful giver."

In the same month of February, the King of England sent his galleys to Naples to meet Queen Eleanor, his mother, Berengaria, the daughter of Sancho, the King of Navarre (whom he was about to wed), and Philip Count of Flanders (son of Theodoric), who accompanied them. But the king's mother and the King of Navarre's daughter put in at Brindisi, where the admiral Margaritus and other of King Tancred's men received them with all honour and reverence. The Count of Flanders however came to Naples, where, finding the King of England's galleys, he went aboard, and arriving at Messina became a supporter of the King of England. The King of France, angered at this, brought it about that the count should leave the King of England and return to him

On the first of March Richard King of England, leaving Messina, came to Catania, where rests the most holy body of the blessed Agatha, virgin and martyr, for the purpose of having an interview with Tancred King of Sicily, who had come there to meet him. Now when King Tancred heard of the King of England's approach, he went out to greet him with the utmost reverence, and brought him into the city with all the honour due to royal worth. As the two kings went in company to visit the blessed Agatha's tomb the clergy and people met them before the entrance of the temple, praising and blessing God, who had made them such close friends.

After prayer at the blessed Agatha's tomb the King of England entered Tancred's palace with that king and there tarried three days and three nights. On the fourth day the King of Sicily sent many and great presents, gold, silver, steeds, and silken cloths to the King of England, who, however, would accept none of them save one little ring as a sign of mutual love. On the other hand, the King of England gave Tancred that best of swords which the Britons call Caliburne, (or Excalibur, as it is called in the *Idylls of the King*), formerly the sword of Arthur, once the noble King of England. Moreover, King Tancred gave the King of England four great ships that they call *ursers* and fifteen galleys; and when the King of England was departing, he brought him on his way as far as Taormina, two stages from Catania. (*Ursers* were round vessels rather than long, went by sail not by oar, and, may on an average have contained 24 men and 40 horses.)

And on the morrow when the King of England wished to be off, King Tancred handed him a certain letter which the King of France had sent him by the Duke of Burgundy. This letter declared that the King of England was a traitor, and would not keep the peace he had made with Tancred. If Tancred himself, the letter went on, would attack the King of England or set upon him by night he (*i.e.*, Philip) and his men would help him to destroy the King of England and his army. To Tancred the King of England made answer:

"I am not a traitor, neither have I been one nor will I be. Moreover, I have not broken the peace I have made with you, nor will I do so as long as I live. But I cannot easily believe the King of France has sent you this message concerning me, for he is my lord and my sworn comrade in this pilgrimage."

To him Tancred replied:

"I hand you the letters which he has himself sent me by the Duke of Burgundy; and if the duke shall deny having brought me these letters on behalf of his lord, the King of France, I am ready to prove my words against him by one of my lords."

And so, after receiving these letters from the hand of King Tancred, the King of England went back to Messina.

On the same day came the King of France to Taormina for an interview with Tancred and, after resting there one night, on the morrow returned to Messina. But the King of England, being wroth, made no pretence to pleasure or good-will, but kept on the lookout for an opportunity of departing with his men. In answer to the King of France's inquiries as to why he was thus treated the King of England sent him by Philip Count of Flanders a copy of all the disclosures the King of Sicily had made to him; and in proof thereof shewed him the aforesaid letters. When this was made clear to the King of France, he was struck speechless by his evil conscience, and had no word of reply. At last, coming to himself, he said:

"Now I see plainly how the King of England is seeking occasion to malign me; for all these words are forged lies. Truly I believe he is plotting against me thus so that he may put away my sister Alice, whom he has sworn to marry. But he may rest assured that if he discards her and marries another wife, I shall be his enemy as long as I live."

Upon hearing this the King of England swore that he could never marry Philip's sister, because his father the King of England had begotten a daughter on her. Moreover, he brought forward many witnesses who were ready to maintain this by every method (that is were ready to prove it by a judicial oath or by a judicial combat or ordeal).

RICHARD'S GREED TOWARD PHILIP.

This is a French account of the transactions, and to be compared with the English accounts above.

Rigord.

When King Philip came to Messina in August, (Philip really reached Messina Sept. 16, 1190) he was lodged with great honour in the palace of King Tancred, who gave him abundantly of his own provisions; and would have given him a countless sum of gold if he or his son Louis would have married one of his daughters. But King Philip, because of the friendship he had for the Emperor Henry, declined either engagement. (Henry VI, from whom Tancred seized the crown, was the son of Frederick Barbarossa and father of Frederick II.)

Later on the strife between the King of England and Tancred for his sister's dowry was terminated in the following way, thanks to King Philip's intervention and efforts:—

The King of England received 40,000 ounces of gold from King Tancred. Of this King Philip had only the third part, when he ought to have had the half. Yet for the sake of peace was he contented with the third.

PHILIP BEGS RICHARD TO SAIL AT ONCE.

Rigord.

Now when some days had passed the King of France begged the King of England to get ready to make the March passage with him. But the King of England replied that he could not cross before August.

★★★★★★★★

Passagium was the name given to the voyage to and from Jerusalem. There were ordinarily reckoned two great '*passagia*' in the course of the year from the towns of the Mediterranean coast to the Holy Land. They usually took place in the early spring (*passagium Martii*) and the late summer or beginning of autumn (*passagium Augusti or Septembris*);

36

but it is not very easy to assign them exact dates.

★★★★★★★★

Then the King of France sent once more urging him as though he were his own vassal to cross the sea along with him. If he would he might marry the King of Navarre's daughter . . . . at Acre; but if he would not go he must wed his (the King of France's) sister, as he was bound to do by oath.

The King of England flatly refused to do anything of the kind; upon which the King of France called on those who had given sureties for this oath to do as they had sworn. And Geoffrey de Rancogne and the Viscount of Châteaudun, in the name of all the rest, declared they would do as they had sworn and go whenever he wished it. At this the King of England was vehemently wroth and swore to disinherit them—a threat which the subsequent course of things brought about. And from this moment envy and quarrels began to rise between the two kings.

MARCH, 1191.—AGREEMENT MADE BY PHILIP AS TO HIS DISPUTE WITH RICHARD.

Rigord, Rymer.

This was the final arrangement between the kings before they parted.

In the name of the Holy and undivided Trinity, Amen. Philip by the grace of God King of France:

Know all men present and to come that a firm peace hath been made between us and our friend and faithful liege Richard, the illustrious King of England:—

1. Of a good heart and will we grant the aforesaid king to marry whomsoever he will, notwithstanding the covenant made between ourselves and him regarding our sister Alice whom he ought to have married.

5. If the King of England have two male heirs or more, he hath willed and granted that the elder shall hold of us in chief all that he ought to hold on this side the sea of England; while the other shall hold in chief one of the three baronies, to wit that of Normandy, of Anjou and Maine, or of Angouleme and Poitou.

6. And by reason of the aforesaid covenant the King of England hath granted us 10,000 silver *marks*—Troy weight; 3,000 *marks* of which he will pay us or our true representative on the feast of All Saints at Chaumont, (in the Vexin); and another 3,000 at

the next feast of All Saints; 2,000 more at the third and 2,000 more at the fourth feast of All Saints.

11. If the aforesaid terms as above written be observed on both sides, we will and grant the King of England to have and hold in peace all the tenements, both fiefs, and domain lands that he held on the day when he started for Jerusalem

14. Moreover the King of England hath agreed to send back to France without any let or hindrance our sister Alice, within a month after his return whether we be alive or dead...

All which things, that they may be lasting, we confirm with the authority of our seal. Given at Messina in the month of March in the year 1190 of the Incarnate Word.

THE KING OF FRANCE GOES TO ACRE AND RECONNOITRES. 13 OR 20 APRIL, 1191.

L'Estoire d'Eracles.

Philip the King of France came straight to Syria with all his host and arrived at the harbour of Acre, where the siege was then progressing. The gentlefolk who were already there had been long and eagerly expecting his coming, and on his arrival, he was received with great honour as becomes so high a man as the King of France. The host was overjoyed at his coming. In his train he brought great store of vessels filled with provisions and many other good things; and in his company he had barons and knights as befitted the crown of France: to wit, count Philip of Flanders, Hugh Duke of Burgundy, and William des Banes, on whose account the discord between the two kings in great measure arose.

As soon as he arrived, he got upon his horse and made a circuit of the whole city to see from what part it might most easily be taken. When he had made his survey, he remarked:

It is strange that with so many warriors at the siege, the city has been so long in getting taken.

The King of France might have taken the city of Acre had he wished; but he waited for the coming of the King of England because they were companions and had made alliance from the time, they left their own lands to conquer everything in common. It was for this cause that he waited—*viz.*, that he wished (the King of England) to share in the joy and conquest of the afore-said city of Acre.

MARCH 30, 1191—PHILIP LEAVES SICILY.

Howden iii.

And in the same month of March, Saturday the 30th, Philip with all his fleet set sail from the harbour of Messina, and on the twenty-second, day following, to wit the Saturday in Easter week, (*i.e.*, April 20, 1191), came with his army to the siege of Acre. But the King of England and his army remained at Messina after the departure of the King of France. And on the very day when the King of France left Messina, Queen Eleanor, the mother of Richard King of England, arrived there.

With her she brought Berengaria, the daughter of Sancho King of Navarre, whom the King of England was going to marry. On the fourth day Queen Eleanor went back to England, intending to pass through Rome; and when she had gone the King of Navarre's daughter remained in the guardianship of the King of England, together with his sister Joan Queen of Sicily.

1191, 13 APRIL—KING PHILIP REACHES ACRE.

Rigord

But Philip the King of the Franks, earnestly desiring to finish the journey he had begun, set sail in March and after a few days, having a favourable breeze, reached Acre on Easter Eve (*i.e.,* 13 April, 1191) with all that belonged to him. Here he was received with the greatest joy by the whole army, which had been besieging the city for so long a time. (He was welcomed) with hymns and songs of praise and floods of tears, as though he had been an angel of God. He at once had his house set up so near the city walls that the enemies of Christ often shot their quarrels and arrows right up to it and even beyond. Then, after having erected his stone-casters, his *mangonels*, and his other engines of war, he so battered the walls before the King of England's arrival that it only wanted an assault for the city to be taken. For he was unwilling to storm the city so long as the King of England was away.

RICHARD LEAVES SICILY THE WEDNESDAY BEFORE GOOD FRIDAY, 1191. (APRIL 10, 1191.)

Ric. of Devizes

The fleet of Richard King of the English launched forth and proceeded in the following order:—In the first line went three ships only. One of these held the Queen of Sicily and the girl from Navarre. The other two carried part of the king's treasure and arms; in all three there were men as a guard and food.

In the second line, what with ships, *busses*, and *dromunds* (largest class of ships of burden), there were thirteen vessels; in the third fourteen; in the fourth twenty; in the fifth thirty; in the sixth forty; in the seventh sixty; and last followed the king himself with his galleys, (mediaeval war ships.) Between the several ships and the lines, the space was so wisely arranged that from one rank to another you might hear a trumpet's blast, and from one ship to another a man's voice. (According to Roger of Howden, Richard set sail with 150 great ships and 53 well-armed galleys.) This too was a wonderful thing, that the king was no less hearty and healthy, strong and hale, light and active, on sea than he was wont to be on land. (Richard of Devizes implies that Philip could not well stand a sea-voyage.) From this I conclude that there was not any man in the world stronger than he, either on land or sea.

SHIP OF THE 13TH CENTURY.

THE STORMY PASSAGE OF KING RICHARD, AND HIS FAITH IN THE CISTERCIAN PRAYERS.

Caesar of Heisterbach

In the first expedition against Jerusalem Richard King of England crossed over with a multitude of pilgrims and very great host. Now on a certain day towards twilight there rose a mighty tempest, so that the ships were battered by the storm and driven hither and thither by the force of the winds. But the king and all the others having death before their eyes cried out all through the night:

O when will the hour come for the Grey Monks (Cistercians, of the reformed order of Citeaux), to rise and praise God. For I have done them such great kindnesses that I cannot doubt that as soon as they begin to pray for me God will look down and pity us.

Wonderful was the king's faith; and the Lord who says "If ye have faith as a grain of mustard seed ye shall say to this mountain 'be thou removed' and it shall be removed" rewarded his faith by a clear miracle.

For about the eighth hour of the night, towards morning, the Lord roused by the prayers of the rising monks, and rising himself in all his might, commanded the winds and waves and there was a great calm; so that all wondered at the sudden change. Wherefore the king on his return, in recompense for this miracle, did still more honour to the order, enriching certain of its houses with alms and founding new ones.

1191, APRIL 12-JUNE 8.—K. RICHARD LEAVES MESSINA, ACQUIRES CYPRUS, GOES THENCE TO ACRE.

Manuel I., Emperor of Constantinople, had died 3rd October, 1180. His young son Alexius was soon supplanted by his cousin Andronicus, who murdered him in 1184, but met with a similar fate in September next year. Before his death Andronicus had sent Isaac Comnenus, a nephew of Theodora (the wife of Baldwin III. of Jerusalem and Manuel's niece), to Cyprus, where however he declared himself Emperor, and succeeded in maintaining his power long after Andronicus at Constantinople had been supplanted by another Isaac (Angelus 1185-95).

According to Howden, Isaac Comnenus of Cyprus had been taken prisoner by Rupin de la Muntaine (of Armenia), who delivered him to his lord "Raymond" (a mistake for Boamund III., prince of Antioch). The same writer makes him Manuel's nephew. Boamund demanded 60,000 besants as his ransom . and the men of Cyprus, hearing of his danger and fearing the cruelty of Andronicus sent an offer to pay 30,000 besants down. Hostages were delivered for the other half and Isaac was set free. He died in 1195.

Roger of Howden, iii.

On Good Friday (April 12), about the ninth hour of the day, a fearful wind, coming up from the S., scattered his navy. The king with his part of the *licet* took shelter in the Isle of Crete and then at Rhodes. But a great *buss*, on board which were the Queen of Sicily and the King of Navarre's daughter, with many intimate friends of the king, and along with it two other *busses* were driven by stress of tempest to Cyprus, the king being quite ignorant what had become of them.

****

The author of the *Itinerarium* shews that there were two storms on April 10 and 24. Richard had a huge wax candle lit on board his own vessel as a sign to the rest of the fleet. He was driven to Rhodes (April 22) and stayed there till May 1st. The queen reached Limasol May 2nd, and was on the point of trusting herself to Tancred's generosity three days later, when on Sunday evening (May 5) two ships appeared on the horizon. They were the leaders of Richard's fleet.

★★★★★★★★

When the storm gave over the king sent out galleys to look for the ship that held his sister and the King of Navarre's daughter. And they were found outside the harbour of Limasol. As for the two other ships, that accompanied this one as far as Limasol, they had perished; and many knights and servants belonging to the king's suite were drowned (at the same time). Amongst these, alas! there was drowned master Roger Malus Catulus, the king's vice-chancellor (April 24). The king's seal, which he used to wear hung round his neck, was found (later). Isaac Emperor of Cyprus laid his hands upon the goods of those who were drowned; and at the same time took and imprisoned all who escaped shipwreck, and confiscated their money. Intoxicated with a mad frenzy of cruelty, he went further, inasmuch as he would not suffer the vessel, in which were the queen of Sicily and the King of Navarre's daughter, to enter the harbour.

When this had been made known to the King of England he came to their aid, with all speed, with many galleys and a great store of ships, and found them lying outside the harbour, exposed to the winds and the sea. Being greatly enraged at this, he sent his messengers once, twice, thrice, to the Emperor of Cyprus, humbly begging him for the love of God and reverence for the life-giving Cross to free the captive pilgrims whom he held in chains and to restore with their goods the goods of those who had been drowned. These goods he desired in order that by their aid services might be offered to God for the souls of the dead. To these envoys the emperor made a haughty answer, saying that he would neither restore the pilgrims nor the goods.

Now the king, hearing that the wicked emperor would do nothing for him unless constrained by force, ordered his whole army to take up arms and follow, him, saying:

Follow me and we will take vengeance for the wrongs which this perfidious emperor has done to God and to us in thus unjustly keeping our pilgrims in chains. Do not fear his men, for they are unarmed and fitted for flight rather than for war. We, on the other hand, are well armed; for he who

When asked for simple right says, "No,"
Yields all things to an armed foe.

It behoves us to fight manfully to free God's people from destruction, knowing that we must win or die. But I have confidence in God that He will this day give us the victory over this perfidious emperor and his people. (May 6).

Meanwhile the emperor had lined the sea-shore everywhere with his men. Few of them were armed and almost all were unskilled in battle. Yet they stood on the shore equipt with swords, lances, and clubs, and holding stakes, bits of wood, seats, boxes before them for a wall. When the King of England and his men had armed themselves, leaving their great ships, they rowed ashore in boats and galleys with great speed. The archers went first to clear a way for the rest. And when they had reached land, under the king's leadership, they made an attack all together upon the emperor and his Griffons, and, as a shower upon the grass, so fell the arrows upon the combatants.

When they had been fighting a long while the emperor and his men took to flight, pursued by the King of England, who slaughtered those opposing him at the sword's edge. Many also he took alive, and had not night intervened maybe the king would on that day have taken the emperor himself. But as the king and his folk were on foot and did not know the mountain paths along which the emperor and his men were fleeing, they returned to Limasol and found it forsaken by the Griffons. There they discovered abundance of corn, wine, oil, and flesh.

On the same day, after the King of England's victory, his sister the queen of Sicily and the King of Navarre's daughter entered Limasol harbour accompanied by the rest of the king's fleet. But the emperor, collecting those of his men who were scattered about the valleys and thickets, on the same night pitched his camp some five miles from the King of England's army, swearing with an oath that on the morrow he would again give battle to the King of England. Now when the king's scouts brought him word of this, (Richard) made his army take up its arms a long while before it was light.

Marching along without any noise they came to the emperor's host and found it sleeping. Then with a great and terrible cry the king entered their tents, whilst the enemy, being roused from sleep, became as dead men, not knowing what to do or where to flee, because the

King of England's army was setting on them like ravening wolves (May 7).

But the emperor with a few of his followers, escaping unarmed, left behind him his treasures, his steeds, his arms, his beautiful tents, and his imperial banner all inwrought with gold. This the King of England despatched at once to St. Edmund, (monastery at Bury St. Edmunds), the glorious king and martyr. Then after his great victory and triumph over his enemies he returned to Limasol.

On the third day, (Saturday, May 11th, according to the *Itinerarium*) from this there came to the King of England in the island of Cyprus Guy King of Jerusalem, Geoffrey de Lusignan his brother, (sons of Hugh de Lusignan), Amfrid del Tursin, Raymond Prince of Antioch, with his son, Bohemund Count of Tripoli, and Leo brother of Rupin de la Muntaine.

★★★★★★★★

Guy de Lusignan fled to the Holy Land, was taken prisoner at the Battle of Hittin (4 July, 1187), but set free in the course of the next year. He began the siege of Acre Aug. 22, 1189. He died in 1195.
Geoffrey de Lusignan, the elder brother of Guy, was given Jaffa and Ascalon by Richard I. He played a distinguished part at the siege of Acre.
Henfrid de Toron (Amfrid del Tursin) the recalcitrant barons wished to make him king in 1186, but he escaped and did homage to Guy and his wife. He is said to have died in 1198.
Bohemund Count of Tripoli, should be Boamund III. whose father Raymond died in 1149. Boamund is said to have died in 1201 *A.D.*
Leo, the first King of Armenia, who was crowned as a sovereign dependent on the Western Empire in January 1198. He died 1219 *A.D.*

★★★★★★★★

These offered their services to the king and became his men, swearing fealty to him against all folk. On the same day the Emperor of Cyprus, seeing himself utterly deserted, sent envoys humbly to the King of England, offering him peace on these terms: He (Isaac) would give 20,000 *marks* of gold in recompense for the money of those who had been drowned; those who had been captured after the shipwreck he would set free with their goods; while he himself, in his own person, would go with (Richard) to Jerusalem and tarry there in his service and in that of God with 100 knights, 400 mounted *turcoples*, and 500 well-armed footmen.

★★★★★★★★

The light-armed native horseman of the Greek Armies. They formed a prominent part in the armies of the great military orders in the East. With the Templars their head officer, the *Turcopolier*, had command of all the men-at-arms, as well as of his own special troops, during action. In the battle a *Turcople* bore the Beauseant or Templars' banner, and, in the regulations for food, the *Turcoples* were allowed meat and wine, as compared with the Templar knights, in the proportions of two to three and five to three; as compared with the men-at-arms in the proportion of three to two.

★★★★★★★★

Moreover, (Isaac) promised his only daughter, who was also his heir, as a hostage; he would deliver up his castles as pledges, would swear eternal fealty to (Richard) and his (successors), and would hold his empire of him. When these *terms* had been agreed to on either side, the emperor came to the King of England, and, in presence of the King of Jerusalem, the prince of Antioch, and the other barons, became the King of England's man and swore fealty to him. Moreover, he swore that he would not leave (Richard) till all he had bargained should be accomplished. But the king handed the emperor tents for himself and his men, assigning knights and sergeants to guard them.

But on the same day after breakfast the emperor repented him of his bargain with the King of England, and while the knights who should have been guarding him were taking their mid-day sleep, he went off slyly, sending the king word that he would keep no peace or agreement with him. This, as it turned out, pleased the king very well. For he, like the wise and prudent man he was, at once handed over a good part of his army to King Guy, the Prince of Antioch, and the other newcomers with orders to pursue the emperor, and, if possible, take him prisoner.

The king himself dividing his galleys into two squadrons, instructed Robert de Turnham with one half to surround the island on the one side and take whatever vessels or galleys he might find. This was accordingly done; whilst the king with the remaining half of his galleys coasted the other part of the island. Thus, he and Robert took as many vessels and galleys as they found in the circuit of the whole island. But the guards of the cities, castles, and harbours, fleeing off to the mountains, left their charges empty in every place where the king and the aforesaid Robert came. . .

Meanwhile the emperor's men came pouring in to the King of England, and becoming his men held their lands of him. Now, on a certain day, when the aforesaid emperor and his comrades had sat down to breakfast, one of them said to him:

My Lord, it is our advice that you make peace with the King of England, lest your whole people perish.

And the emperor, being angered at this speech, smote the speaker with the knife he held, cutting off the nose of the man who had given this counsel; whereupon after breakfast he who had been thus smitten went off to the King of England and adhered to him.

On Sunday, May 12, the feast of SS. Nereus, Achilles, and Pancras, Martyrs, Berengaria the King of Navarre's daughter was married to Richard King of England, in the island of Cyprus at Limasol...

Then, after the celebration of his wedding, the King of England moved his army forward, and the noble city of Nicosia was delivered up to him. On the king's coming with his army to the strongly-fortified castle which is called Cerine, (N. of Cyprus, looking towards Armenia), the emperor's daughter who was there came out to meet him, and cast herself prone on the earth before the king's feet, yielding up the castle and praying for mercy. The king, taking pity on her, sent her to the queen; and, as he journeyed on, the following castles surrendered: Paphos, Buffevent, Deudeamur, and Candare. Then all the other cities and fortresses of the empire surrendered.

But meanwhile the unhappy emperor was lying hid in a certain abbey-fortress called Cape St. Andrew; and, when the king came here for the purpose of taking him, the emperor went out to meet him, cast himself at his feet, and placed himself at the king's mercy, life and limb, without making any stipulation as regards the realm. For he well knew that all things were now in the king's power, and therefore he only begged not to be put in iron fetters and manacles. The king having heard his petition, handed him over to Robert Fitz-Godfrey, his chamberlain, with orders to have gold and silver chains made for his safe keeping. All these things were done in the island of Cyprus, on Saturday, the first day of June, which was also Whit-Sunday eve. (According to the *Itinerarium* this should be Friday, 31 May.)

On the same day, to wit on Whitsun eve, died Philip Count of Flanders, at the siege of Acre; and the King of France, laying hands on all his treasures and everything he possessed, from that hour began to seek an opportunity for withdrawing from the siege, and returning to his own lands, in order that he might reduce the county of Flanders.

And on the same day, to wit Whitsun eve (*i.e.,* June 1), the Queen of England, the Queen of Sicily (sister to the King of England), and the daughter of the Emperor of Cyprus, landed at Acre with the greater part of the King of England's fleet. (According to Ernoul, Richard took Isaac's daughter back with him to his own dominions. On his death she was set free and started for Cyprus, but was detained at Marseilles and forced to marry Raymond VI. of Toulouse, who, however, put her away later, so as to marry the King of Arragon's sister.)

JUNE 6 OR 7—RICHARD'S VOYAGE TO ACRE; THE TAKING OF THE SARACEN DROMOND.

Itin. ii.

And so, having concluded these matters, Richard straightway turned his thoughts towards his passage across (to the Holy Land); and, when he had arranged his baggage, set sail with a favourable wind. The queens put out to sea in *busses* with their own equipage. The king had appointed energetic men to be his wardens and captains in Cyprus, leaving them instructions to send after him what victuals were necessary, to wit wheat, barley, and the flesh of all the animals in which Cyprus abounded,

And lo! there now went abroad a report that Acre was on the point of being taken; upon hearing which the king with a deep sigh prayed God that the city might not fall before his arrival, "for," he said, "after so long a siege our triumph ought, God willing, to be one of exceptional glory." Then with great haste he went on board one of the best and largest of his galleys at Famagusta; and being impatient of delay, as he always was, he kept right ahead, though other and better appointed galleys followed him from every side

And so, as they were furrowing the sea with all haste, they caught their earliest glimpse of that Holy Land of Jerusalem. The castle of Margat (great fortress of the Knights of St. John, to whom it had been sold in 1186 by its lord, Reynald), was the first to meet their eyes; then Tortosa, (the ancient Antaradus, an old Phoenician settlement), set on the sea-shore, Tripolis, (originally a colony founded by the three cities of Sidon, Tyre, and Aradus), Nephyn, Botron, (less than half-way between Tripoli and Beyrout), and not long after the lofty tower of Gibeleth, (modern Jebeil, and ancient Byblos).

At last, on this side of Sidon near Beyrout, they descried afar off a certain ship filled with Saladin's choicest warriors the pick out of all his pagan realm, and destined to bring aid to the besieged in Acre. Seeing that they could not make direct for Acre on account of the nearness of the Christians, the Saracens drew back to sea a little and waited their time to make a sudden rush into the harbour. Richard, who had taken note of the ship, calling up one of his galley-men, Peter des Barren, bade him row hastily and enquire who commanded it. Word was brought back that it belonged to the King of France; but Richard, as he drew near eagerly, could neither hear any French word nor see any Christian standard or banner. As it approached, he began to wonder at its size, its firm and solid build. For it was set off with three masts of great height and its smoothly wrought sides were decked here and there with green or yellow hides. Added to which it was so well rigged out with every fitting appointment and so well furnished with provisions of every kind as to leave no room for improvement.

There was a man present on the king's ship who said he had been at Beyrout when this vessel was loaded. He had seen her cargo sent aboard, to wit, a hundred camel-loads of arms of every kind: great heaps of arbalests, bows, spears, and arrows. It contained also seven Saracen *emirs* and eight hundred chosen Turks, to say nothing of a great stock of food exceeding calculation. There was also a supply of Greek fire closed up in vessels and two hundred most deadly serpents, destined to work havoc among the Christians. (Greek fire, the most destructive agent known to mediaeval warfare, was passed on from the Byzantine Greeks to the Saracens.)

The king now sent other messengers to enquire more particularly as to who the strangers were; and this time they received a different reply: that the strangers were men of Genoa bound for Tyre. Whilst all were in doubt as to what this contradiction could mean, one of our galleymen kept confidently affirming that the ship belonged to the Saracens. He told the king he might cut off his head or hang him on a tree if he failed to make good his assertion by incontrovertible proof, he said:

> Let us, now that they are skurrying away, send a second galley after them without giving them a single word of greeting; in this way we shall see what their intention is and what faith they hold.

Accordingly at the king's command a galley started after the strange ship at full speed. Seeing this, its sailors began to hurl arrows and darts against the crew of the galley, as it drew up alongside of them without offering any greeting. Noting this, Richard gave the word for an immediate onset. On either side the missiles fell like rain and the strange ship now went on at a slower rate, for the oarsmen had to slacken their efforts and there was not much wind. And yet, frequently as our galley-men made their circuits round the enemy, they could find no good opportunity of attacking; so strongly was the vessel built and so well was it manned with warriors, who kept on hurling their darts without a pause.

Our men, on the other hand, were grievously bestead by these darts, falling, as they did, from a vessel of such extraordinary height; for it is no little advantage to have the blind forces of nature on one's side; and it is much easier for a dart to do damage to things beneath it, if it is hurled from above, seeing that it falls downwards of its own accord. For these reasons our men began to falter and relaxed their efforts, wondering what the peerless courage of the unconquered King Richard himself would deem the best course under these circumstances. But he boldly called out to his own men as follows:

"What! are you going to let that vessel get off untouched and unharmed? Shame upon you! After so many triumphs will you let sloth get hold of you now and give way like cowards?—

ever so long as any foes
Remain, are you to seek repose.

—Well do you know, all of you, that you will deserve to be hung on a gallows and put to death if you suffer these enemies to escape."

On hearing these words our galley-men, making a virtue of necessity, plunged eagerly into the sea and getting under the enemy's ship bound the helm with ropes so as to make the vessel lean to one side and hinder its progress. Others, pushing alongside with great skill and perseverance, grasped hold of the cordage and leapt on board. The Turks were ready for these and slew them promptly, cutting off one man's arms, another man's hands or head, and pitching the dead bodies out to sea. This sight roused the other Christians to greater valour... so that scrambling over the ship's bulwarks they hurled themselves upon the Turks and gave no quarter to those who offered any resistance.

But the Turks emboldened by despair used every effort to repel the galley-men, and succeeded in cutting off a foot here, a hand or a head there; whilst their opponents, straining every nerve, drove the Turks back to the very prow of the ship. Upon this other Turks came rushing up from the hold of the vessel and, massed into one body with their fellows, offered a stout resistance, being determined to die bravely or repulse their adversaries like men. For these were the very flower of the Turkish youth—a band skilled in warlike exploits and well-armed.

So, the fight continued and warriors fell everywhere on either side till at last the Turks, pressing on with greater vigour, forced our men back and compelled them to quit the ship Our galleymen accordingly betook themselves to their own galleys and again began to row round the ship, looking out for a place suitable for attack.

Meanwhile the king, noting the danger of his men, and seeing that it would be no easy thing to take the Turkish vessel with all its arms and stores intact, gave orders for each of his galleys to prick the enemy with its spur (*i.e.*, with its iron beak). Accordingly, the galleys, after drawing back a space, are once more swept forward under the impulse of many oars to pierce the enemy's sides. By these tactics the ship was stove in at once, and, giving an inlet to the waves, began to sink; while the Turks, to avoid going down with their vessel, leapt overboard into the sea, where they were slain or drowned. The king, however, spared thirty-five of them, to wit the *emirs* and those skilled in the making of warlike engines. All the others perished; the warlike gear was lost, and the serpents were drowned or tossed about here and there on the sea waves.

Had that ship got safe into Acre the Christians would never have taken the city. Thus did God bring disaster upon the *infidels*, while to the Christians who trusted in him, he gave help at the hands of King Richard, whose warlike endeavours prospered without intermission.

Certain Saracens who had been watching all that took place from the distant hills were grieved beyond measure and carried the news to Saladin.

★★★★★★★★

Selah-ad-Din al Malec an-Nasr Abu 'l Modafler Yussuf, the son of Ayub, the Governor of Tecrit on the Tigris. In December, 1168, Saladin unwillingly accompanied his uncle, Shircuh, Nuradin's lieutenant, for the conquest of Egypt. Shircuh died 23 March, 1169, and was succeeded by his nephew. Saladin's growing power soon excited the suspicion of Nuradin, who died while preparing to march against him (ob. 15 May, 1174). By the end of October Saladin was master of Damascus and in 1175 threw off all dependency on Nuradin's son, Al Malec as-Salah Ismail. In November, 1182, he was conquering along the banks of the Tigris. Though he failed to take Mosul, he was now by far the greatest prince in Western Asia and, within a few years, was ready to undertake the conquest of Palestine, a short account of which has been given in the preface. He died on Wednesday, or rather Thursday, 4 March, 1193, after an illness of twelve days.

★★★★★★★★

He immediately, on hearing their story, seized his beard and in his rage plucked out the hair. Then with many sighs he burst out into speech, "*O Alia kibar ychalla*," *i.e.*, "O God Almighty, now have I lost Acre and those chosen men in whom I placed my trust; I am overcome and oppressed by the harshness of my fate."

In the Saracen host—so those who witnessed the whole occurrence tell us—there was great weeping and howling, insomuch that men cut off their hair for grief and tore their garments, cursing the hour and the star that brought them to Syria; for in the ship, we have been talking of there perished the very choicest flower of their youth, in whom they had most trust.

THE SARACEN ACCOUNT OF THE GREAT SHIP'S LOSS.
Bohâdin.

On the sixteenth of *Jomada* I. (*i.e.*, 11 June, 1191) there came to Beyrout a ship of vast size, laden with warlike implements, with arms, provisions, and valiant men. This ship the *sultan* had ordered his people of Beyrout to fit out and furnish with many soldiers that it might force its way into the city, despite the enemy. It held six hundred and fifty valiant men of war; but the English (king) sunk it after surrounding it with a fleet of forty sail. (Howden makes the vessel hold 1,500 men, of whom Richard only spared 200 according to Ralph de Diceto.)

For just as the battle began, by some fatal chance, the wind dropped and the enemy climbed up the sides after much slaughter, though not without loss to themselves. Our men, however, burnt a vessel of vast bulk belonging to the enemy; and all who were within, many though they were, perished to a man.

But, for all this, the enemy, thanks to their numbers, harassed our seamen greatly. Now when the captain, a man of great valour and much warlike experience, saw that all things boded imminent disaster and that there was no way of escaping death, he called aloud:

By *Allah*, we will seek a noble death; and we will not yield even the smallest morsel of our craft into the hands of the foe.

Thus, he spoke; and those on board began straightway with axes to cleave and bore through their own vessel, until they had, as it were, flung wide the gates by which the water might enter on every side. All men on board were drowned and with them there went down the warlike gear, the victuals, and everything else, so that the enemy carried off no booty. Now the name of this captain was Jacob of Aleppo. One only, of our men who were in the water, did they rescue from

51

drowning. Him they took up into their ships and granting him his life they let him go to the city with the news of our disaster. On hearing the misfortune, all the rest were grievously distressed; but the *sultan* accepted this also with the hand of resignation for the sake of God, who will not suffer the reward of them that love righteousness to perish.

1191, JUNE 8.—RICHARD REACHES ACRE. THE ILLUMINATION. THE FRENCH KING BEGINS THE ATTACK.

When Guy de Lusignan was set free in May, 1188, he seems to have spent a year in Tortosa, Antioch, and Tripoli collecting troops for the siege of Acre. On August 22, 1189, he sat down before this city with 700 knights and 9,000 men at arms gathered out of every Christian nation. Two days later the first instalment of warriors from W. Europe came. After more than one futile assault on the city, which they were not numerous enough to blockade completely, they had to trench themselves in from sea to sea, as a protection against Saladin, who was now holding the neighbouring heights. The Christians had thus at the time of King Richard's arrival been themselves besieged for considerably over a year and a half.

Itin. iii.

After destroying this ship King Richard and all his company hastened with joy and eagerness towards Acre, where he longed to be. Thanks to a favourable wind on the very next night his fleet cast anchor off Tyre. Early next morning he hoisted sail once more, and had not gone very far before they caught sight of that place we have mentioned before—Scandalion; thence passing by Casal Imbert the lofty tower of Acre rose up in the distance, and then by degrees the other fortifications of the city.

★★★★★★★★

Scandalion was built by Baldwin I. probably on the ruins of an earlier fortress. Fulcher of Chartres and Marino Sanuto place it between Tyre and Acre, five miles from the former city. The Franks called it by folk-etymology Camp de Lions.

Casal Imbert is said to be now, (1900), represented by the hill-ruins of El Hamsin, lying left of the road between Tyre and Acre, some four leagues (French) from the latter town.

Acre was taken by Baldwin I. 26 May, 1104; surrendered to Saladin about July 8, 1187; recaptured by the Christians July 12, 1191. It was the last Christian stronghold to fall in the Holy Land (17 June, 1291), of which since the taking of Jerusalem in 1187 it had been the capital.

★★★★★★★★

Acre was then girt round on every side by an infinite number of people from every Christian nation under heaven—the chosen warriors of all Christian lands, men well fitted to undergo the perils of war. Now this host had been besieging the city for a long time in spite of hunger, toil, misfortune, and every kind of distress, just as has been related in the earlier parts of this book. Moreover, beyond them lay an innumerable army of Turks swarming on the mountains and valleys, the hills, and the plains, and having their tents, bright with coloured devices of all kinds, pitched everywhere.

Our men could also see Saladin's own pair of lions and those of his brother Saphadin, and Takadin (Saladin's nephew), the champion of heathendom. Saladin himself was keeping a watch on the sea-coasts and harbours without however ceasing to contrive frequent and fierce attacks upon the Christians. King Richard too, looking forth, reckoned up the number of his foes; and as he reached the harbour the King of France, together with the chiefs of the whole army, all the lords and mighty men, welcomed him with joy and exultation; for they had long been very eager for him to arrive.

It was on (June 8) the Saturday before the feast of the blessed Barnabas the apostle, in Pentecost week, that King Richard with his followers reached Acre. On his arrival the whole land was stirred with the exulting glee of the Christians. For all the people were in transports, shouting out congratulations and blowing trumpets. He was brought ashore with jubilant cries; and there was great joy because the desired of all nations had come. The besieged Turks on the other hand were in the utmost terror and distress because of his arrival; for they saw well that all chances of entrance to and egress from their city were at an end, owing to the number of the king's galleys.

The two kings came down from the harbour together and shewed their respect for one another by graceful courtesies. Then King Richard, withdrawing into the tents that had been prepared for him, set about arranging his affairs, giving special consideration to the question as to what kind of engines were best fitted for taking the city. No pen can describe the joy of the people at his arrival; no tongue can express it.

Even the cloudless night was thought to smile upon his coming with a clearer air than usual. Here the trumpets thundered and there the clarions blared. Here the flutes mingled their shriller tones with the din of drums and the harsher murmurs of the "troinae" till it seemed that all these many discordant sounds blended together in a symphony very pleasant to the ear. Nor was it easy to find anyone who did not share in the general joy and welcome; to which all bore witness by thundering out popular songs or—

Ringing out the praise
And deeds of earlier days,

—enumerated old achievements as incentives to the men of their own day. Some served the minstrels with wine in precious goblets, others, the mean mingling with the mighty, welcomed all comers indifferently and passed the night in utmost glee. Moreover, the fact that Richard had reduced Cyprus was an additional cause of joy; for this island was very handy and well furnished with all things needful for an army.

Lastly, as a proof of the delight that was now springing up in all hearts, the gloom of night was everywhere dispelled by the gleam of waxen lights, till, as the number of the candles increased, night seemed to have borrowed the brightness of day and the Turks thought the whole valley was in a blaze.

The Pisans, wondering at Richard's magnificence and glory, came to him, offering their homage and fealty and, of their own free will, binding themselves to his rule and service. But the crafty Turks early on the Sunday morning (June 9) made a show of attacking us. . . .

And now that the host of both kings was united the whole Christian army, vast as it was, became as one. With the King of France, who had reached Acre on the octave of Easter, there had come the Counts of Flanders and St. Pol, William de Garlande, William des Barres, Drogo de Amiens, William de Merlo, and the Count of Perche, (son of Rotrode II. one of the warriors in the first Crusade.) With them also returned to Acre the marquis of whom we have spoken before, who now held Tyre and aspired to the kingdom of Jerusalem. There was no man of great power or fame in France who did not come then or later to besiege Acre.

King Richard arrived about Whitsuntide with his host and warlike stores. When he learnt that the King of France had paid each of his knights three *aurei* a month, and by this means had gained great popularity, King Richard that he might not be outdone or equalled in generosity, made heralds proclaim throughout the whole army that upon certain terms he would give knights of any land four gold pieces a month if they needed pay. (An *aureus*, or gold piece, was the *bezant* of the Greek Empire, about the size and weight of a Napoleon. It formed the regular gold currency of all Europe, for the Western States practically did not coin gold but used a silver currency. See note A on Mediaeval Coinage.)

For this cause all people gave open praise to King Richard, saying that he must excel all other men in worth and kindly feeling because he surpassed them in his gifts and magnanimity. They would say:

> This is the man, for whom we have so eagerly waited. How soon then, now that he is come, will the assault be made? At last, the most peerless of kings has arrived, the most skilful warrior among Christian men; now let God's will be done.

For, of a surety, the hope of all rested on King Richard

Now when the king had tarried at Acre but a few days he fell ill of a grievous sickness commonly known as *Arnoldia*. (Philip was taken ill of the same disorder. William le Breton attributes this disease to poison.) This disemper is due to the climate of an unknown region that sorted ill with his constitution; but, none the less for this, did he during the whole course of his illness continue the construction of his *petrariae* and *mangonels* (instruments for casting great stones) and the erection of a castle before the city-gate. For he devoted his whole energies to the preparation of warlike engines.

Then the King of France, wearied at so long a delay in commencing the attack, sent word to King Richard that now was a fitting time to begin and to move up the army to the onset by herald proclamation. Richard, in reply, said he was not yet at leisure for carrying out such a plan, because of the serious illness that was on him and also because adverse winds were keeping back his men; nevertheless, he trusted they would come with the next fleet and bring with them materials for making engines of war. The King of France, however, deeming this no sufficient ground for delaying the execution of his project, ordered the heralds to proclaim the attack throughout the army.

So, on the Monday after St. John's Nativity, (if this date is right, it should be July 1, 1189), the King of France, having his engines of war ready, bade all his soldiers arm. Then might one see an innumerable host of men, all fairly armed, with many a bright coat of ring-mail, and many a glittering crest. Then might you see noble steeds covered with their shining trappings and neighing (for the combat); and chosen knights—in such numbers as had never been beheld there before: so many henchmen of great valour, so many pennons, so many banners wrought with different devices.

Itin, iii..

Now while the army, owing to the sickness of the two kings, pined away from excessive grief at having no prince left to be its leader in the battles of the Lord, its misfortunes were aggravated by the unexpected death of the Count of Flanders. The general grief was however somewhat assuaged by the arrival of several fresh vessels, which, after a prosperous voyage, brought many bishops and great lords—each with his own train of followers—to the Christians' aid.

The names of the newcomers were the Bishop of Evreux, Roger de Tooney, several brothers and kinsmen surnamed de Corneby, Robert de Newburgh, Jordan de Humez, the Chamberlain de Tankerville, Count Robert of Leicester, Gerard de Taleboz, Ralph Taisson; also the knights called Torolenses, the Viscount of Châteaudun, Bertram de Verdun, Roger de Hardencourt, the Knights of Préaux, Warin Fitz Gerald, Henry Fitz Nicholas, Ernald de Magneville, the men of Stutteville, William Marcel, William Malet, Andrew de Chavigny, Hugh Brown, &c, &c, and Hugh de Fierté. This latter had been present at the conquest of Cyprus, whence he had come to Acre. The two kings continued ill, but yet God had preserved them to take the city.

When the King of France got well from his sickness, he devoted himself to preparing his engines and setting up his stone-slings in fitting places, from which he kept them working night and day. He had one very good engine of war called "The Bad Neighbour"; and, within the city, the Turks had another which they called "The Bad Kinsman," by whose assistance they frequently managed to destroy the "Bad Neighbour." The King of France on his part kept rebuilding the latter machine till by constant blows he had partly overthrown the chief wall of the city and shattered the "Accursed Tower." On one side the stone-sling of the Duke of Burgundy used also to work, and not without effect; on the other that of the Templars wrought the Turks vast injury, whilst that of the Hospitallers—equally dreaded by the Turks—kept plying always.

Besides all these there was a certain stone-sling, built out of common funds, which they used to call God's stone-sling. Close by it a certain priest, a man of the greatest integrity, was always preaching and at the same time begging money for its reconstruction or for the payment of those who collected the stones it discharged. By its blows the wall near "the Accursed Tower", (see note C on the topography of Acre), was shaken for a length of two perches. The Count of Flanders, too, had a peculiarly choice stone-sling, to say nothing of a smaller one. King Richard took possession of the former on the count's death. These two stone-slings kept plying at a tower near one of the gates, much frequented by the Turks, till it was half smashed in.

Moreover, King Richard had made two other new stone-slings of remarkable material and workmanship, and these hit the mark at an incredible distance. He had also built an engine of the strongest construction of beams. It had steps fitted to it for getting up, and was commonly known as the belfry. (See Note D.) This engine was covered with closely-fitting hides, with ropes, and strong planks of wood, so as not to be destroyed by the blows of the stone-slings or even by Greek fire. (Richard) had also got ready two *mangonels*—one of them of such power that it could hurl its charge into the very middle of the city market.

King Richard's stone-slings were plying night and day, and it is a known fact that a single stone discharged from one of this king's engines slew twelve men. This stone was sent to Saladin for him to look at. The messengers who carried it said that that devil the King of England had brought from the captured city of Messina (a store of) such sea-flints and most lustrous stones for doing execution on the Saracens. Nothing, they went on, could resist the blows of these stones without being shattered or ground to powder. Meanwhile the king, whose fever was getting worse, lay on his bed, chafing sorely when he saw the Turks challenging our men, whilst his sickness prevented him from attacking them. For the constant onsets of the Turks caused him keener pangs than the most fiery throes of his fever.

Acre seemed a city very hard to take, not only because of the natural strength of its position, but also because it was defended by the very choicest Turkish troops. It was all to no purpose that the French had spent so much pains on constructing engines of war and implements for pulling down the walls; because the Turks by a sudden volley of Greek fire would destroy everything their enemies had prepared, no matter at what expense, and consume it utterly with fire. Now, among the other engines made by the King of the French was one which he had constructed with the utmost care. It was intended for scaling the walls, and for this reason was called "The Cat," because after creeping up in the manner of a cat it got a grip of the wall and stuck last to it.

He had also finished another contrivance of hurdles very strongly fastened together with twigs, and this the people used to call the *circleia*. Under this little hurdle, covered with raw hides, the king used to take his seat anxiously discharging bolts from his cross-bow and watching his opportunity to strike any unwary Turk on the battlements of the city. Now it chanced one day, while the French were drawing too close to the walls in their eagerness to bring up the *cat*, that the Turks cast a heap of dry wood over the walls on to the *cat*. Then, without any delay, they discharged a quantity of Greek fire down upon the *circleia* that had been prepared with such great care. After this they set up a stone-sling, taking aim at the same place, when lo! suddenly everything is in flames or destroyed by the blows of the stone-sling.

Upon this the King of France, madly wrath, began to curse with horrid oaths at all who were under his rule and to chide them with shameful reproaches for not taking vengeance against the Saracens who had done him such a wrong. In the heat of his anger, as evening drew on, he proclaimed an attack for the morrow by herald's voice.

Early next morning chosen guards were set at the outer ditches to keep off sudden attacks of the Saracens (outside). For Saladin had bragged that on the same day he would cross the trenches in full force and shew his valour, to the destruction of the Christians.

But he did not keep his word; for he did not come himself, but his fierce and persistent army, under his lieutenant Kahadin, (Takadin), hurling itself in great masses against the trenches, was valiantly opposed by the French. There was no small slaughter on either side. The Turks, dismounting, advanced on foot. The fight went on at close quarters with drawn swords, daggers, and two-headed axes, not to mention clubs that bristled with sharpened teeth. The Turks press on; the valorous Christians, drive them back; each side rages with a two-fold fury; for it was the time of summer heat.

That part of the army destined to take the city continued hurling darts, undermining the walls, pounding away with engines or creeping up to scale the walls. The Turks, dreading the courage of these assailants, signalled to their fellows outside by raising aloft the standard of Saladin in the hopes that (their friends) would come to their aid at once or draw off the enemy by an attack (in the rear). Seeing this Kahadin and his Turks, pressing on with all their vigour, filled the ditch, but were resisted and driven back by our men, who, thanks to God, stood like an impenetrable wall. Meanwhile the King of France's diggers gradually burrowing by subterranean passages reached the very foundations of the walls and filled the chasm they had made with logs, to which they set fire.

Then, when the fire had consumed the beams upholding the wall, a great part of it gave way, sloping down by degrees, but not falling flat. Very many Christians ran up to this spot in the hope of entering, whilst the Turks came up to drive them back. Oh! how many banners might you then see and devices of many a shape, not to mention the desperate (valour) of the Turks as they hurled Greek fire against our men. Here the French brought up ladders, and attempted to scale the wall that was not quite prostrate; there the Turks on the other hand used ladders to defend the breach.

A noble exploit wrought on this occasion must not be passed over in silence. (Howden dates this Wednesday, 3rd July. Bohâdin seems also to place this attack at 2nd-3rd July.) There was a man famous for his valour, Alberic Clements by name. He, seeing the French sweating from their urgent efforts and yet profiting little, called out "Today I will either die or, with God's will, enter Acre." So, saying he boldly climbed the ladder, gained the top of the wall, and slew many of the Turks, who rushed upon him from every side.

When the French were on the point of following him up the ladder it broke, (a frequent occurrence at mediaeval sieges), owing to the numbers on it; for it could not bear so many. Some of them were crushed to death, others were drawn off heavily wounded. The Turks surrounded and overcame Alberic Clements, who, being left alone on the top of the wall, was pierced with countless wounds. He thus made good his promise to die a martyr. At this misfortune the Turks were as much delighted as the French were downcast.

1191, July 5.—K. Richard besieges Acre and forces it to yield.

Itin. Ric.

King Richard was not yet quite recovered from his illness; yet, anxious to be doing something, he turned his thoughts to the capture of the city, and had it attacked by his men in the hopes of gaining some success with God's assistance. Accordingly, he had a kind of hurdle-shed (commonly called a *circleia*) made and brought up to the ditch outside the city wall. Under its shelter were placed his most skilful crossbow-men; whilst, to hearten his own men for the combat and to dispirit the Saracens by his presence, he had himself carried there on silken cushions.

From this position he worked a crossbow, in the management of which he was very skilful, and slew many of the foes by the bolts and quarrels he discharged. His miners also, approaching the tower against which his stone-casters were being levelled, by an underground passage dug down towards the foundations, filling the gaps they made with logs of wood, to which they would set fire, thus causing the walls, which had already been shaken by the stone-casters, to fall down with sudden crash. (On the night of Friday, 5th July, according to Howden.)

Thereupon the king, seeing how difficult the work was and how valiant were the enemies, knowing also how needful it was to kindle men's valour at critical moments, thought it more fitting to encourage the young (warriors) on by promises of reward than to urge them on by harsh words. For who is there whom the prospect of gain will not entice? Accordingly, he proclaimed that he would give two gold pieces to anyone who would detach a stone from the wall near the before-mentioned tower.

★★★★★★★★

Richard, who was well-read in history and romance, may possibly in this piece of magnificence have aimed at emulating that of Raymond of St. Giles at the siege of Jerusalem; Raymond offered a penny for every three stones cast into the ditch he wanted to fill up for his "*machina*" to cross.

★★★★★★★★

Later he promised three and even four gold-pieces for each stone. Then might you see the young men with their followers leap forth and rush against the wall and set themselves zealously to lugging out the stones—and this as much for the sake of praise as of pay. The height of the wall was very great and it was of no slight thickness; yet, dispelling danger, by courage, they extracted many a stone. The Turks rushing against (the assailants) in bands strove to cast them down from the walls; and, while thus engaged in driving back their enemies, unwarily exposed themselves to darts; for in their haste, they rashly neglected to put on their armour. One of the Turks who to his cost was glorying in the arms of Alberic Clements, with which he had girded himself, did King Richard wound to death, piercing him through the breast, with a dart from his cross-bow.

Grieving over the death of this warrior the Turks recklessly rushed forward for vengeance, and, just as though energetic action were a cure for pain, showed themselves so bold that it seemed as if they feared neither darts nor any other missile. Never were our men engaged by warriors—of any creed whatever—more valorous or apter at defence. Memory staggers at the recollection of their deeds. In the press of this conflict neither armour of strongest proof nor twofold coat of mail nor quilted work was strong enough to resist the missiles hurled from the stone-casters. Yet, for all this, the Turks kept countermining from within till they compelled our men to retreat; and then they began to raise a furious cry as though their object had been attained.

CRUSADERS ATTACKING FORTRESS. *From a MS. of William of Tyre (early half of 13th cent.) in the library of M. Ambr. Firmin Didot.*

At last, when the tower had fallen prostrate before the blows of our stone-casters and when King Richard's men began to stop digging, our men-at-arms, (Thursday, 11th July, according to Howden or Saturday, July 6th *Itinerarium*) in their greed for fame and victory, began to don their arms. Amongst the banners of these were the Earl of Leicester's; that of Andrew de Chavigni and of Hugh Brown. The Bishop of Salisbury also came up, equipt in the noblest fashion, and many more. It was about the third hour, *i.e.*, about breakfast time, when these valorous men-at-arms began their work, going forth to storm the tower, which they boldly scaled at once. The Turkish watchmen, on seeing them, raised a shout, and lo! the whole city was soon in a stir.

The Turkish warriors, hurriedly seizing their arms, came thronging up and flung themselves upon the assailants. The men-at-arms strove to get in; the Turks to hurl them back. Rolled together in a confused mass they fought at close quarters, hand against hand, and sword against sword. Here men struck, there they fell. Our men-at-arms were few, whereas the numbers of the Turks kept on increasing. The Turks also threw Greek fire against their enemies, and this at last forced the men-at-arms to retreat and leave the tower, where some of them were slain by weapons, others burnt by that most deadly fire.

★★★★★★★★

Joinville describes the method of discharging Greek fire as follows:—
"Now the way of discharging Greek fire was such that it came on like a vessel of verjuice, while the tail that issued thence was big as a big lance. As it came on it would make a noise like a thunder-bolt; it seemed as if a dragon were flying through the air. So clear a lustre did it shed round that, throughout the army, one could see as if it were day by reason of greatness of the fire that cast forth this great light. Thrice did they cast the Greek fire against us that night, and four times did they shoot it from the *arbalestre à tour*."

★★★★★★★★

At last, the Pisans, eager for fame and vengeance, scrambled up the tower itself with a mighty effort; but bravely as they comported themselves, they too had to retreat before the onset of the Turks, who rushed on as if mad. Never has there been such a people as these Turks for prowess in war. And yet, for all the enemies' valour, the city would on that day have been taken and the whole siege finished if the entire army had displayed an equal valour. For, you must know, by far the larger part of the army was at that hour breakfasting; and, as the attack was made at an unsuitable time, it did not succeed.

Though its walls were partly fallen and partly shaken, though a great part of the inhabitants were slain or weakened by wounds, there still remained in the city 6,000 Turks. With these were the leaders, Mestoc, (Meshtub a Curdish chief), and Caracois, (Kara-kush Governor of Acre) who began now to despair of receiving aid. They imagined the Christian Army had been very keenly touched at the death of Alberic Clements and at the loss of sons and kinsmen who had fallen in the war; and had determined to die or master the Turks—holding that no other course was consistent with honour. So, by common consent and counsel, the besieged begged a truce while they sent notice of their plight to Saladin, hoping that, in accordance with their Pagan ways, he would ensure their safety—as he ought to do—by sending them speedy aid or procuring leave for them to quit the city without disgrace.

To obtain this favour, these two noble Saracens, the most renowned (warriors) in all Paganism, Mestoc and Caracois, came (Friday, 12th July, according to Howden), to our kings, promising to surrender the city, if Saladin did not send them speedy aid. They stipulated, however, that all the besieged Turks should have free leave to go wherever they wished with their arms and all their goods. The King of France and almost all the French agreed to this; but King Richard utterly refused to hear of entering an empty city after so long and toilsome a siege. Wherefore, perceiving King Richard's mind, Caracois and Mestoc went back to Acre without concluding the business.

Saladin, meanwhile, having received envoys from the besieged, bade them hold out stoutly in the certainty that he would shortly send them efficient aid. He declared that he had certain news of the approach of a mighty host of warriors from Babylon (*i.e.*, Cairo) in ships and galleys. These he had sent for some time ago and had given orders to Muleina (their leader) to come within eight days at the furthest. Moreover, he swore that, if these reinforcements should not arrive, he would do his best to get the besieged honourable terms and liberty to depart. So, the envoys returned to the city; and, after the publication of Saladin's promises and exhortations to hold out, the Turks remained anxiously looking out for the succour they expected.

Meanwhile, the Christians' stone casters never ceased battering the walls night and day. Seeing this a panic seized the inhabitants and some, in utter despair, giving way to fear, threw themselves headlong from the walls by night, (July 3rd-4th, according to Bohâdin.) Many of them humbly begged to be baptised and made Christians. There is considerable doubt as to the real merits of these (converts), and not without due reason, since it is to be presumed that it was terror rather than divine grace that caused them to make this request. But the ways of salvation are many.

Meanwhile, frequent envoys kept Saladin well-informed of the danger involved in continuing the defence; for the city could no longer be held against the Christians. So, Saladin, seeing that further delay would be perilous, at last granted the petitions of the besieged; and this he did the more readily because his *emirs*, his *satraps*, and his powerful friends urged him in the same direction; for (many of) these were friends and relatives of the besieged. They alleged that Saladin was bound by the oath he had taken to protect the besieged (Mohammedans) according to the forms of their law, and to secure honourable terms for men who were in such extreme peril, and who otherwise might, by the law of war, be put to a shameful death.

This would be to break, so far as lay in his power, the Mohammedan law—so carefully observed by his predecessors; while it would be most dishonouring to his fame if he suffered the Christians to capture the worshippers of Mahomet. They begged Saladin to consider how, in obedience to his commands, the flower of the Turks had endured so long a siege and defended his city. Let him remember their wives who were cooped up (within those walls) and their miserable families whom they had not seen since the beginning of the siege, three years before.

By such prayers Saladin was persuaded to consent to make a peace with as good terms as he could get; and, when the envoys brought back Saladin's reply, there was great joy in the city. And lo! the chief men of the city came out to our kings offering, by an interpreter, to give up Acre, to restore the Holy Cross, and set free two hundred and fifty noble Christian captives whom they had. But, as these terms did not seem satisfactory to our kings, they offered two thousand noble Christians and 500 captives of inferior rank, whom, they added, Saladin would have sought out throughout his whole land. In return for this, the Turks merely stipulated for leave to quit the city, without arms or food, and carrying nothing save their shirts. Moreover, they would give the two kings 200,000 Saracen *talents* for their life; and as a pledge for the faithful observance of these terms, they handed over the noblest Turks in the city as hostages. These terms our kings, after consulting their wise men, with the consent of all determined to accept.

Thus, on the Friday after the translation of the Blessed Benedict (*i.e.*, July 12), the wealthier and nobler *emirs* were proffered and accepted as hostages, one month being allowed for the restoration of the Holy Cross and the collection of the captive Christians. When the news of this surrender became known, the unthinking crowd was moved with wrath; but the wiser folk were much rejoiced at getting so quickly and without danger what previously they had not been able to obtain in so long a time. Then the heralds made proclamation forbidding anyone to insult the Turks by word or deed. No missiles were to be hurled against the walls or against the Turks if they chanced to appear on the battlements.

On that day, when these famous Turks, of such wonderful valour and warlike excellence, began strolling about on the city walls in all their splendid apparel, previous to their departure (our men) gazed on them with the utmost curiosity. They were wonder-struck at the cheerful features of men who were leaving their city almost penniless and whom only the very sternest necessity had driven to beg for mercy: men whom loss did not deject, and whose visage betrayed no timidity, but even wore the look of victory. It was only their superstitious rites and their pitiful idolatry that had robbed such warriors of their strength.

At last, when all the Turks had quitted Acre, the Christians entered the city in joy and gladness, glorifying God with a loud voice and yielding Him thanks for having magnified His mercy upon them and brought redemption to His people. Thus did the kings set their banners and varied ensigns on the walls and towers; while the city, together with all it contained in the way of victuals and arms, was equally divided between them. The captives too they reckoned up and halved by lot. To the King of France fell the noble Caracois and a great host of other folk; to King Richard, Mestoc and many more.

Moreover, the King of France had the noble palace of the Templars with all its appurtenances, while the royal palace fell to King Richard, who established the two queens there with their maidens and attendants. Thus, each king had his own part of the city in peace, whilst the army was distributed over its whole area, enjoying pleasant rest after so long and continuous a siege. On the night that followed our entry, Saladin retreated with his army from the place where he had camped and settled on a more distant hill.

On the day of its surrender the city had been in the hands of the Saracens four years. (Acre was really taken by Saladin almost immediately after the Battle of Hittin, and apparently between 8-20 July 1187.) It was surrendered, as has been already said, on the morrow of the translation of St. Benedict. But not without horror could the conquerors see the condition of the churches within the city; nor can they even now remember the shameful sights they witnessed there unmoved. What faithful Christian could, with tearless eyes, see the holy features of the crucified Son of God, or even of the saints, dishonoured and defiled? Who would not shudder when he actually saw the insulting way in which the accursed Turks had overthrown the altars, torn down and battered the holy crosses? Ay, and they had even set up their own images of Mahomet in the holy places, introducing foul Mohammedan superstitions, after casting out all the symbols of human redemption and the Christian religion.

THE SIEGE AND CAPTURE OF ACRE (SARACEN ACCOUNT).
Bohâdin.

From this moment (*Rabia* I. A. H. April 1191 *A.D.*), the war commenced afresh; for the milder weather gave either army an opportunity of renewing the Holy War. Soliman, an old man, famous for his rights and victories, was the first to arrive from Aleppo. He was no less skilled in counsel than in warfare, for which reason the *Sultan* held him in great honour and reckoned him a close friend. Next came the

Prince of Baalbec, after whose arrival our troops came up from every side. As regards the enemy, they, in the same manner, so often as they approached our cavalry kept threatening us with the speedy coming of the King of France. Now the King of France is a great ruler among them and pre-eminent above all their other kings in valour and majesty. To him they saw all the Christian forces would yield obedience as to an arbiter of supreme authority. At last, this king, with whose arrival we had so often been threatened, came with six ships, carrying himself, his comrades, food, and horses. He reached Acre on Saturday, the 23rd of *Rabia I.* (20 April, 1191.).

We must now speak of the King of England. Amongst our enemies he was a man of great activity, and of high soul, strong-hearted, famous for his many wars and of dauntless courage in battle. He was reckoned somewhat less than the King of the French so far as regards his royal dignity; but as much wealthier as he was more renowned for his warlike valour. When he reached Cyprus on his way, he deemed that he ought not to pass it by without conquering it, and so, leaving his ships, he attacked the island. Thereupon the lord of Cyprus advanced against him with huge forces, and a fierce battle was fought; after which the Englishman sent to Acre for King Guy and his brother Geoffrey, who came to aid him in his project with a hundred and sixty knights. Meanwhile the Frenchmen waited the issue of this undertaking at Acre. On the last day of *Rabia II.* (26 May) there came letters to Beyrout telling how five of the English ships had been captured while engaged on an expedition against our host. There was also taken a swift vessel laden with men, women, provisions, wooden beams, engines of war and various other things. It also contained forty horses. So signal a victory the Mussulmans regarded as a most joyful omen.

On Saturday, the thirteenth day of *Jomada I.* (8 June), the King of England, after having arranged matters with the lord of Cyprus and subduing the island, arrived (at Acre) with a great show of splendour and might. For he brought with him twenty-five ships of war all stored with men, arms, and weapons. For joy of his arrival the Franks broke forth into public rejoicings, lighting mighty fires in their camps all night long. These fires, being great and terrible to behold, denoted the vast number of our new enemies.

Now the kings (Guy of Jerusalem as well as of Philip Augustus) of our enemies had been threatening us constantly with the arrival of the King of England, and fugitives had brought us the same kind of news as to how the hostile army was delaying to undertake the siege till he had come. For he was a warrior old in war and wise in counsel. Wherefore the hearts of the Musulmans were lessened for fear and dread; but the *Sultan* took all things, as they came, with unmoved soul, relying on that God who always gives amply to the man who trusts in Him.

THE BESIEGED SENT TO THEIR FRIENDS. WHY SALADIN WOULD NOT MEET RICHARD. THE HARD STRAITS OF THE BESIEGED. 14 JUNE—C. 28 JUNE.

Bohâdin

On Friday the 19th day (of *Jomada I., i.e.,* 14 June) the enemy commenced a fierce attack on the city and pressed it hard. Now it had been agreed between us and the townsmen that they should beat their brass drums whenever the enemy made an assault. These now began to beat; and, the *Sultan's* drums making answer, our armies were soon in motion and bearing down upon the foe with such vigour that the Musulmans crossed the fosse and bursting into the tents beyond, carried off the pots with the food in them. Part of this booty was brought to the *Sultan* while I was looking on.

On Monday the 23rd (*i.e.,* 18 June, which however was a Tuesday) the town drum was heard going again; the *Sultan's* drum made answer and a fierce contest waged once more

When the enemy saw the valour of the Musulmans and the wonderful way in which they held out against their misfortunes, they sent a special messenger to beg that passage might be given for an envoy. The permission was granted and the envoy betook himself first to Al-Malek Al-Adil, and in his company went to the *Sultan's* quarters. At this time Al-Malek Al-Afdal was with the *Sultan.* Then (the envoy) told his message and instructions which amounted to this, that the King of England desired an interview with the *Sultan.* On hearing this the *Sultan* made answer straightway, without any thought or counsel:

"Kings, do not meet for purposes of speech except a treaty has been already struck; it would not be seemly for them to wage war one against the other after they have talked and banqueted together. If (your king) desires an interview we must first agree on terms of peace. An interpreter must also be found to go between us in order that we may understand each other; and he must be a man in whom we can both feel confidence. If these conditions be rigidly fulfilled, we will with God's will have a meeting."

On the Sunday, the 29th of *Jomada I.,* (June 24, a Monday not a

Sunday) the enemy came forth again with his footmen in close array along the bank of the Nahr-al Halou. (See note C.) A squadron of our cavalry met them and an engagement followed. . . . They slew a Musulman whom they had taken prisoner and burnt him. Our men soon returned the compliment by burning one of the enemy whom they had in like manner captured. I myself saw the two pyres burning at one and the same time.

Meanwhile there was no lack of frequent messengers from the besieged townsmen who brought us news of their distress and made complaints of the close attack that lasted night and day. They told us also how wearied they were from such a stern and lengthened series of misfortunes as had befallen them from the time when the Englishman arrived. He indeed, they reported, was now afflicted with a grievous disease and lay at death's door. The King of France also had been wounded. And yet by these pieces of good fortune they gained nothing but this, that the siege was pressed on with more vigour than ever.

Now the King of England's sister had two slaves who had been in her service in Sicily while she was wife of the King of that island. These slaves were secretly attached to the Musulman faith. When, after the King of Sicily's death, the queen's brother had crossed over into that island, he had carried her away to his army. About this time these two slaves fled to us, were received into fealty by the *Sultan*, and treated with great generosity

Meanwhile (c. 3 *Jom. II.*, *i.e.*, 28 June) the King of England's illness had grown so much worse that, because of its vehemence, the Franks were drawn off from besieging the city. This was a plain token of the Divine favour towards us; for the town and all who were within it were in the very last stage of weakness, and were being as it were strangled without power to utter a cry, because the engines were beating the walls down to a man's height.

During this time Arab robbers hired by the *Sultan* used to enter the enemy's tents and rob them of what they could find. They even used to take prisoners without any fighting. And this was the way they did it. They would enter a man's tent while he was asleep and wake him by putting a dagger at his throat. Then by signs they would give him to understand that if he said a word, they would finish him off; after which they led him outside the camp bound and brought him to our army, while the prisoner dared not open his mouth. This took place several times.

RICHARD'S NEGOTIATIONS WITH SALADIN.

Bohâdin

I have made mention above of the envoy who begged an interview with Saladin on the part of the Englishman. I have also told on what pretext the *Sultan* refused the petition. Sometime after he presented himself anew on the same business. He had an interview with Al Malec al Adil first, and this prince carried all he said to the *Sultan*. At last, it was decided that Al Adil should have a meeting with the Englishman in the plain. Both the armies were to be present and an interpreter was to be found. When all had been arranged the envoy made a delay of some days on account of the Englishman's illness. And now it became noised "abroad that the princes (of the enemy) had gathered together and reproached him (*i.e.*, Richard) vehemently, saying that he had been the cause of a most urgent peril to the Christian religion. But his envoy returning (to us) a little later delivered us this message in his name:

> Do not imagine that I have been delayed in this business for the reason that is currently reported. For the reins of my rule have been delivered into my hand; and I am the arbiter of my own affairs and subject to the will of no one. But at this time a grievous distemper has seized me so that I am not able to stir. This is the sole cause of my delay. Now it is the wont of kings when they are near to send one another gifts, and I have a present that will not be unpleasing to the *Sultan*, whom I beg to grant me an opportunity of offering it.

To this proposal Al Adil consented on condition of being allowed to make a present in return; and the envoy, agreeing, began again:

> Our gift consists of certain falcons which have been brought from beyond the sea. These are unwell now; and it would be advisable that pullets and hens should be sent us. By such diet may our birds recover their strength and be sent to you.

To this Al-Adil merrily made answer, (for being a wise man he knew well what reply he ought to make):

> Your king himself wants some fowls for his own table, and is trying to wheedle them from us on this pretext.

The interview was then brought to an end in such a manner that the envoy asked:

Pray, then, what is it that you demand of us. Come, tell it out if you really have anything to say, so that we may hear it.

To him we made answer:

Nay, we seek nothing of you; it is you that ask of us? Wherefore if you have anything to say tell it out that we may hear it.

Then was that negotiation broken off till the sixth of the later *Jomada* (*i.e.*, 1 July), when the envoy of the Englishman went forth bringing with him a certain man from Maghreb (*i.e.*, West Africa)—a Musulman whom the enemy had held captive for a long time, but whom they now set free as a gift to the *Sultan*. This captive the *Sultan* received with honour, and after bestowing splendid gifts upon him sent him back to his lord. It was the intention of that (Englishman) by sending these embassies to find out whether we were strong-hearted or weak; moreover, our aim in admitting them was the same.

On Friday, the 17 of *Jomada* II. (*i.e.,* 12 July), a swimmer arrived from the town with letters. These announced that the garrison being reduced to the last extremity was now too weak to defend the breach in the wall which had now become very large. The inhabitants saw nothing but death before them and did not doubt that they would all be massacred if the town fell by assault. For which reasons the garrison had concluded a treaty of peace according to the terms of which the town, with all the warlike engines it contained, was to be delivered to the Franks. They were also to pay 200,000 pieces of gold and to restore five hundred prisoners of ordinary condition and a hundred others of noble rank, whom the Franks might ask for by name.

They engaged also to give up the Holy Cross. If these terms were accepted the Musulmans might go forth without any harm, carrying their money and their personal effects with them, and accompanied by their wives and children. It was bargained in addition that the marquis should have 4,000 pieces of gold for effecting the treaty.

★★★★★★★★

Conrad had left Acre June 25. Howden assigns him a similar payment. Conrad, a younger son of William III., Marquis of Montferrat, started for the East in 1186, where his elder brother, William Longsword, had in 1180 married Sibylla, the daughter of Amalric I. of Jerusalem. Contrary winds drove him to Constantinople where he succeeded in maintaining Isaac Angelus on the throne, during a dangerous rebellion, and received his sister Theodora in marriage. Leaving Constantinople by stealth next year he reached Acre only to find it already in the hands of the Saracens. Falling back upon Tyre he persuaded this city to hold out against Saladin, and thus saved the Holy Land from entire conquest. In Nov., 1190, he was married to Isabella, Amalric's other daughter, who had just been divorced from her first husband, Henfrid of Toron. For this act he was excommunicated by Archbishop Baldwin of Canterbury. During the siege of Acre, the Christians accused him loudly of treachery, and attributed their famine in the winter of 1190-1 to his neglect. He was murdered by the envoys of the Old Man of the Mountains. as will be seen later on, April 28, 1192.

★★★★★★★★

The *Sultan*, after learning the contents of these letters from the town, was much annoyed and, calling together a council, took advice as to what he should do. Opinions varied and no conclusion was arrived at. In his distress he made up his mind to despatch the swimmer by night with another letter, expressing his formal disapproval of the conditions agreed on. He was still in this troubled state when suddenly the Musulmans saw the banners of the enemy with their crosses and distinguishing emblems fixed on the walls. Fires of joy were also gleaming from the ramparts. All this took place on Friday, 17th of the later *Jomada*, in the year 587 (12 July, 1191), at midday. The Franks uttered cries of joy, but the Musulmans, stunned and saddened by so sudden a blow, made their camp resound with their groans and lamentation.

The marquis entered the town with the kings' banners and on the same Friday planted them where the banners of Islam had stood. One was set on the castle; another on the minaret of the great mosque, a third on the Templars' tower, and a fourth on the Tower of Combat. The Musulmans were forced to dwell in a separate quarter of the town. At that moment I was in attendance on the *Sultan* and, seeing him as much dejected as a mother who has just lost her child, I tried to console him with the commonplaces so often used on such occasions, bidding him think of what would happen to the other towns along the sea-coast (if he did not bestir himself) and consider means for the deliverance of the Musulman prisoners in Acre. All this took place on the night preceding Saturday the 18th.

THE HOSPITAL AND CEMETERY OF S. THOMAS AT ACRE.

Ralph of Diceto, ii.

Towards the beginning of the siege of Acre, a certain Englishman, William by name, chaplain to Ralph de Diceto, the Dean of London, bound himself on his way to Jerusalem by a vow that if he came speedily and safely to the harbour at Acre he would build there, so far as his means permitted, a chapel to St. Thomas the Martyr, and would get a cemetery consecrated in the same place in honour of the martyr. This he did and, when many people from all parts began to offer themselves for service at the said chapel, William took the title of prior and, though he proved himself to be Christ's knight by the devotion of his whole self, took special care for the poor and for the burial both of those who fell victims to the sword and disease.

So earnestly and diligently did he busy himself in these works that to men's sight he seemed the nearest counterpart of the great Tobit. There is also at Acre another cemetery which is called the Hospital of the Germans, and a third, more ancient than the other two, called the Hospital of St. Nicholas, in which, before the siege was over, 124,000 men were buried in the course of one year.

QUARRELS BETWEEN THE KINGS (FRENCH ACCOUNT).

Eracles, 179.

After this Philip Count of Flanders fell ill of a severe sickness of which he died. Now he, dreading the illness in which he was, sent for the King of France, having a great longing to speak with him before he died. So, the king came to where the count lay ill and, while they were speaking together, the count warned the king to be on his guard, because there were many people in the army who had sworn his death. I cannot tell who they were, (but) the king, keeping this word in his heart, was sore troubled and angered till he too fell very ill of a double tertian.

So severely did this ailment attack him that he was well-nigh dead. Now, while he lay thus sick, King Richard conceived a great felony, casting about how he might slay the King of France without laying a hand on him. For he felt that he was guilty towards that king whose reproaches could not help reaching his ears. . . .

While the King of France lay sick of this illness the King of England went to pay him a visit. Now, in visiting him, he made inquiries as to how he was, to which the king replied that he was in the hands of God, but felt very much weakened by his illness. Then said King Richard, "And how do you console yourself (in the matter of) Louis your son?"

Then the King of France demanded:

"What then hath hapt to Louis my son, for which I should need consolation?"

"For this very reason am I come," said the King of England, "to comfort you; because he is dead!"

Then said King Philip, "Needs must I now take heart all the more seeing that, if I die in this country, the realm of France will be without an heir."

From that moment his illness abated and the fever left him, while King Richard took leave of him and departed. Full well he deemed he had achieved his end; but malice cannot prosper where God is minded to be merciful. Foul felony it was that King Richard had meditated against the King of France; yet did he not rejoice in success but shame fell upon him and his heirs. When King Richard had departed (King Philip) called the Duke of Burgundy and William des Barres and others of his privy council and demanded 1 of them on their oath and the fealty they had done him to let him know if they had had news of his son Louis' death. Then answered him the Duke of Burgundy:

> Since you came to the siege of Acre there has arrived no vessel from beyond the sea that could bring such news. But the King of England has told you this in felony and malice, thinking to grieve you in your illness from which he would have you not recover.

KING PHILIP'S SICKNESS (ANOTHER ACCOUNT).

Will, le Breton, Philippeis, iv.

While these things were doing Philip lay sick in Acre attended by but a few followers; for he was taken with a fierce fever and frequent tremblings. Such violent irritation, so fierce a heat, laid waste his bones and all his limbs that every nail fell off his fingers and all the hair from his brow; wherefore it was then thought (nor is this rumour at rest even now) that he had been poisoned.

But the divine grace spared him to us, lest France, too soon robbed of her horn, should mourn one through whose ceaseless care she was in later times to enjoy the ease of lengthened peace. And thus, though he long lay sick, afterwards he began to recover by slow degrees; and since he could not be entirely healed where he was, on the kindly advice of his nobles and leeches he became eager to return to his own land and his native fields.

But before starting he told out from his private means pay to support 500 knights for three years. To these he added 1,000 foot soldiers, whose business it was watchfully and faithfully to fight in his stead for the Lord's Sepulchre. The leadership of these troops he entrusted to the Duke of Burgundy.

1191, JULY.—KING RICHARD AND KING PHILIP QUARREL OVER THE CLAIMANTS TO THE THRONE OF JERUSALEM. PHILIP SWEARS TO RESPECT RICHARD'S RIGHTS IN EUROPE AND GOES HOME, SAILING FROM ACRE, JULY 31 (ENGLISH ACCOUNT)

Itinerary iii.

As time went on there arose a fierce quarrel between the two kings. Of this quarrel the marquis was the occasion. For the King of France favoured his claim and was minded to grant him all that he had acquired or might yet acquire in the Holy Land; whereas King Richard, out of pity for King Guy's misfortunes, would not agree to this, thinking that the latter had the better claim.

After a long dispute, the chiefs intervened and the two kings were pacified on the following conditions: That the marquis, who seemed to be heir to the kingdom in virtue of his marriage and who had been of such assistance during the siege, should receive the county of Tyre—to wit Tyre, Sidon, and Beyrout; while King Guy's brother, Geoffrey de Lusignan, should have the county of Joppa—to wit, Joppa and Ascalon—in payment for all he had done. If King Guy should die before the marquis, then this latter, who had, although nefariously, taken the heiress to wife in the hopes of reigning, should be crowned as his successor. Moreover, the ultimate disposal of the kingdom should be left to King Richard, if Guy, the marquis and his wife should all die while he was still in those parts. So, under these terms the contention was ended.

In this state of affairs, towards the end of July within which (month) the Turks had promised to restore the Holy Cross, there ran a rumour through the army that the King of France, on whom the hopes of the people were fixed, wanted to return home, and was making great preparations for his departure. Oh! how shameful, how disgraceful a thing it was to entertain such a project while the great aim (of the expedition) was yet unattained. Oh! why had he come so long a distance if he intended to return so soon, almost before he had accomplished anything? It was truly a noble fulfilment of his vow to have just set foot on the land and to have gained this meagre triumph over the Turks!

And why forsooth did the King of France wish to go home? Because he alleged that sickness demanded his return; and that he had fulfilled his vow so far as he was able. But his chief plea was that when he assumed the cross with King Henry between Trie and Gisors he was in full health. No one was found to credit this assertion. However, it is not to be denied that the King of France had worked well at the siege, and spent money and given good assistance, so that he was rightly deemed of all Christian kings the one most powerful. . . . Now when it became known to all that the King of France's will in this matter was firmly fixed and that he would not give way at the tearful entreaties of his followers, the French loathed his lordship and would have thrown off his rule, had it been possible.

But though they invoked all kinds of misfortune upon his head, the king hastened on his preparations, leaving however the Duke of Burgundy with a great host in the (Holy) Land. He begged King Richard to let him have two galleys; and this king sent him two of his best. (See Rigord French account further on.) His thanklessness for this service appeared later on.

King Richard got the King of France to covenant that they should keep peace with each other. He exacted from the King of France an oath that he would not wittingly or wilfully do any harm against his men or lands so long as King Richard continued in his pilgrimage. (The text here seems very corrupt, and I have accordingly translated so as to make sense, though not, by any means, in harmony with the literal meaning of the words.) And if King Richard, after his return, should seem to be distinctly reprehensible in any matter, he should be allowed forty days for correcting the wrongs complained of, before the King of France should proceed against him.

All these things did the King of France swear that he would faithfully observe, giving as hostages the Duke of Burgundy, Count Henry, (*i.e.,* the Count of Champagne, afterwards King of Jerusalem), and some five others whose names I forget. How faithfully he kept this oath and agreement all the world knows well enough. For directly he reached home (the King of France) stirred up the whole land and threw Normandy into confusion. What need for more words? Among the curses and malisons, not benisons, of all, he took leave and left the army at Acre.

It was on the day of St. Peter-ad-Vincula (Aug. 1) that the King of France went aboard ship and sailed for Tyre, leaving the greater part of his army with King Richard. (Philip went home by way of Rome. He was at Fontevraud by Dec. 25.) With him also there went that wicked marquis and Caracois and all the Saracen hostages that had fallen to his share; for whose redemption the King of France reckoned he would receive 100,000 gold pieces or more, which would help to keep his army in the (Holy) land till Easter. But, when the time for payment came, the (Saracens) seemed to care nothing about the release of their (fellows). Thus, it happened that the greater part of them perished, it being a known fact that not a farthing or even an egg had been paid for their ransom.

Nor, on the plea of having to maintain them, did the French get anything at all, nor even the half of the victuals found when the city was taken. Wherefore the French kept it green in their memory that they received no remuneration from the King of France; and, by reason of this, there arose no small strife and murmur until King Richard, at the request of the Duke of Burgundy, lent him 5,000 silver *marks* to pay his people with.

How Philip went home.

L'Estoire d'Eracles

The King of France knowing what was in the mind of the King of England no longer hid his intentions but sent to seek leeches, to whom he gave fair jewels, praying for their advice as to the best way of curing his malady. The leeches took counsel together and God gave them His grace, so that he recovered of his ailment. Then at once he gave orders that they should make ready his galleys for his passage across the sea. When this was done, he called the Duke of Burgundy and all the knights of France, bidding the latter hold themselves at the bidding of the duke, to whom he gave a great part of his treasure and the right of ruling in his stead. Then the king set forth in his galleys over the sea.

Now when they were in the gulf of Satalie (*i.e.,* of Attalia, so called from the ancient city of Attalia in Pamphylia), a great tempest came down upon them for a day and night. Then the king demanded what hour it was and they told him midnight. Then said the king:

Have no fear! At this very moment are the monks in France awake and praying God for us. Let us have no further fear of danger.

Then the sea grew calm and they proceeded by due stages till they reached Brindisi, whence the king went to Rome. There he spoke with the Apostolic, (the Pope Coelestine III., 1191-1197), to whom he shewed the progress of the army in the land of Jerusalem. People said he was hastening lest anyone should lay hands on the county of Flanders, which, now that count Philip was dead, had fallen to him.

(*Ernoul omits the story, but agrees that Philip was desirous to get Flanders.*)

Why Philip went home (another French account).

Rigord, 35.

What provisions were found (at Acre) the Christians divided among themselves, giving a greater share to the many and a less to the few. But the kings had all the captives for their part and divided them equally. The King of France however handed over his half to the Duke of Burgundy, together with much gold and silver and an infinite quantity of provisions. To the same duke he also entrusted his armies. For he was then sick of a very grievous illness, and besides this looked upon the King of England with much suspicion because the latter king was sending envoys to Saladin and giving and receiving gifts.

For which cause, taking familiar counsel with his chiefs and receiving their permission, he set his army in order and, entrusting himself with sobs and tears to the sea, was carried by God's will to Apulia. He had only three galleys and these Rufus de Volta, of Genoa, had got him.

1191, August.—King Richard's negotiations with Saladin and the injustice of them.

Itin. Ric. iv..

King Richard now distributed gold and silver in great abundance to the French knights and to the strangers of every nation, by means of which they recruited their strength and redeemed their pledges. Moreover, while the King of France was hastening home, King Richard was paying heed to the repair of the city walls, building them higher and stronger than before. He himself was always making the round of them, encouraging the workmen and masons, just as if his sole business were to regain God's heritage. He was still awaiting the end of the time fixed upon between himself and the Turks, occupying himself in the meanwhile with collecting his *mangonels* and baggage ready for carrying them away.

After the period agreed upon for the return of the Holy Cross and the captives had been overpassed by three weeks to see if Saladin would keep his word; when the Saracens kept demanding a further delay, the Christians began to enquire when the Holy Cross was coming. One said "Already has the Cross come!" another said: "It has been seen in the Saracens' Army." But each was deceived, for Saladin was not even setting about Its restoration; nay, he neglected the hostages, in the hope that he would get better terms if he kept it in his possession. And all the while he kept sending frequent presents and envoys, while he made it his aim to waste time in long talks and ambiguous words.

Meanwhile word was sent to the marquis at Tyre bidding him return to the (main) army, and bring with him the hostages the King of France had left in his charge. On his arrival he was to receive his share of the ransom, *viz.,* the King of France's half. On this mission were sent the Bishop of Salisbury (*i.e.,* Hubert Walter), Earl Robert (of Leicester), and Peter de Préaux, a very excellent knight (Aug. 5, 1191). To them the marquis made reply that he would not come on any account—pretending that he feared to venture into King Richard's presence.

Moreover, he bragged that if the Holy Cross ever was recovered he would have half for the King of France; nor was he going to resign the captives till he had got it. When soft words would not prevail, the envoys offered to leave one of their number as a hostage for his safe return; but not even so would he agree, swearing with an oath that he would never go. So, the envoys returned having effected nothing, and the king was very wroth.

Yet at the king's request the Duke of Burgundy, Drogo de Amiens, and Robert de Quenci were despatched on a second mission; for in that he was a claimant for the kingdom the marquis's presence seemed necessary, notwithstanding all his slackness in the efforts made for its conquest. It was also wished that he should give facilities to those sailing with victuals by way of Tyre; for after his wonted fashion the marquis had been hindering their arrival. When the envoys prayed him in King Richard's name to come to his help in Syria—a country over which he hoped to rule—he replied arrogantly that he would never come, but would stay and look after his own city. At last, after long discussions, it was agreed that the three envoys should take back the Saracen hostages to King Richard.

When the term was far overpast and it was evident that Saladin was not going to redeem the hostages, a council of the chiefs was called, at which it was declared useless to wait any longer. Orders were then given to cut off the heads of the hostages with the exception of a few of the nobler prisoners, who perhaps might yet be relieved or exchanged for captive Christians. King Richard, always eager to destroy the Turks, to confound the law of Mahomet utterly, and vindicate that of Christ, on the Friday after the *Assumption,* (*i.e.,* 16 Aug. 1191), bade 2,700 Turkish hostages to be led out of the city and beheaded.

Nor was there any delay. The king's followers leapt forward eager to fulfil the commands, and thankful to the Divine Grace that permitted them to take such a vengeance for those Christians whom these very (captives) had slain with bolts and arrows. (Tuesday, 20 Aug., 1191, according to Howden, who tells us that Saladin had two days previously beheaded all his Christian prisoners).

When evening came on the herald made proclamation that the army should proceed on the morrow and cross the river of Acre advancing, in the name of God the giver of all good things, on the way to Ascalon, conquering the coast as they went. So, they put on board ship ten days' provisions for the army, to wit, bread, biscuit, flour, flesh, and wine. Strict orders were given to the seamen that they were to sail along shore with their cargo-vessels and smacks. These, carrying victuals and armed men, were to keep close to the army that marched by land. (In a similar way the warriors of the first Crusade marched along the coast from Tripoli to Caesarea, accompanied by a small fleet.) So, the army proceeded in two battalions, one going by sea, the other by land; for in no other way could they possess themselves of the land occupied by the Turks.

AUGUST 2, 1101.—SARACEN ACCOUNT OF NEGOTIATIONS. MASSACRE OF MOSLIM PRISONERS BY RICHARD.

Bohâdin, 240.

The same day (*i.e.,* August 2nd), Hossam ad-Din Ibn Barîc issued from Acre accompanied by two of the Englishman's officers. He brought news that the King of France had set out for Tyre, and that they had come to talk over the matter of the prisoners and to see the true cross of the Crucifixion if it were still in the Musulman camp, or to ascertain if it really had been sent to Bagdad. It was shewn to them, and on beholding it they shewed the profoundest reverence, throwing themselves on the ground till they were covered with dust, and humbling themselves in token of devotion.

These envoys told us that the French princes had accepted the *Sultan's* proposition, *viz.,* to deliver all that was specified in the treaty by three instalments at intervals of a month. The *Sultan* then sent an envoy to Tyre with rich presents, quantities of perfumes, and fine raiment—all of which were for the King of the French.

In the morning of the tenth day of *Rajab,* (*i.e.,* 3rd August), Ibn Banc and his comrades returned to the King of England while the *Sultan* went off with his bodyguard and his closest friends to the hill that abuts on Shefa 'Amr. . . . . Envoys did not cease to pass from one side to the other in the hope of laying the foundation of a firm peace.

These negotiations continued till our men had procured the money and the tale of the prisoners that they were to deliver to the French at the end of the first period in accordance with the treaty. The first instalment was to consist of the Holy Cross, 100,000 *dinars* and 1,600 prisoners. Trustworthy men sent by the Franks to conduct the examination found it all complete saving only the prisoners who had been demanded by name, all of whom had not yet been gathered together. And thus, the negotiations continued to drag on till the end of the first term. On this day, the 18th of *Rajab*, (*i.e.*, August 11th), the enemy sent demanding what was due.

The *Sultan* replied as follows:

Choose one of two things. Either send us back our comrades and receive the payment fixed for this term, in which case we will give hostages to ensure the full execution of all that is left. Or accept what we are going to send you today, and in your turn give us hostages to keep until those of our comrades whom you hold prisoners are restored.

To this the envoys made answer:

Not so. Send us what is due for this term and in return we will give our solemn oath that your people shall be restored you.

This proposition the *Sultan* rejected, knowing full well that if he were to deliver the money, the cross, and the prisoners, while our men were still kept captive by the Franks, he would have no security against treachery on the part of the enemy, and this would be a great disaster to Islam.

Then the King of England, seeing all the delays interposed by the *Sultan* to the execution of the treaty, acted perfidiously as regards his Musulman prisoners. On their yielding the town he had engaged to grant them life, adding that if the *Sultan* carried out the bargain, he would give them freedom and suffer them to carry off their children and wives; if the *Sultan* did not fulfil his engagements, they were to be made slaves. Now the king broke his promises to them and made open display of what he had till now kept hidden in his heart, by carrying out what he had intended to do after he had received the money and the Frank prisoners. It is thus that people of his nation ultimately admitted.

In the afternoon of Tuesday, 27 *Rajab*, (*i.e.*, August 20th), about four o'clock, he came out on horseback with all the Frankish Army, knights, footmen, *Turcoples*, and advanced to the pits at the foot of the hill of Al 'Ayâdîyeh, to which place he had already sent on his tents The Franks, on reaching the middle of the plain that stretches between this hill and that of Keisân, close to which place the *sultan's* advanced guard had drawn back, ordered all the Musulman prisoners, whose martyrdom God had decreed for this day, to be brought before him. They numbered more than three thousand and were all bound with ropes. The Franks then flung themselves upon them all at once and massacred them with sword and lance in cold blood. Our advanced guard had already told the *Sultan* of the enemy's movements and he sent it some reinforcements, but only after the massacre.

The Musulmans, seeing what was being done to the prisoners, rushed against the Franks and in the combat, which lasted till nightfall, several were slain and wounded on either side. On the morrow morning our people gathered at the spot and found the Musulmans stretched out upon the ground as martyrs for the faith. They even recognised some of the dead, and the sight was a great affliction to them. The enemy had only spared the prisoners of note and such as were strong enough to work.

The motives of this massacre are differently told; according to some, the captives were slain by way of reprisal for the death of those Christians whom the Musulmans had slain. Others again say that the King of England, on deciding to attempt the conquest of Ascalon, thought it unwise to leave so many prisoners in the town after his departure. God alone knows what the real reason was.

AUG. 22.—THE FRANKS LEAVE ACRE. THE SARACENS RETIRE BEFORE THEM.

Bohâdin.

On the 29th of *Rajab* (*i.e.*, Thursday August 22nd), the Franks mounted their horses and after loading their beasts of baggage with the tents they had just taken down, they started to cross the river and camp on its western bank near the road that leads to Acre. Whilst thus shewing his intention of following the sea-coast the Englishman sent back the rest of his people to Acre, whose fortifications he had repaired. The army that was now setting out on its march included a great many persons of high rank and had the Englishman himself for leader.

On the first of *Shaban*, (*i.e.*, August 24th), at daybreak, the enemy lit several fires, according to their custom on breaking up the camp. The *Sultan*, on learning from his advanced guard that the Franks were in movement, gave orders to pack up the baggage, while his troops remained in the saddle. On this occasion a great many traffickers who followed the camp lost much of their goods and other possessions; for they had not enough horses or other beasts of burden to carry all their possessions. A single man can carry enough to supply his needs for a month; but every one of these traffickers had such great stores that it would have taken them several journeys to transport them elsewhere. Now this time no one could stay behind because of the Franks at Acre.

1191, AUGUST 20 TO AUGUST 30.—FULL REPORT OF KING RICHARD'S MARCH ALONG THE COAST TO CAESAREA.

Itin., Ric, iv.

After the execution of the Turks, and the recovery of his health, King Richard, leaving Acre with all his followers had pitched his tents in the plains outside the city. He compelled all his own men, even though they were unwilling, to leave the city, and so his army tarried in the aforesaid plains—beyond our trenches—till things were ready for the march. Some of the French too he induced by fair words, some by money; and others by violence he compelled to come forth. The king made a host of foot followers remain in their tents round his pavilions, as an extra protection against the frequent attacks of the Turks. It was the king's custom always to be first in attacking the Turks and doing them damage if the divine will suffered it.

On a certain day the Turks, as their manner was, threw our camp into confusion by a sudden onset. While our men were arming the king advanced on horseback at a greater speed than the rest, and with him a certain warrior from Hungary, and several Hungarians. These pursued the Turks further than was expedient; owing to which some of our men, despite their valour, were taken prisoners.

Amongst the captives was this Hungarian count, a man of great worth and fame. With him there was carried off a knight of Poitou, Hugh by name, the king's marshal. On this occasion the king, taking no heed for his own safety, urged on his horse, sparing no effort to rescue his marshal who was, however, swept away by the superior speed (of his enemies). . . . The Turks are not weighted with armour like our men, and for this reason, thanks to the quickness of their movements, they often inflict severe damage on our men. They are almost weaponless, carrying only a bow, a club furnished with sharp teeth, a sword, a lance of reed with iron head, and a lightly hung knife.

When routed they flee away on the swiftest of horses—than which none in the world are fleeter—horses that may be compared for their speed to the flight of swallows. It is a Turkish habit, to cease fleeing when they see their pursuers slacken in the pursuit, like a pertinacious fly, which, though you may drive it off, will return directly you cease your efforts; which will keep its distance so long as you make it, but is ever ready (to renew the attack) should you cease (to be on the alert). It is no otherwise with the Turks. When you stop your pursuit and return, the Turk follows you up.

King Richard was dwelling in his tents waiting for the army to leave the city; for they left it slowly and surlily, not of their own will. Owing to this his numbers swelled but slowly, while the city was still filled with a very great host. Now the whole army, including those who had not yet left the city, was reckoned at 300,000. The people given up to sloth and luxury were loath to leave a city so rich in comforts, to wit, in the choicest of wines and the fairest of damsels. Many, by too intimate an acquaintance with these pleasures, became dissolute, till the city was quite polluted by the luxury of these foolish folk and the inhabitants, whose gluttony and wantonness put wiser men to the blush. To remedy this reproach, it was ordered that no woman should leave the city with the army, except the washerwomen who would go on foot, and could not be a burden or an occasion of sin.

On the appointed day the host armed early, and ranged itself in decent order. At the very rear went the king to guard against the Turks who hung threateningly near. That day's journey was but short. From the very moment this accursed race saw our army on the move, like mountain torrents they began to rain down the heights in many separate bands: here may-be by twenties, there by thirties, and so on. And being so scattered they took every opportunity of doing our army what damage they could, for they grieved sorely at the death of their relatives, whose mangled bodies they had seen; wherefore they harassed our army more keenly, constantly following it up and annoying it by every means in their power.

But by the divine grace our army crossed the river of Acre unharmed, pitched on the other side not far beyond the river, and waited here till the whole army should be collected on Friday, the eve of St. Bartholomew (23 Aug., 1191). On the following Monday two full years had passed since the Christians began to besiege Acre.

So, on Sunday, the morrow of St. Bartholomew (25 Aug.), at early morn the army was ranged in battalions for its march along the seashore. King Richard led the van-guard. The Normans stood like a wall round the Standard which it will not be amiss to describe in order that it may be better known. It consists of a very tall pole, as it were the mast of a ship, made up of most solid timber work well jointed, cunningly carved, and covered with iron, so as not likely to fall a prey to sword, or axe, or fire. On the very top of this mast floated the royal flag—commonly called the banner. There is usually a chosen body of knights appointed for its guard; especially when the fight is upon the open plain, lest it should be prostrated or damaged by any hostile attack; for if by any chance it is cast down, the army is thrown into confusion and flight.

For the timid-hearted know not where to rally if they believe their leader overcome when they do not see his sign erect. It is not easy for any people to offer strong resistance, if, from the fall of their banner, they have reason to fear for their leader's safety, whereas so long as that standard remains upright, they have a safe refuge to which they may betake themselves. To it the sick and the wounded are brought for cure; aye, and even those men of rank or renown who have been cut off in the fight. Wherefore, because it stands so strongly fitted together as a sign for the people, it is, from its thus standing, called the Standard. It is set on wheels with no small advantage, in that, according as the fortune of the battle varies, it can be brought forward if the enemy give way, or drawn back if they press on. Round this standard stood the English and the Normans.

The Duke of Burgundy and his French who were in the rear followed at less speed, and, thanks to their delay, came near to suffering a most terrible loss. The army was marching having the sea on its right, whilst from the mountain heights on the left the Turks kept a watch on all our movements. Suddenly there swelled up a black and dangerous cloud, and the air grew troubled. The army had now reached a narrow passage along which the provision wagons had to go.

Here on account of the narrowness of the way there was some confusion and disorder, which the Saracens noting swept down upon the packhorses and wagons, cutting off unwary men and steeds, plundering much of the baggage, breaking through and dispersing those who offered any resistance, and driving them in flight and slaughter to the brink of the sea. There both sides fought with manful courage for dear life. On this occasion when a Turk had cut off the right hand of a certain Everard, one of the Bishop of Salisbury's men, he without changing countenance, seized his sword with the left hand and, closing with the Turks, stoutly defended himself against them all, brandishing his weapon.

The rear of the army was exceedingly perturbed at this onset till John Fitz Luke, urging his horse forward at full speed bore news of all that had happened to King Richard, who, coming up with a band of his own men, brought aid to the rear and thundered on against the Turks, slaying them right and left with his sword. Nor was there any loitering, but right and left, as of old the Philistines fled from the face of the Machabee, (known as a mediaeval true patriot), so now did the Turks scatter and flee from the face of King Richard till they gained the mountain heights, leaving, however, some of their number headless in our hands. In this conflict one of the French, William des Barres by name, who had formerly incurred Richard's displeasure, was now restored, thanks to his signal valour, to his former favour.

Saladin was not far off with all the flower of his army; but, after this repulse, the Turks, despairing of gaining any advantage, contented themselves with watching our movements from a distance. Accordingly, our army, resuming its line of march, came to a river and cisterns, which they found to be good. There, in a pleasant plain, they fixed their tents; for they saw indications that Saladin had pitched there before them and, noting the way in which so wide a district was trodden down, judged his army to be very large.

Saladin with his Turks was ever on the look out to do us harm; for which purpose he would seize the narrow precipitous pathways, by which our army had to pass, in the hope of slaying or capturing some of our men as they straggled in the rear. But our people proceeded from this river warily and in good order till, after a moderate march, they came near Cayphas, (the modern Haifa), where they pitched their tents and waited for the crowd that followed. Here, between the sea and the town, our army tarried for two days, overhauling the baggage, part of which they threw away seeing that they could do without it. For the crowd of footmen was very heavily weighted with food and arms, on which account very many of them had endured much toil and thirst in the late battle.

On the Tuesday, that is on the third day after the delay at Cayphas (i.e., 27 Aug.), the army advanced again in due order, having the Templars in the van and the Hospitallers in the rear, both of which orders bore themselves so manfully as to be a very pattern of virtues. On this day the army went more warily than usual; for there stretched a great way before them, so covered with bushes and rank growth of herbs that the (soldiers') faces were being constantly torn, especially those of the footmen. Also, in these sea places there was found a great abundance of wild animals, that were constantly leaping out from beneath our feet in places thick set with grass and shrubs.

Of these they used to catch many without the trouble of chasing. (This was the jerboa, *Dipodida C*, a little rodent that leaps like a kangaroo. It is thought to be the "coney" of the Bible.) When the king had come somewhere near Capharnaum—which the Saracens had laid level with the ground—he dismounted to eat; and whilst the army was waiting, those who wished took a snatch also. Immediately after they proceeded on their way to the Casal of the Narrow ways, where the roads become narrow. Here they fixed their tents and rested.

Now it was a custom in the army that every evening, before men went to rest, a certain person, deputed for this very purpose, should cry out in the middle of the host the common exhortation "*Sanctum Sepulchrum adjuva*" (Help us, O Holy Sepulchre!) On hearing these words, the whole multitude would take up the cry, stretching out their hands to heaven and, with copious tears, praying God for aid and mercy.

Then a second time would the herald repeat the same words, calling out as before, "*Sanctum Sepulchrum adjuva*," after which the words were repeated by the whole host; likewise, when he cried aloud for the third time all imitated him with the utmost sorrow of heart and bursts of tears. Who would not have acted thus in such a strait, seeing that the very mention of this custom can draw pious tears from the hearers? By this cry the army seemed to be refreshed in no small degree.

Every night, certain creeping insects, commonly called *tarentes*, (known to us as tarentula), used to annoy our men with burning stings. By day they did no harm; but, as night drew near, they pressed upon (us), armed with the most baleful stings. After they had stung a person, the wound swelled out with the poison they had planted, and the patient suffered the most acute agony. Noble men and wealthy could assuage these tumours at once by ointments, and ease their pangs by an effectual antidote.

Afterwards the wiser folk, learning that these plaguing insects were put to flight by any great noise, began, whenever the tarantulas drew near, to make a frightful din and clatter by clashing together shields, helms, saddle-gear, poles, jars, flagons, basins, pans, plates, and anything else that was handy for making a noise; for on hearing the clatter these insects decamped.

At this Casal the army stayed two days, (*i.e.,* Aug. 28 and 29, according to Dr. Stubbs); for it was a large place and a very convenient one in which to await the arrival of the ships they expected; to wit, barges and galleys laden with the victuals they had need of. These ships, sailing near the coast, alongside of those marching by land, carried food

The army advanced to the town of Merle, (Aug. 30 according to Dr. Stubbs, See Note F.) where the king had passed one of the previous nights; but here it had to guard against the Turks, who threatened from one side. The king had determined to lead the first rank in person on the following day to guard against the expected attacks of the Turks. The Templars, however, were still to guard the rear, for the Turks were ever threatening. On that day the king, putting spurs to his horse, was borne against the Turks and, but for the sloth of his followers, would have reaped great glory. For as he went ahead, driving the Turks before him, some of his men stayed their pursuit. For this slackness they were rebuked in the evening, and rightly too; because had they helped the king to pursue the fleeing Turks they would have accomplished a right noble feat-of-arms. Yet (for all this slackness of his own men) the king drove the Turks wholesale before his face.

Now the journey along the sea-shore was very grievous to the army by reason of the great heat; for it was summer and they were making a very long stage. Many, fainting from the heat and out wearied by the labour of the long march, dropped down dead and were buried where they fell. But on many others who were exhausted by the journey the king took compassion, and had them transported in the galleys and ships to the halting place. At last, after a toilsome day's march, the army came to Caesarea, where the Turks had already partly destroyed the town with its walls and towers so far as they were able. But at the approach of our men, they fled.

Pitching their tents here our people passed the night (August 30), close to a river very near the city. This river is called the River of Crocodiles (the Nahr-Zerka, 3 miles N of Caesarea), because the crocodiles had formerly devoured two knights who were bathing in it. The city of Caesarea (20 miles from Cayphas), is very large and its buildings are constructed with wonderful art. Christ used to come here oftentimes with his disciples, and he made the city illustrious by his divine miracles. The king gave orders for his ships to join the army at this place.

THE MARCH FROM CAESAREA TO ARSUF; THE BATTLE OF ARSUF, SUNDAY, SEPT. 1ST—SUNDAY, SEPT. 8, 1191.

Itin. Ric., iv.

Meanwhile the king had issued a proclamation in the city of Acre that all the slothful folk tarrying there should get aboard the ships he sent and come to the army for the love of God, for the honour of the Christian faith and the fulfilment of their vow. In accordance with the king's mandate, very many came with the royal fleet to Caesarea. And he made arrangements for the fleet, which was well stocked with victuals, to advance alongside of the army.

So, a great multitude of ships being united, and the army being armed and arranged in squadrons, on a certain day (*i.e.,* Sunday, September 1), about the third hour they advanced from Caesarea, going at a steady pace because the Turks were always threatening them. For (the enemy) whenever the army began to move forward—every day alike—pressed as close as they dared, doing what damage they could. And on this day, they harassed us more persistently than usual, though, with God's help, we issued safely, forcing them to leave behind them one of their *emirs*, whose head our men cut off.

★★★★★★★★

The Crusaders seem to have cut off the heads of their slaughtered enemies much as the Red Indians take scalps. At the siege of Antioch, they sent two mule-loads to the *Caliph* of Babylon; and at the siege of Nicaea they flung the heads of a defeated party of rescue over the city walls; and Albert of Aix tells us how Godfrey and his comrades, after having driven off an ambush, rode into Antioch with the heads of their slaughtered foes hanging from their saddle-bows. The custom prevailed in Ireland and Scotland as well as among the Turks, from whom Guibert of Nogent thinks the Crusaders borrowed it (see Note K).

★★★★★★★★

He was a warrior of the greatest courage, of signal valour, and the most illustrious name. He was said to have been a man of such strength that no one had ever been able to unhorse him, and hardly anyone dared even to attack him. For he bore a lance thicker in the shaft than any two of ours. His name was Aias Estoy. At his fall the Turks were afflicted with such grief that they cut off their horses' tails and would gladly have carried off the *emir's* corpse had they been permitted. But our men proceeded thence to the stream which is called the Dead River which the Saracens, before our arrival, had covered over so that we might not see it and so might run the risk of tumbling

88

in. (The Nahr Akhdar according to Dr. Stubbs, but according to the Palestine Exploration Fund's Survey Report it is the Nahr al Mefjir, which reaches the sea between 2 and 3 miles S. of Caesarea.) But here too God preserved us, and our men drank out of the river when laid open; and stayed there two nights. (Nights of Sept. 1 and 2.)

On the third day (Sept. 3) the army proceeded from the Dead River slowly over a waste and empty land. On this day the army was forced to journey along the hills because they could not make any way along the coast, as it was obstructed with grass which flourished in greatest luxuriance. The army marched in closer array than usual, the Templars still bringing up the rear. And on this day the Templars lost so many horses from the attacks of the Turks, that they were almost in despair. The Count of St. Pol (see Note P) also lost very many horses there; and truly so great was his valour on that day in guarding the line of march that he gained exceeding great favour and applause of the whole people.

On the same day was King Richard wounded with a spear in the side whilst slaughtering the Turks. Yet did this light wound serve rather to excite him against the enemies, by making him more eager to avenge the pain he suffered. Wherefore he fought right fiercely throughout the whole day, vigorously driving back the Turks as they came on.

The Turks, pertinaciously keeping alongside of our army, strove to work us all the harm they could, by hurling darts and arrows thick as rain. Alas! how many horses fell down here pierced through with darts; how many, being once severely wounded, died a little later on. Aye, and so thickly fell the rain of darts and arrows there that you could not find so much as four feet of earth all along the army's route entirely without them. This grievous tempest overhung us all the day until, as night came up, the Turks drew off to their own tents; whilst our folk pitched theirs near a certain water called the Salt River, (*i.e.,* Nahr Iskanderueh, it reaches the sea 7 or 8 miles S. of Caesarea,) and there abode two days. It was on the Tuesday after St. Giles' day (*i.e.,* Sept. 3) that they arrived here.

At this place there was no small run upon the bodies of the fat horses that had died of their wounds; and the people in their greedy contention for the right of purchasing the flesh—though at a high price—came to blows. Upon this the king proclaimed, by voice of a herald, that he would give a live horse to anyone who would divide his dead steed among the most valiant of the needy men at arms. And so, men ate horse flesh as though it were the flesh of deer, and, having hunger to season it instead of sauces, they deemed it a most pleasant food.

On the third day (*i.e.,* Thursday, Sept. 5) about the third hour the army proceeded in ordered ranks from the Salt River; for there was a rumour the Turks were lying in wait for them in the forest of Arsuf. This wood it was said they were going to burn so as to prevent our men from passing through it; who however, issuing unharmed, chanced on a pleasant plain near the river that is commonly called Rochetailie. Here they pitched tents for the night, and the scouts who were sent out brought back news that an innumerable host of Turks, reckoned at 300,000, covered the face of the whole land, and awaited our coming at no great distance. The Christian Army did not exceed 100,000. It was on the Thursday (*i.e.* Sept. 5) before the Nativity of the Blessed Mary that (our) army came to the River Rochetailie (Nahr Falaik, or River of the Cleft, is nearly 16 miles S. of Caesarea and 9 S. of the Salt River); where it tarried the next day.

On Saturday (Sept. 7) the eve of the Nativity of the Blessed Mary, at earliest dawn all prepared themselves most carefully as though the Turks were going to attack immediately; for they knew the enemy to have forestalled our path, and that the insolence of the Turks would not abate before a very severe contest had taken place. Indeed, the Turks were already setting their men in order, and always drawing a little nearer.

For this reason, all our men looked to their own affairs very carefully, and the ranks were ranged with the utmost precaution. King Richard, who was very skilful in military matters, drew up the squadrons according to a special scheme, arranging who had better lead the vanguard, and who bring up the rear. With this intent he appointed twelve squadrons; and arranged (his whole army) into five battalions, assigning to each men of great skill in warfare—warriors whose betters were not to be found on earth had their hearts only been firmly staid in God.

On this day the Templars led the first rank; after them went the Bretons and the men of Anjou in due order; next went King Guy with the men of Poitou; in the fourth rank were the Normans and the English, with the royal banner under their charge. Last of all went the Hospitallers in due rank. This last array of all was made up of choice knights divided into squadrons, and its members marched so close together that an apple could not be thrown to the ground without touching the men or their horses. Our army occupied the whole space between Saladin's and the sea-shore.

There might you see (the squadrons each) with its appropriate badge, banners of different forms, various ensigns, and a (whole) people full of vigour, bold and very apt at war. There was the Earl of Leicester, Hugh de Gurnay, William des Barres, Walkelin de Ferrars, Roger de Tony, James de Avesnes, Count Robert de Dreux and his brother the Bishop of Beauvais; William des Barres, William de Guarlande, Drogo de Merle, and very many of his kin.

★★★★★★★★

James de Avesnes arrived at Acre with the Bishop of Beauvais, the Count of Dreux, two days after the commencement of the siege, i.e., on Aug. 24, 1189. He is described as better than Nestor in counsel, than Achilles in valour, and than Regulus in faith. He had been leader of the Crusaders at the siege till the arrival of Henry, Count of Champagne, in July 1190.

Robert II., Count of Dreux, was the son of Robert I. and grandson of Louis VI. He succeeded his father in the country in 1188. He was brother of Philip mentioned below, and is said to have died 28 Sept., 1218 or 1219. His father had taken part in the Crusade of Louis VII., whose brother he was.

Philip, Bishop of Beauvais from 1175 to 1217, was grandson of Louis VI. He had been in the Holy Land in 1178. He was a great warrior, and is elsewhere compared by our author to Archbishop Turpin. Twenty-three years later he distinguished himself, fighting with his mace at the Battle of Bouvines. In 1196 he and his archdeacon had both been taken prisoners by Richard's mercenary captain, Marcadeus, who presented them armed as they were to the king. The Pope wrote for the release of "his son," and Richard sent back the bishop's coat of mail asking if he recognised his son's tunic.

★★★★★★★★

Count Henry of Champagne kept guard on the side of the mountains: as did also the followers on foot. Last of all were drawn up the bowmen and the crossbow-men closing the rear. The packhorses and wagons carrying provisions, baggage, &c., journeyed between the, army and the sea so as to be safe from attack.

Thus did the army advance at a gentle pace so as to guard against separation; for, if loosely scattered, the battalions would be less able to resist the enemy. King Richard and the Duke of Burgundy with a choice train of knights went hither and thither, to right and left, observing the position and bearing of the Turks, that they might regulate the course of the army according to circumstances. And indeed, their watchfulness was very necessary.

The third hour was now drawing on, when lo! a host of Turks, 10,000 in numbers, swept rapidly down upon our men, hurling darts and arrows, and making a terrible din with their confused cries. After these came running up a race of daemons very black in colour; for which cause, because they are black, they are not unfittingly called the negro pack (*nigreduli*). (Then too came on) those Saracens who live in the desert and are commonly called Bedawin, rough, darker than smoke, most pestilent footmen with their bows and round targets—a people light of foot and most eager for battle. These were ever threatening our army.

And beyond those we have mentioned, you might see along the smoother ground well-equipt *phalanxes* of Turks advancing with their several ensigns, banners, and emblems. They seemed to number more than 20,000 men. On steeds swifter than eagles they thundered down upon us, till the whirling dust raised by their rapid flight blackened the very air. Before the *emirs* there went men clanging away with trumpets and clarions; others had drums, others pipes and timbrels, rattles, gongs, cymbals, and other instruments fitted to make a din. To raise these noises was the special business of certain men; and the louder their din the fiercer did their comrades fight. Thus, from every part, by land and sea, did these accursed Turks press upon our army, so that for two miles there was not a hand's breadth of space where this hostile race was not to be found.

That day our own losses and the sufferings of our horses, who were pierced through and through with arrows and darts, shewed how persistently the enemy kept up the attack; and then indeed we found out the use of our stalwart cross-bowmen, our bowmen, and those closely-wedged followers who at the very rear beat back the Turkish onset by constant hurling of their weapons so far as they could. Yet for all this, the enemy in a little while rushed on them again like a torrent of waters, redoubling their blows and so drunk with fury that at last many of our cross-bowmen could hold out no longer, but, throwing away their bows and cross-bow, in sheer dread of death, gave way before the intolerable onset of the Turks and forced a path within the close ranks of our main army, lest they should be cut off from their comrades.

But the better men and bolder, whom shame forbade to yield, faced about and strove against the Turks with unflagging valour. So, they marched backwards in their anxiety to keep themselves from the danger they would run by advancing too confidently in the ordinary method; and all that day they went on, picking their way rather than marching, with their faces turned toward the Turks, who threatened at their rear. Ay! in the stress and bitter peril of that day there was no one who did not wish himself safe at home, with his pilgrimage finished. And of a truth our little (handful of) people was hemmed in on every side by so vast a multitude of Saracens that it could not have escaped had it been so minded; and, like a flock of sheep within the very jaws of the wolves, our men, cooped up as they were, could see nothing around them excepting the sky and their pestilent enemies (swarming up) on every side.

Lord God! What were then the feelings of that weak flock of Christ? Whoever had to bear up against such cruel oppressors? Who was ever ground down by such want of all things? There you might see our soldiers, after losing their good steeds, march along on foot with the footmen, shooting arrows or anything else that chance supplied them with. The Turks, too, whose special pride it is to excel with the bow, kept up the shower of arrows and darts till the air resounded and the brightness of the sun itself grew dark, as with a wintry fall of hail or snow, by reason of the number of their missiles. (Our horses were transfixed with arrows and darts, which covered the surface of the ground so thickly everywhere that a man could have gathered twenty with a single sweep of his hand.

The Turks pressed on so stoutly that they nearly crushed the lines of the Hospitallers, who sent word to King Richard that they could bear up no longer unless their knights were allowed to charge the enemy:

> But he, forbidding, bids them wait
> In closer line and patient state.

Wherefore, for all the peril they were in, they endured on; though with many a heavy gasp, since they were not suffered to breathe freely, so they pursued their way, the excessive heat adding to their toil. Men might well augur that ill things were in store for so small an army hemmed in with so great a host. And now our assailants smote on the backs of our men as they advanced, as if with mallets; so that it was no longer a case for using arrows and darts from a distance, but for piercing with lances or crushing with heavy maces at close quarters: for hand to hand attacks with drawn swords, whilst the blows of the Turks resounded as if from an anvil. The battle raged most severely in the rear rank of the Hospitallers because they might not repay the enemy, but had to go along patient under their sufferings, silent though battered by clubs, and, though struck, not striking in return. At last, unable to bear up against so vast a host, they began to give way and press upon the squadron ahead of them. They fled before the Turks, who were madly raging in their rear.

Who can wonder at their failing to bear up against so persistent an attack, forbidden as they were to strike back or make an onset on their foes: and such foes too! For the very flower of all Paganism, from Damascus and Persia, had gathered here; from the Mediterranean Sea to the East there was no bold warrior even in the most distant corner, no valiant race or people whom Saladin had not called in to his aid by prayer, or pay, or right of dominion, and all in the hope of utterly sweeping the race of Christians from off the face of the earth. But in vain; for, thanks to God, he was not strong enough to achieve his wish. And the best flower of all the youth of Christendom—a soldiery tried in war—had flowed thither (to oppose him) and, like the finest grain shaken from the ears, was united there from the furthest ends of the earth.

If anyone had broken and exterminated this host without a doubt there would have been no one left in the world able to offer resistance. At last more than 20,000 Turks made a sudden confused rush, battering at close quarters with clubs and swords, redoubling their blows against the Hospitallers and pressing on in every way, when lo! one of this brotherhood, Garnier de Napes, cried out with a loud voice:

> O illustrious knight St. George, why dost thou suffer us to be thus confounded? Christendom itself is now perishing if it does not beat back this hateful foe!

****

St. George was *par excellence* the warrior Saint of the Eastern Crusades. In 1097 he was seen issuing with two other saints from the mountains to help the Christian army at the Battle of Dorylaeum and, when almost within sight of Jerusalem, the army tarried at Lydda to restore his ruined church there. Even the Saracens feared his valour, and at the Battle of Nazareth (May 1, 1187) deemed they had slain the Christian Saint in the person of Jakelin de Mailly, the Templar. St. George was represented as riding on a white steed in glittering white armour, like Spenser's Red Cross knight whose prototype he was.

****

Thereupon, the Master of the Hospital going off to the king said:

Lord king, we are grievously beset and are likely to be branded with eternal shame as men who dare not strike in their own defence. Each one of us is losing his own horse for nothing, and why should we put up with it any longer?

To whom the king made reply:

My good master, it must needs be endured, (seeing that) none can be everywhere.

So, the master returned to find the Turks pressing on and dealing death in the rear, while there was no chief or count who did not blush for very shame, saying one to the other:

Why do we not give reins to our horses? Alas! alas! we shall be convicted of cowardly sloth for evermore, and deservedly too. To whom has such a thing ever happened before? Never has shame of so dark a dye been inflicted on so great an army. Unless we charge them speedily, we shall earn ourselves everlasting ignominy; and the longer we delay the greater will be our disgrace.

O how blind is human fate! on what slippery joints it totters! Alas, on what doubtful wheels it rolls along, evolving human events in uncertain succession. Truly an incalculable host of Turks would have perished if matters had been carried out according to the previous arrangement. . . . For whilst our men were treating together and had at last determined that the time for charging the enemy had come, two knights, impatient of delay, overthrew the whole plan. For it had been decreed that, when the moment for setting upon the Turks arrived, six trumpets should sound in three several parts of the army, to wit, two in the front and two in the rear, and two in the middle. The object of this was to distinguish the Christian note of onset from that of the Saracens, and to let each (section of our army) know its distance from the other two.

If this plan had only been carried out the whole body of the Turks would have been cut off and routed; but thanks to the over-haste of these two knights the order was not observed, to the great disadvantage of the commonweal. For these two, you must know, breaking from the ranks spurred their steeds against the Turks, overthrowing and transfixing each his man. One of these knights was the Marshal of the Hospitallers; the other was Baldwin de Carro, a stout knight and bold as a lion, a boon companion of King Richard, who had led him hither as his comrade from his own land.

Now when the other Christians saw these two rushing against the Turks so boldly and calling upon St. George for aid in so loud a voice, they all in a body, wheeling round their steeds, in the name of Christ the Saviour followed and flung themselves against the foe with one mind. There was no delay; but the Hospitallers, who all that day had ridden in unbroken order and were much distressed at being set in such close wedges, shot across the intervening ground and manfully attacked the foe in the wake of the two knights. So, each squadron in its appointed order, turning round its horses, charged the enemy in such a manner that those who had been first in the march were brought up last to the attack, according to their position; whereas the Hospitallers who formed the rear joined battle first.

These also sprang forward with the Hospitallers: the Count of Champagne (Henry II.), with his chosen band; James de Avesnes with his kinsmen, Robert Earl of Dreux, and the Bishop of Beauvais his brother, and the Earl of Leicester, whose steed bore him on at a maddening pace towards the sea on the left. But why mention individuals? All the rear advanced boldly and at once; behind them rushed in the swift-footed men of Poitou, the Bretons, the Angevins, and others whose valour was such that they transfixed each Turk as he came against them with their lances and bore him to the ground. In this encounter the air grew black with dust, and the whole body of the Turks who had of set purpose dismounted so as to aim their darts and arrows better had their heads cut off, for our foot soldiers decapitated those whom our knights had overthrown.

King Richard, seeing the army in confusion, put spurs to his horse and flew up to the spot, not slackening his course till he had made his way through the Hospitallers, to whose aid he brought his followers. Then he bore on the Turks, thundering against them and mightily astonishing them by the deadly blows he dealt. To right and left they fell away before him. Oh! how many might there be seen rolled over on the earth, some groaning, others gasping out their last breath as they wallowed in their blood, and many too maimed and trodden underfoot by those who passed by. Everywhere there were horses riderless. How different from and how unlike the peaceful meditation of cloistered monks musing by their pillars!

Then King Richard, fierce and alone, pressed on the Turks, laying them low; none whom his sword touched might escape; for wherever he went he made a wide path for himself, brandishing his sword on every side. When he had crushed this hateful race by the constant blows of his sword, which mowed them down as if they were a harvest for the sickle, the remainder, frighted at the sight of their dying friends, began to give him a wider berth; for by now the corpses of the Turks covered the face of the ground for half a mile.

At last, the Turks are (really) routed; they leap from their saddles; a dust, full of danger to our men, rises from the combatants. For when our warriors, fatigued with slaying and eager to catch even a breath of air, left the thick of the fight, they could not recognize one another owing to the cloud of dust; but began to lay about them indifferently to right and left, slaying friends in mistake for foes.

But still the Christians pounded away with their swords till the Turks grew faint with terror, though the issue is doubtful yet. Oh! how many banners and standards of many shapes, what countless pennons and flags might you see falling to earth; aye, and just as many good swords lying everywhere, lances of reed tipt with iron heads, Turkish bows and clubs bristling with sharpened teeth. Twenty or more wagon loads of *quarrells*, darts, and other arrows and missiles might have been collected on the field. There you might see many a bearded Turk lie maimed and mutilated, but still striving to resist with the courage of despair until, as our men began to prevail, some of the enemy, shaking themselves free from their steeds, hid among the bushes or climbed up the trees, from which they fell dying with horrid yells before the arrows of our men.

Others leaving their horses strove to slip off by circuitous ways toward the sea, into which they plunged headlong from the promontories, some five perches high. Truly in a notable manner was that hostile race driven back, so that for two miles you could see nothing but the flight of those who just before had been so pertinacious in attack, so haughty, and so fierce. But with God's aid, thus did their pride perish. And indeed our whole army, ranged in its several ranks, had borne down upon the Turks. The Normans and English chosen to guard the Standard drew up gradually and with cautious steps towards that part of our army that was fighting, keeping no great distance from the battle, so that all might have a sure place of refuge.

At last, having finished their slaughter our men paused, but the Turks continued their flight till, seeing our slackness, they regained their courage, and immediately more than 20,000 strong fell upon our men in the rear, threatening them with clubs in the hope of releasing our captives. With deadliest effect they kept launching forth their darts and arrows; smashing, lopping, bruising the heads, arms, and other limbs of our knights, till these bent stupidly over their saddle bows. At last our men recovering their courage, fierce as a lioness robbed of her whelps, rushed upon them again, forcing a way through them as if they were merely tearing through meshes. . , .

Over this host of Turks there was a certain *emir*, a kinsman of Saladin. This warrior had a banner marked with a wonderful device, to wit, a pair of breeches. These he bore—a device well known to his men. This Takeda pursued the Christians with a peculiarly fierce hatred; and he had with him on this occasion more than 700 choice and sturdy Turks, attached to his person. They were selected from Saladin's special followers. Each squadron of this body carried a yellow banner in front with a pennon of a different colour. And now, coming on at full speed, with noise and pride they fell upon our men who began to turn off from them towards the Standard, . . . Our men held out unmoved, repelling force by force. . . . Yet could not this part of our army easily make its way back to the standard, hemmed in as they were by so great a host of enemies. . . .

At last William des Barres, seeing their plight, and breaking through the line galloped headlong against the foe, attacking them with such energy that, after he had slain some with his sword, the rest took to flight. Then the king, sitting on his peerless Cyprian steed, with his chosen band made towards the hills, routing all the Turks he met; helmets clinked as the enemy fell before him, and sparks leapt out from the battery of his sword. So fierce was his onset this day that the Turks very soon all turned off from his irresistible attack, and left a free passage to our army. Thus, at last, despite their wounds, our men reached the Standard, the ranks were formed again, and the host proceeded to Arsuf, outside which town it pitched its tents.

Whilst busied in this work a huge mass of Turks fell upon our rear. Hearing the din of conflict King Richard, calling his own folk to battle, gave reins to his horse, and with only 15 comrades rushed against the Turks, crying out with a loud voice "God and the Holy Sepulchre aid us." This cry he uttered a second and a third time and, when the rest of his men heard his voice, they hurriedly followed him, fell upon the foe, and drove them in headlong rout right up to the wood of Arsuf, whence they had formerly come. . . . Then the king returned to his camp, and our men, wearied with so fierce a combat, rested for the night.

Those who were eager for spoil went back to the battlefield and got as much plunder as they desired. Men who in this way returned used to say that they counted thirty-two *emirs* whom they found lying dead—all cut off on this day. These they reckoned to be men of the greatest authority and power, from their splendid arms and costly gear; and the Turks afterwards begged leave to carry them off because of their rank. In addition, they brought back news of 7,000 Turkish corpses, to say nothing of the wounded, who, straggling here and there out of the fight, died later on, and lay scattered over the fields. But thanks to God's protection, hardly a tenth or even a hundredth of this number fell on our side.

Of all whom the Turks cut off James de Avesnes was the one whose loss is most to be lamented. Whilst he was fighting in the deadly stress of combat, his horse staggered and laid its rider on the earth. Then the Turks crowded round and slew him after much labour. But, before his death, according to the report of those who brought back his body, he had slain some 15 Turks. And these were found lying dead in a circle round him. With him were also found slain three of his kinsmen, to whom certain of our men—shame be on them—who were present at the time did not bear aid, but left them struggling against the Turks as they came on.

For this cause the Count of Dreux and his men were stamped with indelible infamy. Oh, how various are the chances of war! how many groans and sighs were there in the army that night because of the absence of James de Avesnes, James that fearless knight, that illustrious warrior whom (his comrades) surmised to have been slain since he was not with the others. By reason of this apprehension was the whole army perturbed and stunned at the thought of so irreparable a loss.

The battle had been fought on the Saturday before the Nativity of the Blessed Mary (*i.e.*, 7 Sept., 1191), and on the day following, Sunday, orders were issued to search for the body so as to give it burial. Then the Hospitallers and the Templars, taking with them many valiant *Turcoples* and others, donned their armour. These reaching the place, made anxious search, and at last found the body. The face was so thickly covered with blood that before washing it with water they hardly recognised the features; so smeared with gore was he, so swollen with his wounds, and so utterly unlike his former self. Then wrapping the body up decently they carried it down with them to Arsuf. There might you see a great host of knights coming forth to meet the body.

The whole army grieved over the death of so great a man, recollecting his valour, his liberality, and his large dower of virtues. King Richard and King Guy were present at his burial; and for his soul mass was solemnly celebrated with no small offerings in the church of our Lady, the Queen of Heaven, whose natal day it was. Afterwards noble men, taking the body up in their arms, laid it in the grave with sobbing and with tears. Then the burial being done, the clergy honoured the day of the Blessed Mary with due solemnity.

SALADIN'S COUNCIL AFTER THE BATTLE OF ARSUF.

Now Saladin hearing that his choicest troops in whom he placed most trust had been thus routed, was full of wrath and confusion. Then calling his *emirs* together he upbraided them thus:

> Lo! truly splendid are the deeds of my comrades, and right well have they, to whom I have given so many gifts, prospered after all their boasts and pride. See the Christian host now wanders at its will over all Syria with no one to resist it. . . . Here you have the war for which you craved ready to hand, but where is the victory of which you vaunted? How miserably do we of this generation fall short of our noble ancestors, who waged such memorable wars against the Christians, and whose memory will last for ever. . . . Compared with them we are as nothing—we are not worth an egg.

At these reproaches the *emirs* stood silent with downcast looks, till one of them, Sanscunsus of Aleppo by name, made answer thus:

> Most sacred *Soldan*, saving the respect due to your presence, you blame us unjustly, for we attacked the Franks with all our might. . . . But nothing is able to injure them, fortified as they are with impenetrable armour that gives no passage to any kind of missile or sword. It is owing to this that all our attempts against them fell as useless as if expended on very flints. Moreover, one there is of their number at whom we have the greatest cause to wonder. He himself confounds and routs our people. Never have we seen his like; or met with his peer. He is ever foremost of the enemy at each onset; he is first as befits the pick and flower of knighthood. It is he who maims our folk. No one can resist him or rescue a captive from his hands. In their own tongue (the Christians) call him *Melec* (king) Richard. Rightly ought such a king to have dominion over the earth; for a man endued with such valour is strong to subdue all lands. What can

we do more against so mighty and invincible a foe?

Then Saladin, in the heat of his anger, called up his brother Saphadin, and spake as follows:

Know that I wish to see how far I can trust my people in this emergency. Therefore, without delay go forth and lay the walls and towers of Ascalon level with the ground; so too with Gaza. But have Darum kept safe to afford a passage to my people. Likewise destroy Galatia and Blancheguard, Joppa, the Casal of the Plains and Casal Maen, St. George (i.e., Lydda, where was the great church of St. George), and Ramula, Beaumont, Toron, Castle Arnold, Belvoir, and Mirabel. Moreover, thou must beat down our mountain strongholds; nor shall thine eye spare any city, castle or village (casal). Destroy everything, lay everything low, saving Crac (or Karak the great fortress near the S.E. extremity of the Dead Sea), and Jerusalem only.

(And Saphadin going forth without delay accomplished all that Saladin bade him.

Meanwhile a certain most renowned and powerful Saracen, Caysac by name, began to urge Saladin to send out spies into the plain of Ramula (Ar Ramleh, in the 10th century the chief town of Palestine, 2½ miles from Lydda), to see where the Franks were turning. "For," said he, "with gallant comrades I have hopes of cutting off a great part of the Franks should they propose to go in that direction." . . . Then at his prompting Saladin sent 30 emirs of might and fame to hold the river of Arsuf, (the Nahr al'Aujeh.) Each emir led well-nigh 500 sturdy Turks, and they kept watch lest the Franks should cross the river.

On the third day after the battle, i.e., on Monday the morrow of the Blessed Mary's Nativity, (Sept. 9th), King Richard set out with his army from Arsuf. The Templars marched warily in the rear in order to guard against a sudden onset. But even after reaching the aforesaid river they found no obstacle; for the Turks lay in ambush hoping to overwhelm the French with darts and arrows as they came on. But 'twas all to no purpose; for which reason, not unmindful of the late battle, they withdrew, and our men pitched their tents for that night above the river of Arsuf.

Thence early (Sept. 10) in the morning the common folk and our foot soldiers who had hardly borne up against the hardships of the way went ahead with the harbourers (men whose duty it was to quarter the army), to Joppa—a place which had already been destroyed so utterly

101

by the Saracens that the army could not dwell there except in its left part. (Joppa lies on the coast some 10 miles S. of Arsuf. It was the port whence the first Crusaders received their provisions at the siege of Jerusalem.) So, the army coming to Joppa fixed its tents in a very fair olive-orchard, and there abode (Tuesday, Sept. 10). But why say more? Three weeks had already passed since the army first left Acre, (*i.e.* reckoning from the day when the Saracen prisoners were massacred.)

Now the army resting outside Joppa in the open country enjoyed an abundance of different kinds of fruits. For in that place was there plenty of grapes, figs, pomegranates, and huge almonds, with which the branches were overladen everywhere. And lo! King Richard's fleet, and with it the vessels of other (chiefs), came up in the wake of the army. And ships went to and from between Joppa and Acre unmolested, bringing victuals and all that was necessary; at which the Turks grieved much, seeing they were unable to hinder it.

Meanwhile Saladin had caused the towers and walls of Ascalon to be pulled down; and certain common folk, fleeing thence to our army by night, brought the news. . . . By the advice of his nobles, King Richard sent Geoffrey de Lusignan and William de Stagno in a swift galley to investigate the truth of these rumours. These and many others with them sailed right up to Ascalon and, staying before the city, noted the truth of these reports, and, finding them to be correct, rowed back speedily to the king. Thereupon King Richard called a council of the chiefs and leaders of the people to consult whether it would be better to set out for Ascalon so as to save it from utter destruction or advance towards Jerusalem. On these points opinions varied; till at last King Richard set forth his own opinion in the presence of the Duke of Burgundy and the other chiefs:

> All seem to be of different minds—a circumstance which may do us no slight harm—though God forbid it. The Turks, who are destroying Ascalon, dare not make war on us; for which reason I would have you know I think it will be the wisest plan to put the Turks to rout and so save Ascalon. For the route through Ascalon is recognised to be of the utmost importance to pilgrims the whole world over.

****

The importance of Ascalon lay in its being the frontier seaport town towards Egypt. So long as it remained in Saracen hands the *Sultan* could at any moment mass his troops by sea or land against the kingdom of Jerusalem.

The French persistently opposed this scheme on the plea that Joppa ought to be restored first; because if this were done the journey to Jerusalem would be shortened. Why waste words? The acclamation of the crowd supported their view. O blind counsel of sluggards; fatal persistency of the lovers of ease! .... For had they but cleared Ascalon of the Turks the whole land would have been freed at once. Howbeit the people's cry prevailed and it was decreed to make a collection for the restoration of Joppa; and straightway men began to set to work at digging ditches and repairing the towers.

There the army rested a long time in ease and pleasure; while day after day its manifold sins increased—to wit, drunkenness and luxury. For the women from Acre began to return to the army and were a source of iniquity to corrupt the whole people whose love for pilgrimage diminished as its religious zeal abated.

Towards the end of September, when Joppa was partly repaired, the army quitted the suburbs and spread its tents near the Casal of St. Habakkuk. (According to Dr. Stubbs about three miles N. of Lydda.) It was lessened in number, because no small part had sailed back to Acre, where it dwelt in taverns. King Richard, noting the general sloth and falling away, despatched King Guy as his envoy to Acre to exhort the pilgrims to return to Joppa; and when only a very few obeyed his bidding, Richard himself took sail for Acre and there he delivered to the people a most moving discourse about faith and trust in God and the remission of sins—if indeed they did not mean to be pilgrims in the name only.

By such words he stirred up many and brought them back with him to Joppa. He also made the queens with their maidens come to Joppa, where it was reckoned that the army waited almost seven weeks whilst (our) people, who had scattered themselves in all directions, were coming together. But, when once collected, the army was much larger than before, (c. Oct.

1191.—(?SEPT. 29)—K. RICHARD RESCUED FROM THE SARACENS BY SIR WILLIAM OF PRÉAUX.

Itin. Ric. iv.

At this time, it happened that King Richard went out attended by a very small company of his friends to take the air along with his falcons. Now he had also intended to note the condition of the Turks should he see any, and seize them if he came upon them unprepared;

but, being worn out with his journey and his exertions, it chanced that he fell asleep.

And lo! of a sudden the Turks, learning this, swooped down at full speed hoping to take him prisoner. The king, however, roused by the noise of their approach, had just time to mount his Cyprian bay, (the famous horse that Richard brought with him to the Holy Land, described as being of unparalleled speed), and his companions to get on their steeds, when the Turks rushed up and attempted to seize him. Drawing his sword, he set upon them whilst they at once, making a pretence of flight, drew him off to an ambush, from which a great host of Turks suddenly burst forth in such numbers as to surround the king and his little band.

But, bravely brandishing his sword, he kept his assailants at bay, notwithstanding all their efforts; and, though it was the aim of each enemy to take him prisoner he soon forced them to hold off their hands. Even then, perchance, he would have been taken prisoner—deprived as he was of all human aid—had the Turks been quite sure which he was. But in the stress and din of the combat one of the king's comrades, William de Préaux, calling out in Saracen tongue that he was the *Melee* (which turned into Latin means *rex*), was at once surrounded by the Turks and carried off captive to their army.

In the same engagement was slain one of the king's comrades, Reynier de Marun, an illustrious knight, but (on this occasion) almost unarmed. His nephew Walter was also slain, as were Alan and Luke de Stabulo. When this incident was bruited abroad all our army was thrown into confusion; and, hastily seizing its arms and pricking on its steeds, went out to look for the king, until they fell in with him as he came back. On meeting him they rejoiced exceedingly over his safety, while he, going on with them, pursued the Turks precipitately. But their endeavours were vain, for they could not overtake the enemy, who had gone off at full speed with their captive William, exulting mightily at the thought of having taken the king prisoner.

But the king, thanks to God's mercy, was reserved to accomplish greater deeds. At last, seeing that the Turks galloped off too quickly, our folk returned to the army delighted that they had recovered the king safe and whole, and rejoicing in the Lord all the more because they had so nearly lost him.

But there was great sorrow for William de Préaux who by so generous a sacrifice of his own body had purchased the safety of his lord the king. O fealty worthy of all renown! O rare devotion that a man should willingly subject himself to danger in order to spare another! Now some of the king's most intimate friends, out of their great love, reproached him for his frequent rashness and prayed him not to ride abroad in this lonely way anymore for fear of falling into the enemy's hands. For, they said, the safety of all depended on that of the king. . . With such words and with all the daring of friendship they strove to convince the king.

But he none the less delighted to be first in all onsets and last in all retreats; for "who can entirely turn his nature out of doors, even with a pitchfork?" And, whether by reason of his valour or by Divine aid, things almost always turned out according to his wish, so that he would bring back with him a number of Turkish prisoners, or, if they offered any resistance, beat them down and maim them.

1191, OCT. 1.—KING RICHARD'S LETTER HOME, TELLING OF HIS PROGRESS AFTER THE KING OF FRANCE LEFT.

Roger of Howden, iii.

"Richard by the grace of God King of England, Duke of Normandy and Aquitaine, and Earl of Anjou, to N. his beloved and faithful (servant), sends greeting. Know that after the taking of Acre and the departure of the King of France, who there, against the will of God and to the eternal dishonour of his kingdom, so shamelessly failed in his vow, we set out for Joppa. And as we were nearing Arsuf Saladin came fiercely swooping down upon us. But, of God's mercy, we lost no man of importance that day, saving one only—James de Avesnes— a man right dearly beloved by the whole army; and rightly so too, for he had proved himself, by many years' service in the Christian host, to be vigorous, devout, and, as it were, a very column (of support) in holiness and sincerity of word.

"Thence by God's will we came to Joppa, which we have fortified with ditch and wall in our desire to do everything that can promote the Christian cause. On that day, to wit on the Vigil of the Nativity of the Blessed Mary, Saladin lost an infinite number of his greatest men; and being put to flight, in the absence of all help and counsel, he has laid waste the whole land of Syria. On the third day before Saladin's defeat, we were ourselves wounded with a spear on the left side; but, thanks to God, we have now regained strength. Know also that by twenty days after Christmas we hope, through God's grace, to receive the Holy City of Jerusalem and the Lord's Sepulchre, after which we shall return to our own land. Witness our own (hand) at Joppa, 1st

1191, OCT. 1.—KING RICHARD'S LETTER TO THE ABBOT OF CLAIRVAUX RESPECTING HIS PROGRESS AND ASKING FOR AID.

Roger of Howden, iii.

(After greeting his correspondent, Richard tells his story thus.)

Within a brief space of time after the arrival of the King of France at Acre we reached the same place under the Lord's guidance. There after a great lapse of time the city of Acre was restored to the lord King of the French and to us, who granted life to the Saracens on this understanding—fully signed on Saladin's part—that he would restore us fifteen hundred captives. A day was set for the fulfilment of all these conditions, and, as it passed by without the terms of the treaty being carried out, about 2,600 Saracens whom we had in custody were put to death. We spared, however, a few of the nobler ones, in the hope of recovering the Holy Cross and certain captive Christians in exchange for them.

Now when the King of France had gone back to his own land, and after we had repaired the walls of Acre, we proposed to go to Joppa, in company with the Duke of Burgundy and his men, Count Henry and his followers, many other counts, barons, and an innumerable host of people. . . As our fore-guard was pitching its camp near Arsuf, Saladin swooped down upon our rear, but in God's mercy was put to flight by the four squadrons, who alone were opposed to him. On that day, to wit, on Saturday the eve of the Nativity of St. Mary the Virgin, there was so great a slaughter of Saladin's best Saracens as he has never experienced for forty years. . . . After this defeat Saladin, not daring to encounter the Christians, laid snares for them afar off, lying hidden like a lion in his cave.

And having heard that we should go steadily on to Ascalon, he laid that town level with the earth; for which reason with God's aid, we have good hope of speedily recovering the heritage of the Lord. And now that the heritage of the Lord is partly recovered; now that, with this object in view, we have borne the burden and heat of the day; now that we have spent not only all our money, but our strength and our flesh too, we signify to you our utter inability to stay in the parts of Syria beyond Easter. The Duke of Burgundy and his Frenchmen, Count Henry and his men, and other counts, barons, and knights who have spent their (wealth) in God's service, will also go home unless by your activity in preaching to the people (at home), means are provided for peopling the land, and money procured to be spent more freely in God's service.

Wherefore, falling at your knees, we beg you with tears and earnest prayers to stir up the chiefs and noble men and the (common) folk throughout all Christendom to the service of the living God. Make it your business (to ensure their arrival) after Easter in defence of God's heritage, for with His favour, we shall hold till then what we shall win. .. Do you therefore, in this extremity, rouse the people of God to the same vigorous action as you urged upon us and God's other people for the restitution of His heritage, before we started. Signed with our own (hand), at Joppa, 1st Oct.

CIRC. OCT. 29 TO C. NOV. 14.—RICHARD LEAVES JAFFA AND MOVES IN THE DIRECTION OF RAMLEH, REBUILDING TWO FORTRESSES ON THE WAY.

Itin., iv.

Now when the army had regained its strength the king decreed an expedition of the whole host for the reconstruction of the Casal of the Plains—a movement that was deemed very needful to secure a safe passage for pilgrims. The king appointed men to guard Joppa and to complete its walls; with orders to keep the gates most closely lest anyone, excepting the merchants who brought provisions, should get away. To this office he deputed the Bishop of Evreux, the Count of Châlons, and Hugh Ribole, with some others.

RICHARD RESTORES CASAL MAEN (OCT. 30—C. NOV. 14).

Itin, Ric. iv.

Now on the Wednesday before All Saints, as the king was roving in the plains of Ramula, he set upon some Saracen scouts whom he chanced to see, and, thundering on like a wild boar, put them to flight, slaying some. Amongst the dead he left a certain very noble *emir* lying headless on the plain. But the Turks fled. On the morrow, to wit on All Saints Eve, the king, after a short journey, pitched his tents between the Casal of the Plains and Casal Maen. (These are somewhere between Jaffa and Ramleh or Lydda.) The Turkish Army was then at Ramula, from which place their men often made sudden sallies against us. In this place the king dwelt fifteen days or more and restored Casal Maen to its old strength. The Templars rebuilt Casal of the Plains, despite the incessant attacks of the Turks.

One day when a great number of the enemy, together with near a thousand horsemen, threatened us, the king, mounting his horse, went out to meet them. Our army was thrown into confusion and, as they were rushing to arms, the Turks were routed; twenty-six of them slain and sixteen taken prisoners. But the others, scampering off on their fleet steeds, were not captured, though the king followed them with the utmost persistence till he came within full sight of Ramula where the Turkish Army was camped. Then our men returned to the army.

1191, Nov. 6—K. Richard rescues a company of Templars.

Itin., Ric. iv.

On the sixth day after All Saints, that is on the Feast of St. Leonard, (*i.e.*, Wednesday, Nov. 6, 1191), there went out into the country certain camp followers and men-at-arms to seek grass for the horses and fodder for the mules. The Templars went ahead of the men-at-arms so as to ensure them safety as they wandered away from one another over the valleys on the look out for grassy places. For they were wont to scatter themselves in this way when in quest of herbage—herbage which they not seldom washed with their blood owing to their lack of caution.

While the Templars, as we have said, were keeping a watch over the men-at-arms, suddenly from the direction of Bombrac some 4,000 Turkish horsemen, orderly drawn up in four squadrons, leapt forth and attacked the Templars boldly. So closely did they hem the Templars in as to bid fair to destroy or take them captive. This band of Turks was constantly being increased by fresh-comers, till the Templars, hedged in as they were, and seeing it was a case of emergency, dismounted from their steeds. Then, setting back to back firmly, and turning their face Ti

A Party of Crusaders returning from a Foraging Expedition.
From a Thirteenth Century MS. of William of Tyre.

Then might be seen indeed a fierce fight, and blows most valorous. Helms rang and fiery sparks darted out where sword clashed with sword; armour rattled, and there was a din of (many) voices. The Turks pressed on like men; the Templars (as) firmly hurled them back: the one body threatened; the other repelled. The Turks came on bravely; the Templars defended themselves with the utmost courage. At last, the Turks, swarming up in greater numbers, put out their hands to seize the Templars who were now almost overpowered, when lo! Andrew de Chavigni, coming up to their aid at full speed with 15 knights, rescued them from the hands of their foes. Most valiantly did the same Andrew bear himself on this occasion, as did also his comrades when they set upon this crowd of enemies and routed it. But, for all this, the host of the Turks kept on growing larger; now they pressed on; now they fled; then once more the battle was renewed. Meanwhile King Richard' who was carefully supervising the fortification of Casal Maen, hearing the din of conflict, bade the two Earls of St. Pol and Leicester ride with all speed to the Templars' aid. With them he sent William de Cageu and Otho de Trasynges.

As these knights were on the point of starting there rose a cry for help from the before-mentioned men-at-arms. Hearing this the king bade the earls make speed and, seizing his own arms as fast as he could, followed in their wake. Now, as the two earls were hastily riding along, on a sudden about 4,000 of the enemy, leaping out of an ambush from the neighbourhood of a certain stream, formed themselves into two masses. Of these two thousand attacked the Templars, while the other two thousand turned against the two earls and their comrades. Seeing this the earls, drawing up their men in fitting order, got ready for battle.

It was then that the Earl of St. Pol made an unseemly proposition to the noble Earl of Leicester: to wit that the Earl of St. Pol should engage with the enemy, whilst the Earl of Leicester should watch the action from a distance and bring aid if necessary; or that the Earl of Leicester should engage with the Turks, leaving the Earl of St. Pol to look on, watching over the safety of his fighting comrade, but standing apart from the battle. The Earl of Leicester chose to attack, for he could not brook to watch the battle and do nothing. And so, taking his own men with him, he hurled himself where the crowd of Turks was densest, and manfully rescued two of our captive knights from the hands of the enemy. So valorously, so stubbornly did he combat, here laying men low, there lopping off their limbs, that by his achievements on that day his glory was largely increased.

The battle was already waging more fiercely on either side, when

Richard came up trembling (with wrath). Some of his followers reckoning the men he led too few to attack so vast a host of enemies, said to him:

> Lord king, we judge it unwise to begin what we are not sure of being able to carry out. We do not judge it safe to attack so great and so valiant a force with only a few (warriors). Even if you are minded to make so bold a venture you will not be able to bear their onset or to gain your object, if it is your intention to succour our friends by driving off their assailants. For our numbers are not sufficient against so many. Surely it were better to let these men—surrounded as they are by our foes—perish than for thee to get encompassed by the Turks. For, in that case, the very hope of Christendom would perish, and the mainstay of all our confidence fall. We deem it the wiser counsel to secure your safety and decline the fight.

To their persuasion the king replied, changing colour:

> When I sent my loved comrades out to war it was with the promise of bringing them aid. And if I fail to do this, so far as I can, I shall deceive those who trusted to me. And should they meet with death in my absence—which I pray may never happen—never more will I bear the name of king.

Uttering no more words he spurred forward his steed, bursting upon the Turks with wonderful fury, by his vigorous onset scattering their close ranks like a thunderbolt, and laying many low by the mere vigour of his movements. Then, turning back to his own men he scattered the whole body of the enemy, brandishing his sword, going hither and thither, backwards and forwards, bold as a lion. . . . Amongst others, he smote and slew a certain *emir* of gigantic strength and great fame, Ar-al-chais by name. Why recount details? When the enemy had been routed and pursued our men returned to their own quarters with very many captives. Thus was the battle waged on this day without any aid from the French. On the same day three Turkish apostates, renouncing their vain superstition and becoming Christians, submitted to King Richard—it may be through fear of death.

1191, c. Nov. 6.—KING RICHARD'S NEGOTIATIONS WITH SALADIN AND SAPHADIN.

Itin. Ric., iv.

When these two *casals* were repaired . . . . Richard sent noble and wise envoys to Saladin and his brother Saphadin demanding the whole realm of Syria with all its appurtenances just as the Leper King, (Baldwin IV.), had held it. He also demanded tribute from Babylon (*i.e.*, Cairo) just as the kings, his predecessors, had received it. (Egypt according to William of Tyre, paid tribute to Baldwin III.) He claimed by hereditary right all that had from any time (however remote) belonged to the kingdom of Jerusalem, by right of kinship to the preceding kings who had acquired and held it. When the envoys had clearly put forward the substance of the king's demand, Saladin would not acquiesce, he said:

> Your king demands what I cannot assent to without dishonouring Paganism. Nevertheless, I will send by my brother Saphadin, offering him the whole land of Jerusalem, to wit from the River Jordan to the Western Sea, on this one condition, that neither Christian nor Saracen shall ever rebuild Ascalon.

Now when Saphadin came to King Richard with these proposals, the king would not have an interview with him that day, because he had just been bled. (In the Middle Ages bleeding was part of the recognised cure for almost all ailments.) But, at the king's order, Stephen of Turnham entertained Saphadin at breakfast with all manner of delicate foods. This banquet took place between the Casal of the Temple and that of Josaphat.

On the morrow Saphadin sent King Richard seven precious camels and a beautiful tent.

Now when Saphadin, coming to the king, had disclosed Saladin's offers, the king, thinking matters were in a troubled state and that the chances of war were doubtful, saw fit to temporize; for he did not perceive the guile with which they were spinning out the negotiations, so that in the meanwhile they might destroy the cities, castles, and strongholds of the land. In short Saphadin so imposed upon the unsuspecting king with his cunningly-fashioned speeches, that they seemed to have contracted an intimate friendship with one another. For the king consented to receive Saphadin's presents; and messengers were always running between them bearing little gifts from Saphadin to King Richard.

The king's conduct seemed very blameworthy to his men, and it was a common saying that friendship with the Gentiles was a heinous crime. But Saphadin declared himself to be anxious to establish a fixed and lasting peace. So, the king deemed himself acting wisely in making an open and fair peace for the enlargement of the bounds of Christendom; more especially because the King of France had already gone away; (and King Richard) had cause to dread his inconstancy and guile, seeing that (Philip's) friendship had sometimes turned out to be a very hollow sham.

When, however, King Richard found all Saphadin's proffers to be mere words and that the negotiations did not turn out as he wished—especially as regards Crac de Montréal, whose dismantling the king sought to secure as part of the treaty—he broke off entirely. Afterwards, when it was notorious that the peace would come to nothing, you might see the Turks attacking us right and left; whereon King Richard went out to fight them more frequently than ever; and to clear his name of the scandal attached to it carried off the heads of those enemies he had slain as a token that no amount of gifts would make him less energetic against the foe.

13 OCT.—ARAB FREEBOOTERS IN SALADIN'S SERVICE.

Bohâdin

On 22 *Ramadan*, (*i.e.*, Sunday, 13 Oct., 1191), some thieves brought the *Sultan* a horse and a mule that they had stolen from the enemy's camp into which they had penetrated. The *Sultan* had taken into his pay three hundred Arab freebooters, robbers by profession, whose duty it was to make their way into the enemy's quarters and steal his money and his horses. They would also carry off men while still alive. This is how they managed. One of their number would creep up to a sleeping Frank and wake him by putting a dagger to his throat; the sleeper, seeing the thief armed with a dagger, dared not utter a word and let himself be carried outside the camp. Some who dared to cry had their throats cut on the spot; others, finding themselves in such a plight, said nothing, preferring captivity to death. This state of things went on till peace was concluded.

13 OCT.-NOV. 15.—NEGOTIATIONS BETWEEN RICHARD AND SALADIN.

Bohâdin

The same day (22 *Ramadan*) there came a messenger from the front announcing the arrival of a body of troops from Acre. These troops our vanguard had attacked and made twenty-one prisoners, who confirmed the news of the King of England's return to Acre, as also of his illness. The garrison at Acre they added was very weak, food was becoming scarce, and there was little or no money. The same day there came up a numerous fleet from Acre (as they say) with the King of England on board. These ships had a great many men intended as a garrison for Ascalon or, according to others, meant to march against Jerusalem. . . . In the evening of the 24th (*i.e.*, Tuesday, Oct. 15), there came a messenger from the King of England with a beautiful horse as a present to Al Adil in return for those he had himself received from the prince.

On *Ramadan*, the 26, (*i.e.*, Thursday, Oct. 17), Al Malec al Adil who was then commanding our advanced guard received an intimation from the King of England to send him a messenger. Al Adel sent a goodly young man who was his secretary. The interview took place at Yazour whither this prince had come with a considerable number of infantry. . . . Sometime was passed in conversation about the peace and the king uttered these words: "I will not withdraw the word I have given my brother and friend"—terms by which he designated Al Malec al Adil, to whom he then despatched the same messenger with the propositions he offered. In the same spirit he wrote the following letter to the *Sultan:*—

Greet him, O my letter, and tell him that both Musulmans and Franks are reduced to the last extremity; their towns are destroyed and the resources of both sides in men and goods are reduced to nothing. Surely, we have had enough of this state of things; and it is only a question of Jerusalem, the Holy Cross and (our old) possessions. Jerusalem we are resolved not to renounce so long as we have a single man left; and, as regards the Holy Cross, to you it is nothing but a worthless bit of wood, whereas it has great value in our eyes and the *Sultan* will be doing us a great favour if he restore it. Everything will then come right of itself and we shall enjoy a pleasant rest after our long toils.

After reading this letter the *Sultan* gathered his counsellors together to consult them as to his reply, which finally ran as follows :—

To us Jerusalem is as precious, aye and more precious, than it is to you, in that it was the place whence our Prophet made his journey by night to heaven and is destined to be the gathering place of our nation at the last day. Do not dream that we shall give it up to you or that we can be so obliging in this matter. As to the land—it belonged to us originally, and it is you who are the real aggressors. When you seized it, it was only because of the suddenness of your coming and the weakness of those Musulmans who then held it. So long as the war shall last God will not suffer you to raise one stone upon another. Finally, as regards the cross, its possession is very profitable to us and we should not be justified in parting with it unless to the advantage of Islam.

Such was ⟨ing of Eng-
land.

INCENSE-BURNER OF THE 11TH CENTURY, representing the Temple
of Jerusalem. *From the treasure of Trèves Cathedral.*

On the 29th day of *Ramadan.* (*i.e.*, Sunday, Oct. 20, 1191), Al Adil sent for me and four others to tell us of the proposal that had been made to him by the King of England's messenger. Its substance was as follows: That Al Adil should wed the king's sister, whom he had brought with him from Sicily at his crossing over; for her husband, the King of Sicily, was then dead. She was to be established in Jerusalem and her brother would yield her all the places he held in the Sahel, (the low plain country bordering the Mediterranean)—to wit, Acre, Jaffa, Ascalon, and their dependances.

The *Sultan*, on his side, was to give Al Adil all that he possessed in the Sahel and declare him King of that country. Al Adil was to retain all the towns and the fiefs he actually owned; but the Holy Cross was to be restored to the Franks. The villages were to be given up to the

114

Templars and Hospitallers, while the strongholds were to be reserved for the newly-married pair. The Musulman and the Frankish prisoners were to be set free and the King of England was to embark for his own land. That is the way, said the king, to settle everything.

Al Adil, who was pleased with the proposal, sent for us and charged us to carry the communication to the *Sultan*. I was to be spokesman for those who accompanied me. Should the *Sultan* approve of this arrangement and see the advantages it brought to the Musulmans, I was to call my colleagues to witness his approbation and consent; whereas, if he rejected the definite offer now made, they might bear witness to his refusal Accordingly we presented ourselves before the *Sultan* and I acted as spokesman, telling him what had happened in the conference; after which I read Al Adil's letter in the presence of my colleagues.

The *Sultan* eagerly gave his consent, knowing full well that the King of England would not hold to the engagement, which was only a piece of trickery or a joke on his part. At my request he gave his formal consent, saying "Yes" three times and calling all the bystanders to take note of it. We then returned to Al Adil and told him all that had passed. My colleagues declared that I had warned the *Sultan* several times that I was going to hold his words in evidence and that he had persisted in approving everything. And, this being so, the proposition might be accepted with his consent.

On the second day of *Shawall*, (*i.e.*, Wednesday, Oct. 23), Ibn al Nahdal set out for the enemy's camp as Al Adil's envoy. When the king heard of his arrival, he sent word that the princess had flown into a passion at the very suggestion of such a marriage, and had rejected it in the most formal manner, swearing that she would never become the wife of a Musulman. Her brother added: "If Al Malec al Adil will only become a Christian we will carry out the marriage." Thus, did he leave the door open for a continuance of the negotiations.

16 *Shawall* (*i.e.*, Wednesday, 6 November, 1191), towards evening Al Adil received a messenger from the King of England. This envoy came to complain of the ambuscade and demand that Al Adil would grant his master an interview.

On the 18 of *Shawall* Al Adil accordingly went to the front, where a large tent had been set up to receive him. He also brought with him delicate meats and drinks, objects of art, and everything that it is customary to be offered by one prince to another. When minded to make gifts of this kind no one, as is well known, could surpass him in magnificence.

When the King of England reached his tent he received him with the greatest honour, ushered him in, and had him served with those dishes of his nation which he believed would be most agreeable to him. Al Adil, the king, and those who accompanied him all ate of the dishes offered. The interview lasted the greater part of the day and they parted with mutual assurances of perfect friendship.

The same day the king begged Al Adil to get him an interview with the *Sultan*, who, on receiving this message, consulted his council as to what reply he should make. But, for all this, the advice of no counsellor resembled the answer sent by the *Sultan*—which ran as follows:

It would be a shameful thing for kings to continue disputing after they have once met. Better let the questions at issue be settled first. . . . Moreover, I do not know your tongue any more than you understand mine; and so we should have to find an interpreter in whom we could each place confidence. Later, when definite terms have been agreed on, we will have a meeting to ratify our sincere friendship.

The King of England was struck with the wisdom of this answer and saw that his end could only be *reached* by conforming to the *Sultan's* wishes.

On the 19 *Shawall*, (Saturday, 9 November), the *Sultan* gave audience to the lord of Sidon in order that he might learn the object of his mission. I was present at the introduction of the envoy and his train. The *Sultan* received him very honourably, said a few words to his suite, and had them served with a magnificent banquet. Then, making everyone else withdraw, he remained alone with them to hear their propositions. . . . After listening to the envoy the *Sultan* promised to give him a reply later on. , . . .

At evening on the same day there arrived at the *Sultan's* quarters the son of Humfrey, (Henfrid IV. of Toron), one of the great Frank lords, with a message from the King of England. In his train was an aged man, said to be one hundred and twenty years old. . . . The king's message ran thus:

I love your uprightness and desire your friendship. You have already promised to give your brother all the coast. . . . But it is absolutely necessary that we should have part of Jerusalem. It is my wish to make such a division, that your brother may incur no blame from the Musulmans and I none from the Franks.

The *Sultan* immediately replied with fair words . . . but his object was to shake the foundations of the treaty. . . . After the envoys had left he turned to me and said:

If we were to make peace with this people nothing would secure us against their bad faith. If I chanced to die, there would be great difficulty in collecting such an army as we have here; and in the meanwhile, the enemy would have grown very strong. And so, it is better to continue the Holy War till we have either driven them from the sea-coast or are ourselves dead.

This was his private opinion, but that of the general public forced him to conclude peace.

On the 21st day of *Shawall* (*i.e.,* Monday, Nov. 11), the *Sultan* called his *emirs* and his counsellors together for the purpose of laying the propositions of the marquis before them. These propositions he was very eager to accept. . . . . At the same time, he laid the propositions of the King of England before them. The king demanded a certain number of towns along the coast by name, but would leave the hilly parts to the Mussulmans, or, failing this, all should be equally divided. In either case the Christians were to have priests in the monasteries and churches of the Holy City. . . . The *Sultan* submitted the conditions of the king and the marquis to his *emirs* . . . . to see which they would prefer. He also charged them to decide which of the king's two proposals was to be preferred.

The council declared that, if peace must be made, it should be with the king; for they could scarcely reckon on a real alliance between the Musulmans and the Franks (of Syria); but must always look out for treachery on the part of the latter. Then the assembly broke up, but the peace conferences continued, messengers never ceasing to pass to and fro till the basis of the treaty was settled. . . . On the marriage question the king, in his last communication with Al Adil said:

The whole Christian commonwealth blames me for wishing to marry my sister to a Musulman without obtaining the Pope's leave. Accordingly, I am sending him an ambassador to treat of this matter and I shall have an answer in six months. If he consents, the business will be done; if not, I will give you my brother's daughter to wife—for in this case there will be no need to ask the Pope's leave.

During all this time the hostilities were going on . . . and the

Lord of Sidon sometimes would ride out with Al Adil to examine the Frankish positions from a hill-top. Every day that the enemy saw these two together they renewed their efforts to get the peace signed. So great was their fear lest the marquis should conclude an alliance with the Musulmans and thus break up the power of the Franks. Things remained in this state till the 25 of *Shawall*, (*i.e.,* till Friday, Nov. 15.)

On the following Friday the *Sultan* had the envoys of the Franks from beyond the sea brought in (before his council). The son of Humfrey acted as interpreter. . . To the new marriage proposals, it was replied:

> If the marriage is to take place let it take place according to the original agreement, for we will not be false to our word. But, if this cannot be, there is no need to search out any other woman.

With this declaration ended the conference. . . And the *Sultan* set out for Jerusalem, the Franks for their own territories. As the winter was rough and rain fell in torrents the *Sultan* went off to the Holy City and we passed the whole winter in Jerusalem. . . The King of England set out for Acre, where he remained some time. He left, however, a garrison in Jaffa.

THE CAMP BETWEEN LYDDA AND RAMLEH.—CIRC. NOV. 14-C. DEC. 5, 1191.
THE CAMP AT RAMLEH AND LYDDA.—CIRC. DEC. 5, 1191 -C. DEC. (31), 1191.

Itin. Ric. iv.

After repairing the two *casals* and leaving guards there the king led his army towards Ramula. On hearing this Saladin, not daring to join battle, issued orders to destroy Ramula utterly; whilst he himself went off towards Darum, having confidence in the hills. Our army pitched its tents between St. George, (*i.e.*, Lydda), and Ramula, and there, abode twenty days waiting for reinforcements and provisions. There we were troubled by constant attacks; moreover, the heavy rains drove us from our position, so that the King of Jerusalem and our people had to remove into St. George and Ramula. . . . At Ramula we dwelt about six weeks.

And truly we were not in pleasant quarters; but a merry ending when it chances makes amends for hard beginnings. . . . On the eve of St. Thomas' day, (*i.e.,* Friday, Dec. 20) when King Richard with only a small following was going from our camp towards the *casal* of Blanche-garde, (from its heights there was an unbroken view of the hostile city), to lay an ambush for the Saracens, he turned back owing, as it is believed, to some divinely sent instinct that warned him of his peril. And lo! at that very hour two Saracens, who had fled to him, told him how Saladin had a little before despatched three hundred chosen warriors to Blanche-garde, whither the king had intended to go....At midnight of Holy Innocents' day, (*i.e.,* Saturday, Dec. 28), the Hospitallers and the Templars left the camp and returned at early dawn with 200 oxen, which they drove in from the mountains near Jerusalem.

THE EARL OF LEICESTER'S ADVENTURE.—DECEMBER.

Ibid.

One day it chanced that the noble Earl of Leicester, with only a few followers, attempted to drive back a large number of Turks who were insolently approaching our line. Three of his comrades pursuing the Turks too hotly were captured and carried off. Seeing this the earl hurled himself against more than a hundred of the enemy in his eagerness to free his friends. And lo! while he was following the Turks up beyond a certain river about 400 Turkish horsemen came up from one side with their reed lances and bows, cutting off the earl and his few comrades at the rear.

Having thus surrounded the earl they made every effort to take him prisoner. Already had they felled Warin Fitz Gerald from his horse and battered him with their iron clubs: . . . and lo! not much later Drogo de Fontenillo and Robert Nigel were unhorsed too; while so great a host of Turks and Persians pressed round the earl in the hopes of seizing him that at last they threw him from his horse, severely wounded him, and almost drowned him in the river.

He, brandishing his sword, dealt blows to right and left; and in that moment of peril there came to his aid Henry Fitz Nicholas and Robert de Newburgh of memorable renown, whose noble self-denial has gained him such eternal fame. He, seeing the earl so cruelly bestead, dismounted from his own steed and offered it to the earl, whose life he deemed more precious than his own. I fear that a deed of this kind begets very few imitations; though, on the contrary, every evil deed is largely copied. Thus, by his brave act did this noble Robert preserve his own life and the earl's. (In accordance with the ideal spirit of chivalry a vassal should at all times be ready to yield up his steed to secure his lord's safety.)

Besides these there were with the Earl Ralph de Sancta Maria,

Arnold de Bosco, Henry de Mailoc, William and Saul de Bruil..... At last, the Turks had so wearied the earl and his few followers that they could no longer bear up against the heavy brunt of the engagement but, clinging on to their horses' necks, stood out motionless receiving all the blows thundered down upon them. Finally, they were almost stupefied and, offering no further resistance, were carried off captives towards Darum.

O how good a thing it is to hope in the Lord! for He who guards Israel does not slumber, nor does He suffer anyone to be tried beyond what he is able. When our army heard the news of these exploits, the knights hurriedly armed themselves and went out, pursuing, attacking, scattering, mauling the Turks. Amongst our men, on this occasion, were Andrew de Chavigny, Henry de Gray, Peter des Préaux, and many other most renowned men of valour. Each slew his Turk at the first outset.

One Turk attacked by Peter des Préaux was of such prowess that Peter, though assisted by several of his comrades, failed to take him prisoner alive; nay it was with difficulty that they managed to get the better of him and slay him. Andrew de Chavigny pierced the *emir* who encountered him through the middle with his lance, and hurled him from his horse smitten with a deadly wound. Never more could he gather his host around him.

The same Turk pierced Andrew's arm with his reed-spear and broke it. On their *emir's* fall, the Turks rushed up together striving hard to rescue his body; but, so far as he was concerned, it was all up with him. Yet, for all this, the Turks pressed on against our men vigorously, and they would probably have prevailed had not our numbers increased.

The arrival of succours renewed the valour of the first warriors despite their fatigue. Then the battle raged fiercely; the earl dealt blows and received them, hurled down the Turks, was battered in his turn, cut off many a head, received many a blow from many antagonists, but for himself had never need to deal a second. Two horses were slain under him; wherefore it is truly said of him that no man so young and of so small stature ever performed such splendid feats of arms. At last, there came up to his aid so great a host of chosen knights from our army that—despite the crowd of combatants—none of our men fell. For, you must know, that the Turks now broke up and scattered in different directions, being pursued by our men until they were tired out and returned to the army in peace.

THE ARMY ADVANCES TOWARDS JERUSALEM AND REACHES BEIT NÛBA (C. DEC. 31) WHERE IT STAYS TILL (C. JAN. 13) 1192.

When Saladin knew that we were ready to advance on Jerusalem the Holy City and were only two miles away from his army, thinking it not safe to fight with the Christians, he gave orders to lay Darum level with the ground and fled to Jerusalem. The Turks too left the plains and occupied the heights, ... while our army in due order set forth (c. Dec. 31 according to Dr. Stubbs), for the Casa of Betenoble, (the present Beit-Nûba), where we were discomforted by heavy rain and unwholesome weather, owing to which very many of our beasts of burden died. Indeed, so great was the tempest and such the downpour of rain and showers, coupled with the blasts of violent winds, that the stakes of our tents were torn up and whirled away, whilst our horses perished of cold and wet. A great part of our food and biscuit was also spoiled; and the swine flesh, commonly called bacon, grew rotten.

Our armour and breastplates became fouled with rust and could not be restored to their original brightness by any amount of rubbing; clothes began to wear out and very many people, from long sojourn in a foreign land, lost health and were afflicted with great ills. This comfort alone sustained them: the hope that they were at last on the point of visiting the Lord's Sepulchre; for beyond measure did they desire to see the city of Jerusalem and finish their pilgrimage. Each man carried his own food so as to get the siege finished soon; and you might see people gladly volunteer in large numbers for any expedition.

Those also who had been lying sick at Joppa had themselves borne down in couches and beds to the army in the hopes of advancing towards Jerusalem. There also kept flowing in from every side an over-numerous host hoping to visit our Lord's Sepulchre with the army. This one hope was strong enough to overcome all inconveniences. But the Turks fell upon the sick as they were being borne down, slaying alike those who carried and who were being carried.

Now was the army glad in heart at the hope of reaching the Lord's Sepulchre which it had so long desired to see. Breast plates were scoured lest any rust should stain them; helms were furbished up with cloths lest the creeping damp should dim their gleam; sword blades are smeared with grease lest any moisture should tarnish their brightness. But why enumerate details? All got ready for the journey, boasting that no hostile attack and no obstacle should hinder them from accomplishing their pilgrimage.

But the wiser set of men did not fall in with the too hasty zeal of the common folk. For the Templars, the Hospitallers, and the Pullani, (those born of mixed Frankish/Syrian parents), having a sharper view of the future, dissuaded King Richard from going towards Jerusalem at that moment; because, they said, if he were to lay siege and set himself with all his might to take Saladin and all the Turks cooped up in the city with him, the Turkish Army that lay on the mountain heights outside would be making sudden attacks. Thus, there would be a double danger in every fight from the enemy in Jerusalem and the enemy outside. (The Christians would be in the same position as they had been at the siege of Acre between two enemies.)

Nor, they continued, if they were successful in capturing the city would their success avail much unless they had very stout warriors to whose care they might entrust the city. And this they did not think was likely to be the case, for, in their opinion, the people were show- ing all eagerness to get their pilgrimage finished, in order that they might get home without delay, being already unspeakably wearied at what they had undergone. For all these reasons they recommended the king in their subtlety to put off the advance in order that their warlike strength and numbers might not be diminished, and their (ranks) would hold together so long as the pilgrimage was not com- pleted. But their plea was not listened to at all.

The new year was already beginning, to wit, the year of the Lord 1192—a *Bissextile* year having D for its second dominical letter. And lo! on the third day after the *Circumcision*, (*i.e.*, Friday, 3 Jan, 1192), while our army was eagerly preparing to advance, a host of hideous Turks, who, during the preceding night had lurked among the thickets near the Casal of the Plains leapt forth at dawn to keep a guard on the road along which our army was about to move. It thus happened that they slew two of our followers, whom they saw going abroad early; for whose death God took a speedy vengeance. For King Richard (who, being forewarned of the Turkish ambush, had that same night lain hid near the Casal of the Baths—now 1900, Umm el Hommâm), came up to them now at full speed, hoping to rescue the two men.

When however, the Turks recognised Richard by his banner, they cut off their prisoners' heads and took to flight at once. They were almost a hundred in number, of whom the king slew or captured seven as they made for the hills. But the king, spurring on his Cyprian bay, caught up eight Turks in their flight towards Mirabel, (1900 the present Mejdel Yâba), and in the first encounter unhorsed two and maimed them, before any of his comrades could come up. Such was the incomparable swiftness of his steed. On this occasion Geoffrey de Lusignan with some other (knights) slew or captured twenty of these Turks and, had they followed up the fugitives closer and further, would assuredly have taken more.

8 JAN., 1192.—THE COUNCIL OF THE FRANKS.

Ibn Alathír, ii.

On the 20th of *Dulheggia* (*i.e.*, Wednesday, 8 Jan., 1192), the Franks returned to Ramleh. And this was the reason of their return.

They used to draw all their supplies from the coast; but when they had moved far inland the Musulmans began attacking their convoys and pillaging them as they went along the road. Then said the King of England to the Franks of Syria who were with them:

> Draw me a plan of Jerusalem; for I have never seen it.

And they drew him up a plan of the city. And, looking thereon, he saw the valley which surrounds the town everywhere except for a small space towards the North. Then began he to question concerning this valley and its depth. And they told him how it was deep and difficult to cross; whereon he said:

> It will be impossible to take this town so long as Saladin lives and the Musulmans are at peace one with the other. For if we lay siege on this side the other sides will be unbeleaguered, and by them will men and provisions be able to enter. Whereas if we divide our host and siege, it on either side Saladin will gather his army and attack one section. Nor will the other party be able to come to help its fellows for fear lest those in the town should make a sally on its quarters.

THE DETERMINATION TO RETIRE FROM BEIT-NÛBA TO THE COAST.—(C. JAN. 13) 1192.

Itin. Ric. v.

In the year 1192, not many days after *Epiphany*, the wise men (of the army) held a council, to which they summoned the more discreet natives of the land, for the purpose of deciding whether they should advance towards Jerusalem or turn aside elsewhere. By the recommendation of the Hospitallers, the Templars, and the Pullani, all idea of an advance was given up on the plea that they ought to busy themselves in rebuilding Ascalon, from which stronghold an eye might be kept on the carriage of food from Egypt to Jerusalem. . . .

Now when the order for retreat became known to the army, the common folk were taken with great grief; all groaned and sighed at finding the dear hope of their heart to visit the Lord's Sepulchre so suddenly cast away. . . . They invoked every ill on the authors of this decree, they cursed the delay and those who brought about such untoward things.

But had they known from what want those who were in Jerusalem then suffered they would have drawn some consolation from the misery of their foes. For the Turks, who were at that time cooped up in Jerusalem, were sorely straitened by reason of the heavy fall of snow and hail and the hillside floods that swept off their horses and mules. In truth, had our men known the true condition of the enemy, beyond a doubt Jerusalem might easily have been taken.

THE RETURN TO RAMLEH. C. JAN. 13, 1192.—THE FRENCH GO BACK TO JAFFA AND ELSEWHERE.

Itin, Ric., v.

The Feast of St. Hilary, (Monday, 13 Jan., 1192), was now drawing on, and so great a grief and anxiety for return urged our people that a good many almost apostatized, cursing the very day of their birth, and grieving it having been destined to such misfortunes. Moreover, sickness and want weakened many to such a degree that they could scarcely bear up; added to which many were not strong enough to carry their own food, whilst, thanks to the cold and rain, the horses and mules were constantly falling down through lack of strength. . . . Many of the sick would have run great peril had not King Richard, moved by a touch of divine piety, taken thought for them. For he sent out messengers in all directions to collect those who were fast perishing and, gathering them all into one body, had them carried down to Ramleh, whither the whole army now returned, though it had left the place so short a time before.

Now, whilst the army was staying at Ramleh in the utmost grief, very many began to desert, either through a distaste for the tiresome march or indignation. Owing to this the army was diminished in no small degree; for the greatest part of the French went off in anger to Joppa, and there, abode at their case. Some also went off to Acre where there was no lack of food. Some also accepted the urgent invitations of the Marquis of Tyre; whilst some, in their wrath and indignation, accompanied the Duke of Burgundy when he turned off to the Casal of the Plains, at which place he dwelt eight days.

19-20, Jan. 1192.—The march from Ramleh to Ascalon.

But King Richard, enraged at the turn matters were taking, set out with his nephew Henry Count of Champagne, and the rest of his diminished army to Ibelin. Moreover, so marshy and clayey did they find the ways that at the time of pitching their tents they could think of nothing but how best to rest their wearied heads. At Ibelin, (identified 1900 with Yebneh or Jamnia), he stayed for one night, outworn with grief and toil such as no tongue nor pen can describe.

At earliest dawn the army went forward in due order, preceded by those whose business it was to pitch the tents. But the misery of the previous day was as nothing to this day's march. For, as our men plodded on wearily, bitter snow drifted in their faces, thick hailstones rattled down, and pouring rain enveloped them.

The marshy land too gave way beneath their feet; baggage, horses and men sank in the swamps, and the more men struggled the deeper they became involved... So battered, so weary, and so worn, cursing the day on which they were born, and smiting themselves they at last reached Ascalon—only to find it so levelled by the Saracens that they could barely struggle through the gates over the heaps of stones. This day was (Sunday) 20th Jan.... Ascalon lies near the Greek sea, nor is any city better situated as regards the strength of its position, its pleasant suburbs or its good harbour, though indeed this last is dangerous because the violence of the sea often breaks the vessels riding there.

Hence it happened that, because of the storm then raging, no ships dared to enter the haven with provisions for eight days. So, there was great want in the army, nor did men or mules taste aught for eight days save the little food they had brought with them. A last, when the weather calmed a little, transports came in with victuals; but the bad weather soon began again, bringing want to the army; for the vessels, that people call barges, and the galleys sent to bring provisions, were wrecked by the violence of the winds, and almost all on board them were drowned. All the *sneccae* (smacks) belonging to the king and others were also broken. Out of their wood the king had his long ships built, in the vain hope of navigating by their aid.

Jan.-Feb., 1192.—The rebuilding of Ascalon.

Itin. Ric., v.

Saladin, hearing that our army was scattered along the coast, suffered his chiefs to return home and see to their private concerns till May—the time fitted for renewing warlike operations—came round.

Meanwhile the Turks, who had now warred at Saladin's side for four years, departed to revisit their families. . . . They grieved inconsolably at the loss of their chiefs—the *emirs*, and others whom Saladin had neglected to redeem according to his agreement and whom King Richard had had beheaded at Acre as we have told before.

Hence, they nurtured an inexorable hate and indignation against Saladin. So, with groaning and lamentation, Saladin's army departed for a season.

As the month of January drew to an end and the weather became more healthful the king, ill-pleased at seeing his army dispersed, sent envoys to the French to induce them to Ascalon that the army might be united and take counsel in common as regards its future movements. . . . .

The French, on hearing these proposals, declared themselves willing to obey the king up to Easter, (Easter Sunday, 1192, fell on April 5), but only on this condition—that they were then to be allowed to return to France, if they wished it, without any opposition.

To all these terms the king agreed, thinking it well to dissimulate for a while. So, the French came back and the army was once more consolidated.

Now it seemed good to repair the walls of Ascalon and rebuild the city by a common effort. But the nobles were so impoverished that they could each do but little; and yet, for all that, each set to work according to his own capacity. . . . . till you might see the whole army toiling together—chiefs, nobles, knights, men-at-arms, sergeants, and all passing stones from hand to hand.

Nor was there any distinction between laymen and clerks, high or low, servants and masters; all shared in the same labour; toil made all on an equality. . . . The king himself was distinguished for his efforts, working at the building with his own hands, urging others on by word of mouth, and distributing money.

At his exhortation each of the nobles took in hand part of the work (engaging) to finish it at his own expense according to his means; and if any had to stop working from lack of money, this high-souled king, whose heart was greater than even his royal dignity, gave them of his own wealth so far as he knew them to be in want.

To sum up, by his earnest endeavours, things proceeded so well and so much energy and money did he expend that three parts of the city were said to have been built at his expense.

1192, Feb.—King Richard's quarrel with the Duke of Burgundy, who goes off to Acre.

Itin. Ric.

These things being done, Richard sent envoys to the marquis, as he had done many times before, bidding him come to Ascalon and take his share in the expense, as was fitting considering the claims he advanced upon the kingdom. And he called upon him to do this by the oath he had formerly taken in the King of France's presence. But that craven and perverse-minded marquis sneeringly made answer that he would not come at all, unless he had an interview with Richard first. To his army however he spoke differently, declaring that he would not budge a foot. But, for all this, they had a conference later at Casal Imbert. (Now 1900, known as Khurbet Hamsîn, the ruins of Hamsîn)

Then while the walls of Ascalon were being rebuilt there rose dissensions between the king and the Duke of Burgundy. For, now that their provisions were for the most part consumed, the French began to ask the duke about the pay he owed them, without which they declared they could not fight any more. The duke, being hard pressed and having no money himself, thought fit to ask Richard for a further loan; for, as we have said before, Richard had lent him a certain sum at Acre—a loan which was to be repaid from the ransom of the captive Turks.

But there had been no repayment, inasmuch as the prisoners redeemed themselves with their heads and not with money; for which reason King Richard did not now accommodate the duke. Now, seeing that some took the duke's part, the matter became a fruitful source of quarrels till the duke, in anger, took his departure for Acre, and the Franks hurriedly followed him.

The quarrel of the Genoese and the Pisans at Acre (c. Feb. 15).

Now when they reached Acre, they found the Genoese and the Pisans in fierce conflict with one another. For the Pisans out of simple generosity and justice favoured King Guy; whereas the Genoese were on the side of the marquis, more especially because of the oath of fealty which bound the marquis to the King of France. From this there arose mutual attacks, slaughter, civil war, and general disturbance in Acre, by which the whole city was thrown into confusion. As the French drew near, they heard a great hubbub and the din of folk urging one another on to fight. Taking note of this, the duke and his

Frenchmen got their arms ready and thus advanced desirous of helping the Genoese, who were above measure delighted at their arrival.

But the Pisans, foreseeing that they would be attacked, went out boldly to meet the new comers, knowing that they came with no friendly intent. Setting upon the Duke of Burgundy, who seemed to be the leader, they surrounded him, pierced his horse with a lance, and flung him to the ground; after which they betook themselves back to the city, closed the gates firmly and waited for what would happen next. For the Pisans had already learnt that the Genoese had sent to the marquis, calling upon him to come to Acre as soon as he could and pledging themselves to deliver up the town to him. Nor was there any delay; the marquis came in his galleys with an armed host, hoping to seize the city suddenly. At his arrival the Pisans plied their *petrariae* and *mangonels* without intermission, and held out for three days relying on their valour and the justice of their cause.

And so, the two parties strove together manfully until the Pisans sent word to King Richard of their state, with a request that he would come up at once. The king had reached Caesarea on his way to a conference with the marquis, when the envoys met him and urged him on behalf of the Pisans to come speedily and preserve Acre. Then, under cover of night, they went back to Acre, while the marquis, having heard that Richard was advancing, turned back to Tyre; for, having an evil conscience, he mistrusted the purpose of the king's coming.

The Duke of Burgundy and his French had already gone off to the same city. The king, who had reached Acre on the first Thursday in Lent, (Feb. 20), next day took upon himself the management of everything, as if he were the only man left in the land. Calling the people together he showed them by the clearest arguments that between colleagues nothing was better than friendship, peace, and unity; nothing worse than quarrels. By such arguments he conciliated the Genoese with the Pisans, and renewed their old friendship with the kiss of peace.

1192, MARCH.—K. RICHARD AND THE MARQUIS OF MONTEFERRAT.

Itin. Ric, v.

Then King Richard sent word to the marquis to meet him for a conference at Casal Imbert, . . where indeed they did have an interview but to little purpose. For the marquis made a pretence of the withdrawal of the Duke of Burgundy and the French; and, by such wordy pretexts, strove to excuse his inaction. And so, alleging the absence of the French as an excuse, he went back to Tyre and hid himself in his wife's chambers, keeping aloof from military affairs. Richard, seeing that the Duke of Burgundy and the marquis had, of their own free will, absented themselves, took counsel with the leaders and more discreet men as to the best course of action; and they, after careful consideration, declared the marquis to have forfeited the privileges formerly assigned to him in the kingdom.

Wherefore, by reason of his prevarication, he was to be deprived of his possessions. Owing to this, the ill-feeling between King Richard and the lords of France, and specially the marquis, took deeper root. The latter, indeed, renewed his old invitation to all the French to leave Ascalon and come to him at Tyre. By these means he threw the kingdom into such confusion that King Richard from the day after Ash Wednesday till the Tuesday before Easter, (*i.e.,* from Thursday, Feb 20.—31 March, 1192), could not leave Acre. . . . On Palm Sunday (March 29) King Richard at Acre in great state girded with the belt of knighthood Saphadin's son who had been sent there for this purpose.

Meanwhile the Duke of Burgundy and the marquis sent envoys to Ascalon bidding those French who still remained there to come to Tyre as quickly as they could to take a share in the plan (concocted there) and to concert one mode of action according to the oath already sworn to the King of France. Then was it made clear how long-premeditated the plot had been, extending indeed from the very time when the marquis had made his treaty with the King of France and his people.

The agreement was that after this king's departure the marquis should have the French as his allies in the accomplishment of his designs. So, the marquis, as though the French were specially bound to him, strove to withdraw them from the (general) expedition in order that King Richard, left alone, might have less power to dispose of the kingdom.

On the Tuesday before Easter the king returned from Acre to the army at Ascalon, very sad and ill at ease. Next day on the Wednesday, (*i.e.,* April 1, 1192), the chief men of the French came before him, demanding that he would give them guides and free leave to depart as he had promised. Agreeing to this he immediately granted them very many comrades in their journey, to wit, the Templars, Hospitallers, earl Henry of Champagne and many others. He also went with them a space, praying them with many tears to stay with him a little while at his expense. As they still refused, he let them go and returned

to Ascalon, whence he sent a swift messenger to Acre with instructions to the guardians of that city not to admit the French. No insult
or harm, however, was to be done them, lest it should give rise to
contention. And so, the French, coming to Acre, had to take up their
station outside the city.

Now on the day of our Lord's Supper, (*i.e.,* Thursday, April 2), the
army was greatly distressed at this departure of the French, by which
its strength was in no small degree lessened. For there had gone off
almost 700 knights, men of proved valour. . . . But the Turks rejoiced
on hearing the news, and Saladin immediately sent off messengers on
horseback to all his subjects, bidding them make no excuse but return
in haste to the land of Jerusalem.

c. April 1.—Conrad of Montferrat negotiates with Saladin on his own account.

Bohâdin.

(*According to Bohâdin Richard still kept sending messages to "his good
brother" Al-Adil begging him to negotiate a peace. Saladin was agreeable to
this on the understanding that, if his brother found out that Richard was not in
earnest, he should drag out the negotiations so as to give time for the reinforcements to come in. Accordingly, Al-Adil left Jerusalem on Friday, 20 March,
1192, and soon wrote word from Keisan that Henfrid of Toron had been with
him and that Richard's terms seemed advantageous, for he offered to leave the
Temple and the citadel in the hands of the Saracens provided the half of the
Holy City was given up to the Christians. On April 1st, however, Al-Adil
returned, and the same evening news came to Jerusalem that the Franks had
been plundering in the neighbourhood of Darum.*)

Joseph the lord of Sidon's page came to demand peace on the part
of the marquis. The *Sultan* consented, but annexed many conditions:
After ratifying the treaty the marquis was to break with his compatriots and make war upon them; he was to keep the towns he might
take from the Franks, and we likewise were to keep what we might
take; those that were taken by the combined forces should (save the
citadels) belong to the marquis, whilst we should have the Musulman
prisoners and the booty.

The marquis was to set free all the Musulman prisoners in his estates; and, if the King of England should grant him the government of
the country, he was to take care that the peace should be continued
on the terms expressed in our treaty with the King of England. We,
however, would except from this the town of Ascalon and the district

beyond it. The territory on the sea-coast was to belong to the marquis, but what we still held should remain ours. The land and the towns lying between the territory of the Franks and the Musulmans were to be divided between the two nations.

1192, APRIL 5.—K. RICHARD KEEPS HIS EASTER AT ASCALON. COUNSELS OF RETURN. NEGOTIATIONS AS TO CROWN OF JERUSALEM. MARQUIS CONRAD CHOSEN KING.

Itin. Ric. v.

The feast of Easter, which this year fell on 5 April, King Richard celebrated with great splendour at Ascalon offering food and drink in abundance to all who desired them. He had his tents fixed in the plains near Ascalon, and for the entertainment of his people got together everything that might help the splendour of the festival. Never was there seen a more lavish, free-hearted expenditure.

On Easter Monday the king zealously renewed his work at the city walls, urging on the rest of the host so earnestly that before long, thanks to his assistance and labours, the work was entirely finished at his expense... On Easter Tuesday the king set out with a few comrades to inspect Gaza, (lying 12-13 miles S.W. of Ascalon and from 2-3 miles from the sea); and on Wednesday he made a circuit of Darum, (now, 1900, the village of Deir-el-Belâh), to see on what side it lay most open to assault.... When the French had gone away those who, at the king's bidding, had escorted them to Acre, returned to the army.

It is not out of our province to note to what kinds of pursuits the French devoted themselves on reaching Tyre. For they, though reported to have made their pilgrimage to the Holy Land out of devotion, nevertheless on quitting the camp abandoned themselves to wantonness, women's songs, and banqueting with harlots. Those who saw them brought us word how they were applauding bands of dancing women, (according to Ibn Alathîr, Richard had himself been entertained in a similar manner at his interview with Saphadin two or three months before), and how the very luxury of their costume bespoke their indolent effeminacy....

Round their necks were jewelled collars and on their heads garlands wrought with every kind of flowers; goblets they brandished in their hands not swords; their nights were spent in potations and profligacy.... Why should I say more? Their outward appearance proved their inward levity. Shame! indeed it was, for the French to devote themselves to such pursuits. Yet, in spite of this, we do not assert that they were all guilty of such folly without exception; some there were whom the dissoluteness of their fellows grieved not a little and who mourned over the quarrel with the king.

When Easter was over and the time of passage had arrived, there came an envoy to Richard with news calculated to stir the whole army. The envoy was the Prior of Hereford in England, and he came with letters from the king's chancellor, William, Bishop of Ely, informing the king how this prelate and those whom the king had associated with him in the government of the realm had been driven out of their strongholds; and how some of the chancellor's adherents had been cut off in seditious disturbance; and how, by the intrigues of Earl John, the king's brother, the chancellor had been driven out of the kingdom whilst there was no money left in the king's treasury or anywhere else, unless perchance what remained hidden in the churches.

Moreover, the prior brought word how the aforesaid earl, after, by many injuries and oppressions, driving the chancellor, who was at once priest and bishop, into Normandy, was steadily exacting the oath of fidelity and submission from the earls and nobles of the realm as well as depriving them of their castles... On hearing these things, the king was thunderstruck and remained thinking much but speaking little; for a deed of such villainy seemed hardly credible... When his trouble came to the knowledge of the rest, they too were disturbed... For, if the king were to depart no one would remain, seeing that there was such strife between those at Ascalon and Tyre; and so, beyond a doubt, all the land now liberated would fall into the possession of the Turks for ever.

On the morrow King Richard laid the news before the chiefs, interpreting the words of the prior, and declaring that he must go home. At the same time, if he went away, he promised to maintain three hundred knights and two thousand choice foot soldiers at his expense . . . . . .After taking counsel together the wise men replied that they thought it specially needful to create a new king, whom all might obey. To him the whole land might be entrusted, he might wage the wars of the people, and lead the whole army. If this were not done before King Richard's departure, they declared that they would all go away, seeing that they were not strong enough to guard the land.

In reply, the king at once asked whether they would elect Guy or the marquis for their king; whereupon, without any delay, the whole people together, weak and mighty, prayed with bended knees that they might have the marquis for their chief and defender. For him they reckoned the more necessary to the kingdom seeing that he was the more powerful man. Then the king, after hearing their petition, reproved them in a quiet way for the fickleness (with which they now chose) the marquis, whom they had so frequently abused before.

King Richard, after weighing the petition of the whole people on behalf of the marquis, gave his assent and had noble envoys despatched to Tyre for the purpose of bringing the marquis with due honour to Ascalon. So, by decree of the whole assembly, Henry Count of Champagne, Otho de Transynges, and William de Cageu, were elected and sent on this mission. With their train of followers these went to Tyre in galleys, hastening to bear to the marquis the news he had so long desired. But as they say in proverbs:

There's many a slip
'Twixt the cup and the lip.

And, it may be, God rejected the marquis as a man unworthy of the kingdom. In proof of his unworthiness, we may note that Richard had many times, both since the King of France's departure as well as before, begged the marquis for aid in conquering the kingdom; but had always met with a refusal.

Moreover, the marquis had contrived things prejudicial to the honour of the kingly crown and detrimental to the army at Ascalon. He had even attempted to strike a bargain with Saladin on these terms: that he (the marquis) should hold half of Jerusalem of Saladin, together with Beyrout, Sidon, and half the land on this side the river. Saladin was well enough inclined to this peace and would have granted it but for the constant opposition of his brother Saphadin, who, as we learnt later, dissuaded Saladin from coming to terms with any Christian unless with the assent of King Richard, he said:

For there is no better Christian to be found anywhere than King Richard, nor any man like him in uprightness. Without his knowledge and his assent, I will be a party to no concord.

Thus, was that wicked plan brought to nought; thus was the progress of treason broken short. That such a bargain had been contemplated was shewn afterwards by the most absolute evidence; for, while two miserable go-betweens in this business—men who were employed in carrying messages between Saladin and the marquis, were issuing from Jerusalem Stephen of Turnham chanced to meet them. Their names were then sufficiently branded with ignominy; one of them being called Balian of Ybelin, (Balian II. of Ibelin, third son of

Balian I., and one of the greatest lords in the Holy Land), the other Reginald of Sidon, (he married Balian's daughter after putting away Agnes, mother of Baldwin IV, his first wife.) But let us pass them by in silence; for like dust that a man throws against the wind all their labour and exertion, as was fitting, came to nothing.

The ambassadors, coming to Tyre, explained their mission, telling the marquis in detail how he had been unanimously elected king with King Richard's assent; that the crown had been granted him to the intent that he might come like a man, with all his army to transact the business of the realm, to inflict vengeance on the Turks, and to take steps for establishing his rule over the rest of the kingdom of Jerusalem which now belonged to him. On hearing this the marquis in the overjoy of his heart, stretching out his hands towards heaven, is said to have prayed thus:

> O Lord God, who hast created me soul and body, thou who alone art the true and tender king, grant I beseech thee that, if thou deemest me worthy of ruling thy kingdom, I may be crowned. But, if otherwise, may I never attain that honour.

After the news was known in Tyre there was great joy among the people, every man busying himself in procuring things to add splendour to the coronation.

1192, MONDAY, APRIL 27.—K. CONRAD ASSASSINATED AT TYRE.

Itin. Ric. v.

Meanwhile Count Henry, after discharging his mission turned off to Acre with his fellow envoys. Whilst they were equipping themselves in comely fashion there, and were on the point of returning to the army at Ascalon, the marquis was cut off by sudden death at Tyre. For, on a certain day, as he was returning in a very happy and mirthful mood a from a banquet given by the Bishop of Beauvais, and had already reached the custom-house before the city, lo! two young men, assassins, who for greater speed wore no cloaks, ran up to him quickly and, whipping out two knives that they held (concealed) in their hands, gave him a deadly wound in the region of the heart and then took to flight. The marquis, falling at once from his horse, rolled over—a dying man.

One of the murderers was cut down on the spot; the other at once betook himself to a church, but, being torn out, was sentenced to be dragged through the middle of the city till life was extinct. Before his death he was diligently questioned at whose prompting he had thus acted, and with what purpose. He confessed to have been despatched for this very object a long time previously. They had undertaken the deed on the motion of and in befitting obedience to the command of another—a fact which was plainly true.

For these young men had been in the marquis' service for a long time, on the lookout for a good moment for committing this crime. They declared themselves to have been sent by the Old Man of Musse, (*i.e.,* the Old Man of the Mountain, chief of the Assassins, see note G), who judged the marquis worthy of death, and had ordered him to be slain within a fixed period.

For, you must know, the Old Man of Musse has all men, whom he judges unworthy of life, cut off in the same way. Indeed, the Old Man of Musse, accordance with hereditary custom, has very many noble boys brought up in his palace. These he has instructed in all prudence and learning, and versed in different tongues to the intent that in every nation they may be able to comport themselves at ease without an interpreter.

The faith of these folk is very cruel and obscure; and its disciples are trained up to its full apprehension with the greatest care and pains. Then the Old Man has those whom he deems to be of full age called into his presence, and enjoins them, for the remission of their sins, to cut off any powerful man or tyrant whom he signifies to them by name.

For the execution of this service, he hands them, each one, a sharp knife of terrible length; and they, applying themselves most earnestly to the fulfilment of his mandate, set forth without any delay until they reach the tyrant designated. In his service they remain until the time of accomplishing their business comes. And it is their hope by such service to merit celestial glory. And of this sect were those who so nefariously cut off the marquis.

But the marquis, already at his last gasp, was gently carried by the hands of his men to the palace. They, walling him round, grieved and wept inconsolably because their time of joy had been so brief. After receiving the last sacraments, the marquis enjoined his wife to keep strict ward over the city of Tyre and not to yield it up to any man except to King Richard or to his own heir in the kingdom by right of hereditary succession.

Then he died and was buried at the Hospital with vehement lamentation. Thus was the happiness of those, who but now were rejoicing so keenly, cut short; thus did the lordship, so long desired, vanish without having been enjoyed.

In the confusion that now ensued there rose a rumour among the French (who fancied they could conceal their own wickedness by such inventions), to the effect that King Richard had wrongfully contrived the marquis's death and had hired these two assassins for the purpose. (This charge is repeated by many other writers of the time.) O shameless envy, that is always carping at what is better than itself, gnawing away at what is good, and striving to darken all noble achievements if so be it cannot utterly extinguish them.

Nor were these jealous folk satisfied with thus defaming King Richard in the Holy Land; they went so far as to send a message to the King of France bidding him, now that the marquis had been slain, be on his guard against the assassin-servants of the Old Man. For, they continued, King Richard had sent four sectaries of this creed to France for the purpose of murdering the king. . . .

When the marquis had been buried, the French who were pitched in their tents outside the city met together. They were almost ten thousand in number and, after having taken consultation, sent an envoy to the marquis' wife bidding her deliver up the city to them without delay, in order that they might hold it for the King of France. She made answer that she would give it up, as her lord had bidden her, to King Richard, when he came to see her, and to no one else, she said:

For there is no other man who has worked so hard to rescue the land from the Turks and to restore it to its former liberty. He ought to dispose of the kingdom because he is more valiant than anyone else.

At this reply the French were very wroth; but, whilst they were thus striving to get hold of the city, lo! Count Henry, not a little astonished at learning of what had happened, came to Tyre. Now, as soon as ever the people saw him in their midst, sent there as if by God, they chose him for prince and lord; and, coming up to him, began to beg him most earnestly to assume the crown and marry the marquis' widow, upon whom the kingdom ought to devolve by right of hereditary succession.

To their prayers the count replied that in this business, to which it seemed God was calling him, he would act according to the advice of the king his uncle; whereupon, without any delay, envoys were sent off to King Richard, telling him how the marquis had been so foully slain, and how the people had duly elected (Count Henry).

Ernoul (unbracketed paragraphs), Eracles (bracketed paragraphs)

It chanced one day that a merchant vessel, belonging to the land of the Assassins, came to Tyre; and the marquis, who was greedy of gain, sent and took of their goods what he pleased. The merchants then disembarked and made complaint to the marquis, telling how they had been robbed in his port and praying him by God to give them back their own. The marquis made answer that they should not have their things back, but had better look to the safety of what was left them. On seeing this, the merchants said they would complain to their lord; and the marquis replied that they might go and complain wherever they liked.

(Then said Bernard du Temple to the marquis: "I will give you a full quittance of these folk; so that no word about them shall ever be heard again." And thereupon he had them drowned in the sea—a thing which, however, could not be concealed from the Old Man.)

(Now when the Lord of the Assassins knew that the marquis had taken his men and his goods he sent to the marquis for their restoration. The marquis replied that he would not give them back. Then sent the Lord of the Assassins a second time warning the marquis that if restoration was not made, he would have him slain. Then went the Lord of the Assassins and bade two of his men that they should go to Tyre and slay the marquis. Accordingly, they went, and reaching Tyre became Christians. One of them entered the service of the marquis, while the other dwelt with Balian, who had Queen Mary to wife.)

(Now it came to pass one day that Isabel, the wife of the marquis, had gone to the baths, and the marquis would not eat till she had bathed. Then the marquis became aware that she was staying too late, and because he was a-hungered he got on his horse with two knights accompanying him, intending to eat with the Bishop of Beauvais if he had not yet eaten.)

(But when he arrived the bishop had already eaten. Then said the marquis: "Sir bishop, I came to eat with you; but, as you have already eaten, I will return home." The bishop replied that, if he would stay, he would give him plenty to eat; but the marquis, answering that he would not tarry, went back. Now, when he was come out from the door of the archbishop's house, which is close to the Change, and when he was in the middle of the narrow road, on either side thereof was there a man sitting. And, as he came towards these two men, they rose to meet him, and one of them, advancing, shewed him a letter, and, as the marquis reached out his hand to take it, he drew a knife and smote him through the body, as did the other also who had leapt on the horse's croup. The latter, stabbing the marquis, in the side struck him dead. He was buried in the Hospital of St. John. These things took place in the year of Our Lord's incarnation, 1192.)

LETTER FROM THE CHIEF OF THE ASSASSINS.

William of Newburgh, ii., Roger of Wendover, iii.

In these days there came to the princes of Europe letters from the Old Man of the Mountain. Now by this name does the chief of a certain Eastern people—the Hansesii—call himrelf. And he bears this title not by reason of his age, but for his wisdom and influence. Now these same letters were writ in Hebrew, in Greek, and in Latin characters; moreover, they were drawn up not with ink—a substance little used of this people—but in murex-blood, as was evident by the writing itself. And, you must know, that a certain trustworthy man declared to me how he had seen and read these letters at the time they were solemnly presented to the King of the French at Paris. Their tenor was as follows:—

Roger of Wendover, iii.

To Limpold, Duke of Austria, the Old Man of the Mountain sendeth greeting: Seeing that many kings and princes beyond the sea accuse Richard, King and Lord of the English, concerning the death of the marquis, I swear, by God who reigneth for ever and by the law we follow, that he had no hand in his death. This is the true cause of the marquis's death:

(*The letter then proceeds to tell how the marquis had slain and robbed an "Assassin" sailing in a ship of Sattalie and driven into Tyre by stress of weather. The "Old Man" sent demanding vengeance and recompense which Conrad refused, throwing the blame of the transaction on Reginald of Sidon. A second messenger, Edrisi by name, Conrad would have drowned had not "our friends" at Tyre hurried out of the city*).

And from this hour did we long to kill the marquis and sent two of our brethren to Tyre who slew him openly and almost in the presence of the whole people. This was the ground of the marquis's death, and we tell you, of a surety, that in this deed Richard had no share, and that men have done him a wrong (in saying that he had). Know also that we slay no man after this fashion for any reward or money, but only if he have injured us first. Know too that we have writ these letters in our house, at our fortress of Messiac, (doubtless the castle of Massiad great stronghold of the Western branch of the Assassins), in the presence of our brethren, mid-September. And we have sealed them with our seal in the year from Alexander 1500.

★★★★★★★★

This dating is a feeble attempt at imitating a system of chronology common in the Byzantine Empire, but misunderstood by the forgers of this document. The era of Alexander dates from the great conqueror's death, 12 Nov., 324 b c. Hence the year 1194, if we may suppose this to be the date of the forgery in question, should be 1519.

★★★★★★★★

(*The letter as given by William of Newburgh is to the same effect, but with less detail and more of vague generalities. Both letters are, of course, to be considered as forgeries, though they are interesting evidence of the extent to which these charges against Richard had poisoned men's minds.*)

CIRC. 1, MAY, 1192.—K. RICHARD AGREES TO EARL HENRY'S ELECTION TO THE CROWN OF JERUSALEM.

Itin. Ric. v.

Now whilst King Richard in those days was pursuing the Turks in the plains of Ramleh, the envoys from Tyre appeared before him . . . with their news. The king, on hearing of the marquis' death remained speechless for a long time, being, as it were, stunned at so strange and unexpected a kind of death. But he was rejoiced at the election of his nephew to the kingly rank, knowing full well that his own followers had desired it keenly.

Seeing that, by the unalterable decrees of fate, the marquis left this world, as you state, what advantage will excessive mourning bring to the living? I agree to the election of Henry with all my heart, and indeed do urgently desire that, by God's will he may rule over the kingdom after we have got full possession of it. As regards his marriage with the marquis' widow I offer no advice; for the marquis himself got her unjustly in her former husband's life time, and so committed adultery with her. But let the count take the kingdom. I grant him the lordship of Acre city in everlasting *seizin*, with all appertaining thereto, Tyre, Joppa, and the whole land which by God's grace we are going to acquire. Bid him from me join our expedition as quickly as

139

he can and bring the French with him; for I have determined to take Darum by force, if indeed any Turks there shall venture to resist me.

Having made this reply the king returned to Ascalon.

After hearing the king's answer, the envoys returned to the count at Tyre. Then gladness revived once more and all people rejoiced. And now, those who surrounded the count began persuading him to marry the heiress of the realm; but he refused, fearing to incur King Richard's displeasure. Yet, for all this, the French and the great lords of the realm urged on the match, on the plea that it would strengthen the general position. By their endeavours it came to pass that the marchioness, of her own accord came up to the count and offered him the keys of the city; whereupon, at the instance of the French, who were anxious to push things on, the Count Henry and the marchioness were solemnly married before the church in the presence of many clerks and laymen.

Those who persuaded the count to this action are believed not to have had much difficulty; for there is no trouble in compelling a man to go the way he wishes. The nuptials were celebrated with regal splendour. All rejoiced at the realization of what all had desired; but the French were exultant. The Normans too were equally well pleased; for the count was nephew both to the King of France and the King of England. Thanks to this agreement, men began to hope for more prosperous times; and for the patching up of old discords. When the marriage was over the count sent men to take charge of Acre, Joppa, and the other cities and castles of the land ... after which he issued an order bidding the whole host set forth without any delay for the expedition against Darum.

1192, MAY 22.—K. RICHARD TAKES DARUM.

Itin., Ric. v.

About the time when the marquis was slain at Tyre, messengers kept coming to King Richard and begging him to return home. Of these messengers some used to assert that things were all right, others that the land of England was on the point of being seized; some persuaded the king to return, others to bend all his energies to gaining possession of the land of pilgrimage to which he had come. With their conflicting accounts his mind was so confused that he was quite at a doubt what course to take. But he could gauge the mind of the King of France by his previous knowledge, as the proverb says, "He who has a bad man for his neighbour is sure to find something wrong in the morning."

In the interim while Count Henry and the French at Acre were getting ready for the siege at Darum, King Richard, who hated sloth, issued from Ascalon, and despatched his stone-casters (after having had them taken to pieces) towards Darum by ship. Having appointed men to guard Ascalon, . . he set forth and arrived at Darum Castle, (about 20 miles from Ascalon), on a certain Sunday, (May 17), having only his personal attendants with him. His own tent and those of his comrades were fixed not far from this castle; but, owing to his scanty numbers, it was uncertain from what side it would be best to begin the siege, seeing that so small a host could not encompass the whole fortress

Wherefore, they settled down together in a certain plain near the town. The Turks, holding the efforts of so tiny an army cheap, made a sally and then, after worrying our men for a while as it were with challenges to fight, finally betook themselves within their stronghold, shot fast the bolts of their gates, and prepared to defend themselves. Just then the stone-casters came up in the ships. These, all disjointed as they were, the king and his nobles shouldered bit by bit, and, not without perspiration, carried on foot for almost a mile, as we ourselves saw. At last, when they were all pieced together, set up, and assigned to their proper guards, the king in person undertook to work one against the principal tower. The Normans had another; and the men of Poitou a third. All three they plied for the destruction of the fortress. The Turks were in despair at the sight of such imminent destruction; but for all this they made manful efforts at defence. Night and day, without intermission, did the king have the stone-casters worked.

Now in the castle of Darum there were seventeen towers of great strength and well-furnished withal. Of these one was taller and stronger than the others, being also girt externally by a deeper moat. Moreover, on one side it was constructed of regularly-placed stone, on the other it was protected by the natural rock. But a coward fear now seized upon this perfidious race of not being able to defend themselves efficaciously or even to make good their escape. The king made his miners dig secretly beneath the earth, thus breaking up the pavement and making a gap in the wall. Meanwhile the stone-casters had kept plying away at one of the Turkish *mangonels* on the chief tower and had broken it up, to the great distress of the enemy. . . .

Their position was already insecure, when suddenly, by the aid of fire and the king's stone-caster, a gate was burst open. . . Then three Saracens came out to the king begging for peace and offering to yield up the fortress and all they possessed there if only their lives were spared. The king, who would not accept these terms, bade them defend themselves as best they could; and, on their return, his stone-caster was worked more vigorously than ever. Just after, a certain tower, which had already been undermined by the king's diggers and been battered with incessant blows, collapsed with a terrible crash.

Our men then followed up the Turks, slaying them as they made for the chief tower, before reaching which however, in accordance with their most abominable plan, they hamstrung all their horses to prevent their being of any use to their enemies. Our men valiantly entered the tower, the first to force his way in being Seguin Barrez with his man-at-arms, Ospiard; the third was Peter de Garstonia. After these came very many others whose names are now lost.

The first man whose banner was erected on the walls was Stephen de Longchamp; the second the Count of Leicester, the third Andrew de Chavigni, and the fourth Raymond son of the prince (*i.e.,* of Boamund III., Prince of Antioch.) The Genoese too and the Pisans set up their banners of various shapes upon the walls. Thus were our banners set up and those of the Turks cast down.

Those Turks whom our men found holding out on the battlements they hurled down into the ditch there to be dashed to pieces. The number of Turks slain in the different parts of the castle was sixty. Those who had taken refuge in the tower, seeing that they were lost . . . surrendered themselves to perpetual slavery on the Friday before Whit-Sunday, (*i.e.,* 22 May, 1192.) This they did the more readily because one of their most powerful *emirs*, Caisac by name, who had been appointed to guard the fortress, had failed to bring them help. Now, when Darum was taken, almost forty Christian captives were found in chains; these were set free. On the Friday night, (text says "on Saturday night), the king made his men keep watch over the Turks who were still in the tower till early on the Saturday morning.

Then on Whitsun Eve the Turks, coming down from the Tower at the king's command, had their hands bound so tightly behind their backs with leathern thongs that they roared for pain. They were three hundred in number, not reckoning little children and women. Thus, before the French came up, with the aid of his own men only did King Richard nobly get possession of Darum after a siege of four days. A hard matter did our men find it to achieve this without the French; but it was a feat of arms all the more glorious for this reason.

When Darum was taken, up there came in great haste Count Henry with the French and the Duke of Burgundy, hoping to assist at its capture; but the affair was entirely over before they arrived. The king went out to meet the count, and with great joy led him into the fortress. He also now, in the presence of very many (chiefs), gave him this fortress and all belonging to it, as the first-fruits of the kingdom. Then they all tarried in Darum for the great festival of Pentecost, (*i.e.*, 24 May, 1192); after which, on the Monday, they left soldiers to guard the fortress and set out for Ascalon, passing through Gaza and Furbia (according to Dr. Stubbs probably Herbia between Ascalon and Gaza) on way, at which last place the king abode for three days. The rest, however, proceeded to Ascalon, where the French were keeping Pentecost. . . .

1192, CIRC. MAY 30.—K. RICHARD RESOLVES TO STAY IN THE HOLY LAND.

Itin. Ric. v.

(*On his way from Darum to Ascalon Richard at Furbia receives news that Caysac is fortifying the Castle of Figs, and on his way there, reaches the Canebrake of Starlings. Here he stays the night of May 28; and next day, finding the Castle of Figs, empty, returns to the Canebrake for another night, when:*)

At the Canebrake of Starlings there came an envoy to the king. This envoy was named John of Alencon, and he had been despatched with news of how England was disturbed by Earl John, the king's brother, who, without paying any regard to the advice of the queen, his mother or of others, was acting after his own will. Messengers were also passing between him and the King of France, and things had already gone so far that, unless means were taken for bridling this treason, England would very soon be lost to the King of England.

On hearing these things, the king was troubled, and, after long and silent consideration as to what was the best course for him to pursue, at last said that he really must go home lest he should be stript of his ancestral soil and the kingdom of his fathers. But before the king's resolution was fully known certain people were going about and saying "that the king was about to depart"; but others said, "No, he will persevere to the end; uncertain rumours will not call him away from the completion of so pious a work, seeing that his departure would diminish our chances of conquering the land, and would not consort with his honour."

Now, being of different minds as regards King Richard's departure, the chiefs and leaders of the army—French, Normans, English, Poitevins, Angevins, men of Maine meeting together bound themselves by a pledge to advance against Jerusalem without any delay, whether the king stayed or went away. When this resolution was made known to the army, there was joy beyond bounds; all people rejoiced in common, rich and poor, mean and mighty. Nor was there any one in the army who did not, according to his means, show some outward signs, as a testimony to the joy of his heart. Wherefore, right on till midnight, numerous lamps were burning and bands of singers went about noisily trolling various kinds of songs,

The while in wakeful glee
They mark night's watches flee.

Only the king's mind was troubled by anxious cares, as he revolved many plans, till tired out by the weight of his thoughts, he sought his couch in angry mood. Yet for all this, at this time, at the beginning of June, the whole army was of one mind and eager to advance.

June 3.—At Beit Jibrin the king is reproached by one of his chaplains for thinking of going home.

Itinerarum v.,

From the Canebrake of Starlings (*Cannetum Sturnellorum*) the king and his army passed down through the plain to Ibelin, (identified with Beit Gibrin, about 14 miles N. W. of Hebron) a fortress belonging to the Hospital near Hebron. Anna, the mother of Mary the mother of God, is said to have been born in a valley close at hand. . . . Here the army were pestered with certain very small flies, called *cincennellae*, that flit about like sparks of fire. The neighbouring district was filled with these insects, which set upon us in the most pertinacious fashion, stinging, and that very sharply, the hands, neck, throat, forehead, countenance—in fact any exposed part of the pilgrim's person.

These stings were promptly succeeded by a very rancorous swelling, so that all who had been stung looked as if they were lepers; and men could scarcely guard themselves against this most grievous visitation by fitting veils to their heads and necks. Nevertheless, exhilarated by their hope and their mutual pledge of proceeding towards Jerusalem, they deemed that all adversities should be borne bravely. Only a wave of care distressed the king because of the news he had heard.

One day a certain Poitevin chaplain, by name William, was deeply grieved at the sight of Richard sitting with downcast eyes in solitary meditation within his tent; but, knowing the king to be enraged at the news of the envoys, he dared not address him, and thus unburden his mind of its weight. So, weeping most bitterly, he kept his pious eyes fixed upon the king and said nothing.

When the king gathered from his attitude that he was desirous of speaking, he called the chaplain up and said, "Lord chaplain, I adjure thee by thy oath of fealty to tell me, without any concealment, the cause why you are thus weeping, if perchance I am in any way to blame."

To him the chaplain made answer, with low voice and tearful eyes, "I will not speak before I am assured that you will not be wroth with me for what I say."

The king then with an oath promised him impunity, on which the chaplain, taking courage, began:

Lord King, all men, especially those who have most regard for your honour, reproach you for your haste to return home. May God forbid that uncertain rumours should turn you aside from acquiring this desolate land. This indeed would be to your eternal shame. Let not the splendour of so bright a beginning be dimmed by too hasty a return; let not after generations reproach you for having meanly departed, leaving your work incomplete. . . . Remember Lord King what things God has already done for thee in prospering memorable acts such as no king of thy age has ever surpassed in number or in glory. Remember, O king, how, when thou wast Earl of Poitou, thou hadst no neighbour who did not yield to your strength; remember the confusion of the Brabançons, whom thou so often routedst with a little band.

Remember how gloriously thou didst drive the Count of St. Giles from the siege of Hautefort; how thou didst receive possession of thine own realm without use of shield or helm; remember how manfully thou didst conquer Messina, utterly crushing the Greek race that dared to war against thee. Remember how God enriched thee at the conquest of Cyprus—an enterprise which, before thee, no one ever dared to undertake: how thou didst subdue it in fifteen days and with God's assistance didst take the emperor prisoner; remember the destruction of that splendid ship near Acre harbour with the drowning of its eight hundred men and its serpents.

Remember how thou didst reach Acre just in time to receive its surrender; and thy recovery from the Arnaldia of which so many other chiefs died. Remember how God has entrusted this land to thy care; how its safety rests on thee alone now that the King of France has gone off so meanly. Remember the Christian captives whom you freed at Darum......But why mention single occurrences..... Remember how, from the moment of leaving the western world, thou hast stood out as a conqueror and how before thy feet enemies have fallen prone and been consigned to chains.....

Already does the *Soldan* dread thee, already are the recesses of Babylon struck with amazement; already does the valour of the Turks fear thy approach. What more! All men say commonly that thou art the father of all, the patron and champion of Christendom, which, if deserted by you, will lie exposed to the plunder of her enemies.

JUNE 4.—RICHARD PROMISES TO STAY TILL EASTER, 1193, AND RETURNS TO ASCALON PREPARATORY TO ADVANCING AGAINST JERUSALEM.

While the chaplain was thus speaking the king remained quite silent, as also did those who sat with them in the tent. By this speech the king's heart was changed ... and lo! on the morrow at the ninth hour he turned back with all his army and settled outside the city of Ascalon in the orchards, every man believing that he was now really on the point of departing in all speed.

But, having changed his mind by God's grace and the chaplain's speech, the king told Count Henry his nephew and the Duke of Burgundy, that no messenger or news or complaint should call him from the land before Easter. Accordingly on the 4th June, that is in Trinity week—sending for his herald, Philip, the king bade him notify through the whole army, that he would certainly remain till Easter. He also bade everyone get himself ready for sieging Jerusalem according to his means.

Then, at the herald's voice, all men began to rejoice as a bird at dawn of day. Without delay they equipt themselves, got things ready for the journey, and with outstretched hands called out "We praise thee O God, and give thee thanks because we shall now see thy city in which the Turks have dwelt so long." ... Moreover, the humbler part of the crowd, urged on by hope, fastened bags of food round their necks, declaring that they were well able to carry a month's provision. So keenly desirous were they of advancing towards Jerusalem....

June 7-12.—1192.—K. Richard and the army march towards Jerusalem, and camp at Beit Nûba for the second time.

(The army then marches to Blancheguard, where it stays from June 7-9, on which last day it starts for Toron of the Knights. On June 10 Richard starts for Castle Arnald. On June 11th the French come up and the whole army sets out for Beit Nûba, there to await Count Henry, whom Richard has sent to call up the loiterers at Acre.)

The king and the army stationed outside Ascalon, being now quite ready for the march, issued from Ascalon on the Octave of Holy Trinity, (Sunday, 7 June), and with early dawn set out for Jerusalem. . . . On the morrow (Wednesday) June 10 after breakfast the army moved from Toron (identified with Latroon, 1 mile S.W. Amwas and 3 miles S.W. of Beit-Nûba), towards Castle Arnald, (apparently the same as Albert of Aix's Castle Arnulf), to the right of which place, on some rising ground, the king ordered his tents to be fixed.

Next day the French came up, and all the army set out for Betenopolis, where it stayed a considerable time waiting for the return of Count Henry, whom the king had sent to Acre to bring up the people who were living there at their ease. For this cause the whole army had to wait a month or more at the foot of the mountain which the pilgrims cross on their return from the Holy City. On Friday, the morrow of St. Barnabas, (*i.e.,* on June 12th), as the king at early morn went out as far as the fountain of Emmaus, (identified with Amwas, 2½ miles S. E. of Beit Nûba, probably not the Emmaus of Luke), and, finding certain Turks unprepared, he fell upon them and slew twenty.

He also took Saladin's herald prisoner. This herald used to proclaim Saladin's edicts. Him the king spared. He also took three camels, horses and mules, and very fine *Turcomans,* (the best war horses of the French knights of the Holy Land). . . . He pursued the Saracens over the mountains, until following one of them into a certain valley, he transfixed him, causing him to fall dying from his horse. On his overthrow the king looked up and saw afar off the city of Jerusalem.

★★★★★★★★

If Richard had pushed his pursuit far enough to come within sight of Jerusalem, he had probably reached Neby Samwil, the Mons Gaudii of the Crusaders, which stands up over 2,900 feet above the level of the sea, some 5 miles N.W. of Jerusalem. It is only 8¾ miles S. E. of Beit Nûba.

★★★★★★★★

How King Richard would not even look upon the Holy City which he might not free from Paynim hands.

A Legend of the Thirteenth Century.

Joinville.

(When King Louis IX. was at Jaffa he was told that the *Soldan* would grant him a safe conduct to visit Jerusalem if he cared to do so. A council was called to consider the proposal which was ultimately rejected on the analogy of the following anecdote, then related of King Richard I. After hearing this narrative St. Louis refused to set eyes on a city he could not rescue from the hands of the Saracens. There is no reason why this legend should not be based on fact; but as it only makes its appearance more than fifty years after King Richard's death it is impossible to feel sure of the details.)

When the great King Philip left Acre for France, he let his folk all remain in the camp with Duke Hugh of Burgundy, the grandfather of the duke who has lately died. Now, whilst the duke was tarrying at Acre and King Richard with him, there came news how that they might take Jerusalem on the morrow if they willed it; for all the *Soldan's* chivalry had gone to Damascus by reason of a war which (Saladin) had with another prince. So, they set out their men, the King of England and his followers forming the first battalion, the Duke of Burgundy with the King of France's men the second.

Whilst they thought to take the town there came word from the duke's camp that he would go no further; for the Duke of Burgundy was turning back because he would not have it said that the English had taken Jerusalem. Now, whilst men were thus talking, there came one of the king's knights to him crying out, "Sire, sire, come hither and I will shew you Jerusalem." But, when the king heard these words, he cast his coat of arms before his eyes. And he wept tears as he called upon our Lord:

Fair Lord God, I pray thee not to let me see thy Holy City, if so be that I may not deliver it out of the hands of thy enemies.

And they told king (Louis) this story for an ensample: (for they argued) that, if he who was the greatest of all Christian kings were to accomplish his pilgrimage without delivering the city, all the other kings and pilgrims who might come after him would hold it enough to do their pilgrimage as the King of France had done his, and so would take no thought for the deliverance of Jerusalem.

c. June 12.—Saladin's Terror. The Discipline of the Religious Orders.

Itin. Ric. v.

Now when the Turks, who dwelt in Jerusalem, heard from the fugitives that King Richard was approaching they were terribly afraid, so much so that, had the king at that moment advanced in full force, the Turks would assuredly have forsaken Jerusalem and left it for the Christians. . . . Even Saladin had called for his best horse and given orders to be furnished with a fleeter *destrier,* so that he might flee from the face of King Richard, whose coming he dared not await.

On the same day while the king was occupied as above, two hundred Saracens, coming down from the heights towards the tents of the French, threw the whole army into confusion before they were themselves routed. For, first of all, they slew two of our attendants, who had gone out to seek fodder for the mules; and, hearing the cries of these two, the French, the Templars, and the Hospitallers sprang forth upon the Turks, who offered a brave resistance. . . . On this occasion a certain knight performed what would have been an illustrious act of valour had it not involved the breaking of the rule of his order. . . . He was a Hospitaller, Robert de Bruges by name.

★★★★★★★★

The Rule of the Templars on which the military rules of the Hospitallers are said to have been modelled: "If a brother on an expedition pricks forward without leave and harm comes of it, he is liable to lose his habit. But if he sees a Christian in peril of death and his conscience moves him to go to the rescue he may do so."

★★★★★★★★

This knight in his eagerness to engage, having passed by the royal standard, set spurs to his noble horse and came to the king, contrary to all rules of discipline deserting his fellows, and was thus hurried alone against the enemies before the advance of the other Hospitallers. Coming up from the opposite part of the field he attacked in full career a certain well-armed Turk with his lance. Despite the strength of his armour the Turk fell to the ground pierced through the body so that the lance stood out behind. . . . At that moment all our men advancing at full speed set upon the enemy.

Then Garner, the master of the Hospital, bade the aforesaid Robert de Bruges descend from his horse and await his punishment. Then did this brother obediently return from the battlefield to the tent, and there stayed till the noble and mighty men of the army fell on their knees before the Master Garner and begged pardon for Robert's fault. Now did each side, straining every nerve, fight on with doubtful success. . . . and our men had already begun to waver under the fatigue of war, when lo! by God's good providence the Count of Perche heard the din of conflict and came up. He, however, was not of much avail; and, unless the Bishop of Salisbury had quickly advanced with his squadron, the French would have been routed on that day.

THE RELEASE OF KARAKUSH AND EL MESHTUB.

From Abulfaragius's *Chronicon Syriacum*; *Leipzig*, 1789

At the capture of Acre, the Franks took two Arab lords prisoners, Bar Meshtub and Kara-kush the Eunuch. The latter was a Roman (*i.e.,* a Greek?) by nation, and Saladin had sent him into Africa where he took many cities. Then he returned into Egypt and built there a wall which remains to this day and is called by his name. Now this man was chief of the Arab host in Acre; and when the French bargained that he should pay the 8,000 *denarii* for his liberty, he asked Bar Meshtub at what rate he was to be redeemed. Then said the Franks: "At 30,000 *denarii.*"

To which Kara-kush made answer: "I, too, will pay 30,000; for Bar Meshtub shall not give 30,000 *denarii* and I only 8,000." At this the Franks laughed and took 30,000 *denarii* from him. And other tales are told of this Kara-kush to the same effect; and a certain poet wrote a whole book about him and published it after his death.

APRIL-MAY, 1192.—CIVIL WAR AMONG THE SARACENS HINDERS SALADIN'S POLICY.

Bohâdin.

It was on Thursday, the first of *Jomada* II., (*i.e.,* 14 June, 1192, which, however, is a Sunday. Probably, we should read 1 *Rebia* II., *i.e.,* Thursday, 16 April), that Saf-Addin Al Meshtub recovered his liberty and reached the Holy City. The *Sultan* was with his brother Al Adil when he saw this *emir* enter suddenly. At sight of him he felt the keenest joy, rose to embrace him, and, after having the hall cleared, held a conversation with him, asking his visitor what the enemy were doing and what he thought of the projected peace. From Al Meshtub the *Sultan* now learnt that the King of England had not a word to say about it.

The same day the *Sultan* sent off a despatch to his son Al Afdal bidding him cross the Euphrates and seize upon the provinces occupied by Al Mansur the son of Taki-ad-din. For this prince had offended the *Sultan* and, fearing his displeasure, had just broken out into open rebellion. He had, however, succeeded in engaging the interest of Al Adil, whom he begged to intercede in his favour. This intercession displeased the *Sultan*, who became exceedingly wrath at being opposed by members of his own family, and all the more that one of those who justly dreaded punishment should dare to demand the confirmation of the pardon he asked for by an oath.

It was this that prevented the King of England from concluding the peace; for the dissensions that had just broken out in the *Sultan's* family seemed likely to trouble the sources of war and oblige his enemy to submit to any terms... On 6 *Rabia* II. (*i.e.,* Tuesday, 21 April), Joseph brought a message from the marquis he said:

> An arrangement is on the point of being concluded between the marquis and the Franks, and if it is concluded soon the Franks will depart for their own land...

Accordingly, the *Sultan*, who was greatly concerned at the course of events in the East, fearing to see Al Mansur make alliance with Bectimor, (Lord of Khelat near the Euphrates), made haste to accept the marquis' proposals

Wherefore he had an act embodying these conditions drawn up and despatched it by Joseph on 9 Rab. II. (*i.e.,* Friday, 24 April.)

(*Al Adil at last succeeded in getting the Sultan's pardon for his great nephew Al Mansur. But even then, when the document was already drawn up, he pressed for his brother's signature so urgently that Saladin in anger at such demands tore up the schedule (May 14). Bohâdin himself was used as the intermediary in this business, and when Saladin finally consented to pardon his great-nephew was despatched to gather the opinions of the emirs serving under Al Afdal, who collected them before the envoy. Bohâdin did his message, and then:*)

The *emir* Hossam replied in these words:

> We are the *Sultan's* slaves and servants ... (yet) it is impossible for us to carry on two wars—one against the Musulmans and the other against the *infidels*—at the same time. If the *Sultan* wishes us to fight with the Musulmans let him allow us to, to make peace with the *infidels*; then we will cross the Euphrates and fight, but it must be under his eyes. If, on the other hand, he wishes us to continue the Holy War, let him pardon the Musulmans and grant them peace.

All the assembly approved this answer. Then the *Sultan* let his anger relax and drew up a fresh act, confirmed by his own oath and sign manual. . . . On 8 *Jomada* I. (May 22) Al Adil set out to conclude this business and assure Al Mansur. (Al Malec-al-Mansur Mohammed was Taki-ad-Din's son and succeeded his father as Lord of Hamah.)

1192, JUNE 17.—ATTACK OF TURKS UPON THE CRUSADERS' CARAVAN. PROWESS OF THE EARL OF LEICESTER.

Itin. Ric, v.

On the seventeenth of June, St. Botolph's Day, Wednesday, our caravan laden with victuals and other necessaries left Joppa for the army. Frederick de Viana was appointed to escort it in the place of Count Henry who should have protected the rear, but had been sent to Acre. So, Frederick asked Baldwin de Carron and Clarembald de Mont Chablon to help guard the caravan that day and preserve us from straggling. But, as they marched along without due caution, they paid the penalty of their carelessness. . . . For lo! not far from

Ramleh the Turkish horsemen, leaping out from the cover of the hills, rushed upon our rear, eager to outrace one another. Those who had the fleetest horses cut their way through our rearguard and Baldwin (de) Carron was unhorsed. He, however, immediately drew his sword and defended himself against his assailants. In the same conflict Richard D'Orques and Theodoric were also unhorsed.

But Baldwin continued to fight bravely on foot till his men got him another horse. . . . As often as the Turks laid any one low, his comrades bearing up against the crowd made him remount and very valiantly gave one another aid. Indeed, with such a multitude of Turks closing round our men, it was no wonder if the bravest warriors got unhorsed. And, moreover, the javelins of the Turks flew so thickly that they wounded the horses and made them very weak.

And lo! Baldwin was unhorsed a second time, whereupon he bade one of his men-at-arms dismount and hand him his horse. Baldwin remounted, and at once saw the head of his follower cut off; although this warrior had borne himself very stoutly so long as he was mounted. Thus did our men stand their ground defending themselves. Philip, Baldwin's comrade, who distinguished himself more than all the rest, was taken prisoner, and with him the Turks were carrying off Richard D'Orques' brother, a most valiant warrior. . . . Moreover, Clarembald de Mont Chablun, on seeing the numbers of the Turks increase, forsook his men, and took to headlong flight. On this the conflict was renewed most fiercely; Baldwin was unhorsed a third time and now was so battered with clubs as to be rendered almost helpless.

Then, jammed close by the increasing crowd of enemies, he called out with a loud voice to that most valiant soldier Manasses de Insula, who was then harrying all the Turks, "O, Manasses are you too forsaking me?" On hearing his voice, Manasses flew swiftly to his rescue. Still closer thronged the Turks, all too many for this pair of warriors, and while they were struggling against innumerable foes, Manasses also was hurled from his horse; and, as he lay prostrate, he was so cruelly battered with their toothed iron clubs, so mauled and so bruised, that one of his legs was cut clean through to the marrow. Thus were Baldwin and Manasses weighted down by the hostile throng, and all the while their own men were ignorant what had become of them.

At this moment lo! God sent the valiant Earl of Leicester as their champion and liberator, though he too was unaware of their position. Now the earl, coming on in full career, unhorsed the first Turk he fell in with; whereupon Anscon, Stephen de Longchamp's comrade, cut off the (fallen warrior's) head and flung it away. Stephen too bore himself manfully in every stress. And lo! our men increased while the courage of the Turks ebbed away, till they were put to flight and driven to the mountains in headlong haste. Then our wounded were gently lifted from the ground and set on horses and brought down to the army. I have deemed this day's achievements worthy of special note, and thus have I told, among other things, how the Earl of Leicester routed the Turks.

Now on the day of St Alban, which is the third day before the festival of St. John the Baptist, (*i.e.,* Monday, June 22), while the army was staying at Betenopolis, it received consolation from a report that reached the king. For to the king there came a most holy abbot, whose very features proclaimed his sanctity. He was Abbot of St. Elias, and had a flowing beard, white hair, and a reverend countenance. This man told the king, that he had been keeping a fragment of the Holy Cross hidden away for a long time past, and (intended to keep it) till by God's aid the Holy Land should be clear of the Turks and restored to its former condition.

He declared that he was the only person who knew where this treasure lay; that Saladin had many times pressed him closely, and narrowly questioned him, seeking by the most cunningly contrived interrogations to become possessed of his secret. He had nevertheless always put off the tyrant with deceitful words; and, when Saladin had given orders for him to be bound with thongs, the abbot stoutly asserted that he had lost the cross when Jerusalem was taken, and so had deceived his tormentor. On hearing this the king with a large host at once set forth to the place of which the abbot spoke; and thence brought back the Holy Cross with due reverence and delight to the army quarters, where the people eagerly kissed it with the utmost devotion and pious tears.

1192, c. June 22.—King Richard is advised to give up the hope of besetting Jerusalem, and the army resolves to go and attack Cairo.

Itin., Ric. vi..

Now when men had been adoring this Holy Cross for some time with no little joy at possessing it, the common folk began to complain again, saying "Lord God, what will come to us? Shall we ever get to Jerusalem? What more shall we do? Shall we (manage to) hold out to the end of this pilgrimage?" And there was much murmuring and complaint, whereupon the king and the great men met together to consult as to the expediency of advancing or not. Certain of the French advocated an advance; for to them this seemed the most advisable course. The king however answered that it was impossible for him to do so, he said:

> You will not find me leading the people in such a way as to lay myself open to reprehension or shame. Truly it would be the mark of an unwary man if I were to lend myself to any such folly. But, if you see fit to attack Jerusalem, I will not desert you; I will be your comrade though not your lord; I will follow but I will not lead. Saladin knows everything that is done in our army, he knows our capacity and our strength. We are far off from the coast, and if Saladin should come down into the plain of Ramula with his host and cut off our provisions by guarding the ways (so as to prevent provisions being brought up to Beit Nûba by way of Joppa and Ramleh), would not this, I ask you, be our utter ruin?
>
> Then, however it would be too late for repentance. Besides, the circuit of Jerusalem, so far as we hear, is very large and, if our little host were to attempt to close it in on every side, our numbers would not suffice for the siege and the protection of those who bring up our stores. Besides, if I were to sanction any such imprudence while I was leader, and if any misfortune

befell us, I alone should be charged with rashness, and be reckoned responsible for the danger of all Moreover I know for certain that there are some here (and in France too) who are most eager for me to act rashly, and lay myself open to some dishonouring charge.

For these reasons I do not think fit to show any hurry in the conduct of such difficult affairs. Besides we and our people are strangers, entirely ignorant of the district, its roads and its passes. ...Therefore I think it better to proceed on the advice of the natives who, we may be sure, are eager to get back to their old possessions, and who know the country. It seems fit to follow the advice of the Templars and the Hospitallers—as to whether we shall advance to the siege of Jerusalem or to siege Babylon, Beyrout, or Damascus. If we adopt their advice our army will no longer be, as it now is, torn apart by such great dissensions.

Accordingly at the king's suggestion it was agreed to follow without any gainsaying whatever should approve itself to twenty sworn jurors. Then there were elected for the decision of this matter five Templars, five Hospitallers, five native Syrians belonging to the land, and five French nobles. These twenty, after having met and consulted together, replied that it would certainly be best to advance to the siege of Babylon (Cairo). To this decision the French, when they heard it, offered a persistent opposition, declaring that they would not move except against Jerusalem. When the king heard of the obstinacy and disloyalty of the French, he was troubled, and said:

If the French will agree to my advice, and consent to advance to the siege of Cairo as the jurors have decided, why! I will lend them my Acre fleet with all its fair equipments to carry food and whatever they want, so that the army may march in perfect confidence along the coast. I will also, at my own cost, maintain seven hundred knights and two hundred sergeants for the expedition in God's name. Moreover, if anyone has need of my help in money or anything else that I have, let him be assured that I will liberally supply his needs.

1192.—23 JUNE.—KING RICHARD TAKES THE SARACEN CARAVAN.

Then King Richard gave immediate orders that they should meet at the tents of the Hospitallers and make careful enquiries as to what each man could contribute for the conduct of the siege and how many men he could maintain. Accordingly, they met there, and the chief men promised along with others that they would be at great expense for the siege—as did also those who had little in their treasure-stores. But in such doubtful circumstances it seemed a very indiscreet thing to aim even at beginning the siege of Jerusalem after the jurors had pronounced against it.

Now, while they were anxiously engaged in seeing how far each man could assist in the siege, Bernard, the king's scout, came up with some other spies, who were all natives of the land. They were clad in Saracen garb and came from the direction of Egypt—differing in no respect, so far as appearance went, from the Saracens. Thus, they were able to study the position of the Saracens at ease and keep the king informed thereon. No one spoke the Saracen tongue better than they; one of them indeed having, in return for his service in this way, formerly received from King Richard 100 silver *marks*.

These scouts bade the king start at once with his people and cut off the caravans that were coming from Babylon (Cairo), promising to conduct him there. The king, being greatly delighted at this news, sent to the Duke of Burgundy, inviting him to come up quickly with his Frenchmen. This he did and the French also, but on the understanding that they should receive the third part of the booty. The king consented, whereupon they set forward at once—about 500 well-armed knights, as was reckoned. The king led 1,000 lightly-armed serving-men at his own cost.

The king went before all the rest and, as the day was now closing, they advanced all night beneath the splendour of the moon to Galatia, (possibly Khurbet Jeledîyeh, 6 miles S. W. of Tell es Safi and 12 N. E. of Ascalon), where they rested a space while they sent to Ascalon for victuals. Meanwhile, until the servants, who had been sent for provisions, returned, they kept an armed watch. Now it chanced that, from the moment when our folk first began to move in the matter of the caravans, a scout told the whole affair to Saladin in Jerusalem, mentioning how he had seen King Richard hastening in the direction of the caravans. Thus was the secrecy of our plan revealed, and Saladin at once sent out 500 choice Turks to the rescue. They were armed with reed weapons and with bows, and, when they had joined those who originally had charge of the caravans, they made up a total of 2,000 horsemen, without counting the numerous footmen.

While Richard and his people were at Galatia a spy came up telling him how one of the caravans was passing through the "Round

Cistern." This caravan he advised the king to seize at once, while holding back (the main body of) his troops. "Whoever," he went on, "gets this caravan will have a very large booty." But, as this spy belonged to the land, the king would not put absolute trust in him, but sent out a certain Bedouin and two *Turcople* servants whom he had dressed up so as to look like the Bedouins. These he despatched to find out the truth of this information. They, going out by night, passed over the hills from which they could get the best views until they caught sight of some Saracens on a lofty site. Now these Saracens were themselves spies, lying in wait for passers-by.

When our Bedouin approached them stealthily, they asked him who he and his companions were: whence they were coming and whither they were going. Our Bedouin, nodding to his comrades that they should not speak a word for fear of being betrayed by their accent, made answer that he was returning from the parts of Ascalon, to which city he had gone on the lookout for booty.

To him one of the Saracens made reply: "Nay, thou hast come to lay snares for us; for thou livest with the King of England." The Bedouin answered, "Thou liest," and, with the words, set off hurriedly in the direction of the other caravans, while the Turks pursued with bows and reed weapons until they were too tired to follow any further. But our spies, finding the report about the caravans to be true, returned to the king in haste with the news that he might certainly capture the caravans if he only set out at once. On hearing this, the king gave his horses a little food and set forth in haste with his own people.

All that night did they march till they reached the place where the caravan had pitched with its guards resting round it. Not far from this spot the king and his comrades paused while arming themselves and forming their line. The king was in the front rank and the French in the rear. Then the king, by his herald, forbade anyone to set about plundering; they were all to strive manfully to penetrate and shatter the Turkish ranks.

Now, when it was already day, a spy came up at headlong speed telling the king that the caravan was making preparations to move on at earliest dawn; for its guards had got note of the king's intended attack. Hearing this the king at once sent forward his crossbowmen and archers to delay the Turkish march by sham challenges. . . .whilst our ranks were drawing near in due order and with what speed they could. Seeing this the Turks betook themselves to the spur of a neighbouring hill and drew up their forces in squadrons, but with less arrogance than usual. Then while the Turks were hurling their darts and arrows, thick as dew, against our forces as they pressed on, and while the caravan was still resting in one place, the king, dividing his army, fell upon them suddenly, piercing through and thoroughly routing their first squadron. Then all took to headlong flight as hares before dogs. The caravan remained behind whilst our men, dealing slaughter indefatigably to right and left, did not cease in the pursuit till the Turks lay everywhere dead on the parching sand. . .

Nobly did the royal troops fight; most vigorously too did the French display their wonted prowess. Moreover, King Richard shone forth with a more illustrious record than all the rest, none of whom could be compared to him. Borne aloft on his horse he was carried against the enemy with signal valour; his ashen shaft gave way beneath his ceaseless onsets till, being made, as it were, rotten with blood, it shivered into bits. Then, without delay, he brandished his sword and thundered on, threatening, overthrowing, taking prisoners, mowing down some, cutting off others, cleaving men from the top of the head to the teeth. No kind of armour was strong enough to withstand his blows. . . .

Thirty Turks in their flight turning round swooped down upon Roger de Tooney, slaying his horse beneath him and almost capturing (the knight) himself. His comrade Jocelin of Maine came up to rescue Roger from their hands, but was also thrown from his horse at once. Thereupon Roger de Tooney came up, and defending himself bravely, all on foot as he was, set his friend free. Meanwhile our men arrived and with them the Earl of Leicester, laying about him to right and left; Gilbert Maleman with four comrades, Alexander Arsic, and some other comrades almost twenty in all. There also came up Stephen de Longchamp who conferred a great service on Roger de Tooney by bringing him a horse, on whose back he might extricate himself from the middle of the Turks.

Then was the slaughter renewed, the heavens thundered, the air was bright with sparks struck from the swords. The ground reeked with blood, dismembered corpses were everywhere: lopt off arms, hands, feet, heads, and even eyes. Our men were hindered in walking over the plain by the corpses of the dead Turks, so thickly were they strewn about; and the bodies, which they had just dismembered, caused our men to stumble. . . . There was the Turks' pride ground down, their arrogance abolished, and their boldness suppressed. With such prowess did our men capture the caravan.

(*The spoils consisted of spices, gold, silver, silks, purple robes, arms of every kind, richly wrought pillows and tents, hides, bladders for carrying water, and cinnamon, sugar, spice, pepper, barley, wheat, flour and wax. There were also taken 4,700 camels, and mules and asses beyond number. Thirteen hundred Turkish horsemen were cut off, without reckoning the foot.)*

23 JUNE, 1192.—SALADIN'S GRIEF AT THE CAPTURE OF THE CARAVAN BY THE CHRISTIANS.

Bohâdin

This caravan had originally been divided into three parts, of which the first escorted by a band of Arabs and the troops of Al Adil had taken the road of Al Carac. The second, also escorted by Arabs, had been led by the road which crosses the desert. The third was that seized by the enemy. . . It was an event most shameful to us; never for a long time had Islam experienced such a disaster. . . According to one report which reached us the enemy had about a hundred knights slain, according to another only ten. Only two persons of any consequence were slain on our side. . . I have heard it said by one of those whom the enemy made prisoner that on this same night a rumour was spread among the Franks that the *Sultan's* army was drawing near.

On hearing this they took to flight, leaving their booty behind. Later on, learning that the alarm was false, they returned to their prey. During their absence several of their Mussulman prisoners managed to escape; and among them the man of whom I speak. I asked him how many camels and horses he thought the enemy had taken, and he replied "About 3,000 camels and nearly as many horses." This terrible event happened on the morning of Tuesday, 11 *Jomada* II. (*i.e.,* on 24 June, which, however, was a Wednesday in 1192.)

On the evening of that day, I was seated near the *Sultan* when one of the young Mamelukes attached to his stables brought him news of what had taken place. No news ever caused him keener grief or troubled his heart more. I did my best to console him, but he would hardly listen to me. The enemy rejoined the main body on Friday, 16 *Jomada* II. (*i.e.,* 29 June). . . . Then they carried their tents to Beit-Nûba and determined to march on Jerusalem in all seriousness. . . .

They posted a body of troops at Lydda to guard the road by which their convoys passed, and despatched Count Henry to bring all the troops that were to be found in Tyre, Tripoli, and Acre. The *Sultan*, on hearing their intention of advancing against Jerusalem, divided the ramparts of the city amongst his *emirs* with orders to get everything ready for a siege. He took care also to corrupt all the water in the vi-

159

cinity of the Holy City, to block up the springs, to destroy the cisterns, and fill up the wells. So, there was not left in all the neighbourhood a single drop of drinking water; such was the energy with which he worked. It is well known that near Jerusalem it is impossible to sink pits for drinkable water, as the ground is nothing else than a huge mountain made up of exceedingly hard rock. The *Sultan* also sent orders into all his provinces for his troops to hurry up.

JULY 1-2.—BOHÂDIN AND THE SULTAN.

Bohâdin

On the night preceding Thursday, 19 *Jomada* II. the *Sultan* called together his *emirs*. With them came Abu al Heja (commander of the garrison of Acre before Al Meshtub) the fat, a man who could scarcely move and had to keep seated in an arm chair. . . The *Sultan* bade me pronounce a discourse to encourage them to persevere in the Holy War. . . . Amongst other things I said, "When our Holy Prophet suffered tribulation his companions swore an oath to fight for him till death. Here is an example that we ought to imitate above all other people. Let us unite then in the Temple and there take an oath to support one another till death. Such an action may perhaps be rewarded by the repulse of the enemy." The whole assembly approved my advice and promised to carry it out.

The *Sultan* remained silent for some time, in the attitude of a man who is thinking, and all the bystanders respected his silence. At last, he broke out with these words:

Praise be to God and a blessing on his messenger. Know that today you are the only army and the sole stay of Islam. Consider how the blood, the wealth, the children of the Musulmans are placed under your protection, and that, among all the true believers, you only are capable of opposing such enemies as we have before! us. If you give way, which God forbid, the enemy will gradually possess himself of the country as easily as a man can roll up a parchment, and you will be responsible, for you have undertaken to defend it. You have received money from the public treasure, and it is on you that the safety of the Musulmans everywhere depends. I have said.

Saf Ad-din Al-Meshtub then took up the word:

Lord, we are your slaves and servants. You have heaped benefits upon us, you have raised us in rank and enriched us with gifts, whilst we have nothing to offer in return except our heads; and these we place at your feet. There is not one of us—I swear it before God—who will cease to aid you so long as life lasts.

The whole assembly made the same declaration, and this oath revived the spirit and quieted the heart of the *Sultan*. He then had them served with the ordinary repast, after which they withdrew. . . In the evening we resumed our service with the prince, as was customary, and watched part of the night with him. But he was not at all in a communicative mood. Then we said the last prayer together.

Now, as this was the signal for everyone to withdraw, I was going out with the rest, when he called me back. Accordingly, I came and stood upright before him while he asked me if I had heard the latest news. I answered "No;" on which he said:

> Today I have received a communication from Abu al-Heja the fat from which I learn that, at a meeting of the *emirs* in his house, I have been blamed for listening to your advice about the siege and for consenting to let ourselves be shut up in the town. They say there can be no advantage in this and that, so closed up, they will undergo the same fate as the garrison at Acre. . . It would be better to risk a pitched battle. Then if God grants us the victory, we shall become masters of all the enemy possess. If we are beaten we shall it is true lose the Holy City, but we shall have saved our army.

Now the *Sultan* bore towards Jerusalem an affection such as you can hardly imagine; for which reason such a communication caused him much pain. This night, the whole of which I passed with him, was one of those when we remained together to watch and pray. The letter he had received contained the following passage:

> If you wish us to stay in the Holy City stay with us yourself, or at least leave a member of your family there; for the Curds will never obey the Turks any more than the Turks will obey the Curds.

It was then decided that the *Sultan* should leave his grand-nephew Meji Ad-din, son of Ferrukh-Chah (son of Saladin's brother, Chah-an-Chah, and the most trusted of Saladin's warriors) and Lord of Baal-bec It was at first suggested that the *Sultan* should let himself be closed up in the city, but he had to renounce this project because of the danger to Islam that might result from it.

At daybreak I found him still watching; and, feeling compassion for him, I begged him to take an hour's rest. I then went off to my own house; but I had scarcely got there before I heard the *Mueddin* (crier of the mosque) call to prayer, and I had only just time to snatch up what was necessary for the ablution as day was beginning to appear already.

Now, as I was in the habit of sometimes making my morning prayer with the *Sultan*, I went off to him and found him renewing his ablution. After we had prayed together, I said to him: "An idea has struck me; may I lay it before you?"

He replied "Speak."

I then proceeded:

Your Highness is overwhelmed with cares such as you can hardly support. Now that earthly means fail address yourself to God, the All Powerful. Today is Friday, the luckiest day in the week, the one on which every prayer is heard, and we are here (in Jerusalem) in the most propitious place. Let the *Sultan* do his ablutions, let him distribute alms in secret so that no one may know whence they come, and let him offer a prayer of two *recas* between the *adân* and the *ikama*. Thus, shall he address himself to the Lord in a low voice, confiding to him the direction of all his affairs and avowing his own helplessness... Perhaps God will have pity on you and hear your supplication.

Now the *Sultan* was a sincere believer in all the *dogmas* of our faith, and was wont to submit himself absolutely to the precepts of the Divine Law. We then left him and, when the hour of divine service arrived, I prayed at his side in the mosque of Al Aksa and saw him make two *recas*, prostrating himself at the same time and calling upon the Lord in a low voice, while the tears ran down upon his prayer-carpet. When the prayer was over the faithful withdrew. In the evening I resumed my customary service at his side, and lo there came up a despatch from Jordic who, at that time, was commanding the advanced guard. In it the *Sultan* read these words: "The whole army of the enemy came out on horseback to post itself on the top of the hill; it then returned to its camp, and we have sent out spies to know what is going on"

On Saturday morning, (*i.e.,* July 4), there came a second despatch of which the following is a summary:

Our spy has come back and tells us that there is dissension among the enemy, some of whom desire to push on to the

Holy City whilst the others are for returning into their own territory. The Franks insist upon marching against Jerusalem. They say, 'It was to rescue the Holy City that we left our own country, and we will not go home before we have taken it.' To this the King of England made answer: 'The enemy has corrupted all the springs till there is absolutely not a drop of water left in the neighbourhood of the town; where then shall we water our horses?'

Someone suggested that they could get water at Tekoua, a river that runs about a *parasang's* distance from Jerusalem. 'How,' said the king, 'shall we manage to water our beasts there?' 'We will divide the army in two parts,' was the answer, 'of these one part shall go out on horseback to the water while the other shall stay by the town to carry on the siege. So, the army shall go once each day to Tekoua.' To this suggestion the king made answer: 'As soon as one division has gone off with its beasts for water the garrison will make a sally upon those that are left, and then it is all over with the Christian host.'' "At last, they decided to choose three hundred persons of influence, who were to deliver their powers to twelve individuals. These twelve were to choose three others to settle the question. The night, was spent waiting for the decision of the *triumvirate*.

Next morning, 21 *Jomada* II. (*i.e.,* July 4), they moved off in the direction of Ramleh agreeably to the decision. . . The *Sultan*, on hearing this, got on horseback with his troops and all witnessed the most lively joy. And yet, as he knew the enemy to have plenty of camels and other beasts of burden, he had fears for Egypt, a land that the King of England had many times shewn an inclination to invade.

Negotiations begin again with Richard and Earl Henry, but are broken off. c. 5 July-19 July, 1192.

Bohâdin

Now the *Sultan*, freed from his cares by the retreat of the enemy, had the envoy from Earl Henry brought in to hear his proposals. This man was introduced and, after receiving leave to set forth the object of his mission, spoke as follows:—

Earl Henry says thus:

The King of England has given me all the towns along the coast and I have them in my hands. Deliver up to me then my other towns that I may make peace with you and be as one of your children.

At these words the *Sultan* was so wroth that he was on the point of using violence against the messenger. He had made him stand upright before him in order to cut off his head, when the man said: "Wait a moment; I have only a word to say. The count demands what part you will give him now the whole land is in your possession." The *Sultan* then reprimanded the envoy and had him led forth.

Then on 23 *Jomada* II. (*i.e.*, Monday, July 6), there came from the Franks Haj Joseph, Al-Meshtub's friend. He said that the King of England had sent for him and Count Henry and, after clearing the hall, had spoken to him as follows: "You must say to your friend on my part, 'We have both of us lost strength, and the best thing we can do is to put an end to this bloodshed. Do not imagine that it is the weakness of my resources that makes me suggest this; it is to the advantage of both sides. Be mediator between the *Sultan* and me; but do not let yourself be deceived by the retreat I have just made. When the Ram goes back it is only that it may strike the harder.'" The king sent two persons with the Haj to receive Al-Meshtub's reply.

The ostensible object of this communication was to negotiate the liberty of Behâ-ad-din Kara-kush, but in reality, it was about the treaty of peace. The Haj informed us that the Franks had left Ramlah for Jaffa, and that they were too weak to undertake any expedition. Al-Meshtub, who had been brought up from Neapolis (Nablus or Shechem, some 30 miles N. of Jerusalem), to hear the message, replied as follows:

> We will make peace with Count Henry in his quality of Lord of Acre; for this city has been given him. As regards the other towns terms must be arranged between the King of England and us.

On Friday, the 27th (*i.e.,* July 10), the Frankish ambassador returned along with Haj Joseph, said he:

> Here, are the very words of the king, *i.e.*, of the King of England—'I desire to merit your affection and friendship. I have no wish to play the Pharoah over this land any more than I suppose you have. You must not make all your Musulmans perish nor I all our Franks. Here is Count Henry, my sister's son, whom I have put in possession of all these countries, and now

I put him and his army at your disposal. If you invite him to accompany you on an expedition to your Eastern provinces he will obey.' The king also said 'Many monks and men of religion have begged churches of you and you have granted their petitions generously. And now I ask of you to give me a church. As to what displeased you in my former communications with Al-Malec Al-Adil I renounce them and entertain them no more. If you will give me a farm or a village, I will accept it and give you an equivalent.'

(*Saladin answered thus—his council having advised him to be conciliatory:—*)

Since you address us in so conciliatory a way, and since one good turn deserves another, the *Sultan* will regard your nephew as one of his sons; and you will soon learn how he has treated this prince. To you he grants the greatest of churches, the Church of the Resurrection, and he will divide the rest of the country with you. The sea-coast towns that you already hold you shall keep; the fortresses that we have in the mountain regions shall remain ours; while what lies between the mountains and the sea coast shall be divided between us. Ascalon and its neighbourhood shall be ruined and belong to neither. If you wish to have some villages from us you shall have them. What I objected to most up till now was the matter of Ascalon.

On the 28th, (*i.e.*, Saturday 11 July)—the day after his arrival—the ambassador left us, completely satisfied. After his departure we heard that the Franks had started for Ascalon on their way towards Egypt. An ambassador also came to us from us Kotb-ad-din, the son of Kalij Arslan, bringing us this message from his master:

The Pope has taken the road for Constantinople at the head of a multitude whose numbers God only knows."

Here the ambassador added that he had himself slain twelve knights on the way.

The prince continued:

Send me someone to whose care I may commit my kingdom; for I am not strong enough to defend it myself.

But the *Sultan* gave no credence to this communication and did not trouble himself about it.

(On 12th July Richard demanded the right of putting 20 soldiers in the citadel at Jerusalem; but his envoy, by word of mouth, said that the king gave up all his claims on the Holy City. Richard sent a couple of falcons as a present to Saladin.)

The *Sultan* convoked his *emirs* to advise on his reply, and they determined to answer that the king had no right over Jerusalem except that of pilgrimage. The ambassador having then demanded that no impost should be levied on the pilgrims, we saw by this that he was no longer in agreement with us. As regards Ascalon and the places round it they must be absolutely destroyed. But when the ambassador observed that the king had spent much money on these fortifications Al Meshtub said to the *Sultan*, "Let him keep the cultivated fields and the villages as an indemnity." To this the *Sultan* agreed, but he insisted on the demolition of Al Darum and other places. . .

As to the other towns and their dependencies the *Sultan* agreed to leave the Franks all that lay between Jaffa and Tyre, adding, "Every time there is a dispute regarding the possession of a village, we will divide it." . . . The *Sultan* gave the envoy rich presents for the Franks in exchange for those they had sent him. And everyone knows that in a matter of presents nobody could surpass him, so great were his heart and his liberality.

Late in the night preceding 3rd *Rajab* (*i.e.*, that of July 14) the Haj Joseph returned with the king's ambassador, and on Thursday morning the 3rd, (*i.e.*, on July 15, which however was a Wednesday). . . . delivered his message.

> The king begs you to leave him these three places (Ascalon, Darum, and Gaza). Of what importance can they be in the eyes of so powerful a prince as you? The king insists on this concession merely because of the ill-will shewn by the Franks, who will not consent to their being surrendered. He has entirely given up Jerusalem. . . . except as regards the church of the Resurrection. Leave him then the towns in question and let there be a general peace. The Franks will keep all they now hold from Darum to Ascalon, you will keep all that is now in your hands. Then everything will come right of itself and the king will be able to depart. Otherwise, the Franks will not let him go and he will not be able to resist them.

See the cunning of this accursed man; who to gain his ends at one time would employ soft language, at another violence. Although he saw that he was obliged to depart he persisted in the same line of conduct. God alone was able to protect the Musulmans against his malice. Never have we had to meet the hostility of a subtler or bolder man than he.

On receiving this message, the *Sultan* called his *emirs* together. . . Here is the substance of their reply:

> As to the villages that the king demands we do not care about them, but the Musulmans will never consent to yield them. As to the fortifications of Ascalon let the king take Lydda, a village in the plain, to indemnify him.

It was on Friday morning, 4 *Rajab*, (*i.e.,* 16 July, really a Thursday), that the ambassador took his leave. . . . On the 7th Haj Yussuf returned alone and told us the king had said to him,:

> It is impossible to let one stone of the fortifications of Ascalon be pulled down; we cannot let such a thing be said of us in the country. The limits of the two countries are well fixed and admit of no discussion.

After this communication the *Sultan* made preparations against the enemy, intending to show by vigorous action his determination to continue the war if need be.

1192, CIRC. 27 JUNE-27 JULY.—KING RICHARD AND THE ARMY RETREAT. SALADIN ATTACKS JOPPA.

Itin., Ric. v.

Then the king and the army returned to near Bethaven which is four miles from Joppa, and there they divided the booty. Thence they proceeded on the next day to Ramula. Meanwhile Count Henry came to Ramula from Acre, leading with him the men he had brought from that city. From Ramula all together set out to Betenopolis, whence they first started. . . . There the king in his munificence distributed his camels among those knights who had stayed behind to guard the army on the same scale as to those who had taken part in the expedition. In this he imitated that most valiant warrior King David. He also divided all the asses among the serving-men.

Then was the army so replenished with camels, asses, and other beasts of burden that they could scarcely be kept together. People gladly ate the flesh of young camels after roasting it and stuffing it with lard; for it was white and pleasant enough to the taste. But before long, after the distribution of the beasts of burden, the people grew dainty and complained that these camels ate up too much barley, and so raised grain beyond its previous price. At the same time the old cry and complaint was renewed about the delay in advancing against Jerusalem

(*The Turks had now stopt up the streams near Jerusalem; it was midsummer—about St. John the Baptist's day—and there was no water to be found within 2 miles of the city.*)

For these causes it was decided not to besiege Jerusalem at that time. But when the army knew that it was not to be led against Jerusalem, each man in his sorrow and bitter distress began to curse the delay and the (blasting of the) hopes he had entertained. Men kept declaring that they only wished to live long enough for the Christians to gain Jerusalem, and for the holy places to be wrested from the hands of the *infidels....* Nor is it a thing to be wondered at that the pilgrims had borne all these misfortunes, as it were to no purpose; and that, for all their sorrow, things did not prosper with them. For, whenever the army was advancing anywhere, about evening the French would gather into one body and, turning aside from the rest of the host, would settle by themselves for the night in a separate place, as though they were too good company for the others.

Nor were they content merely with separating company, but quarrelling amongst themselves, they used to inveigh one against the other. . . And, moreover, above all other things of this kind Henry Duke of Burgundy, led on by the arrogant prompting of an evil soul, or perhaps by envy had a song composed and sung publicly. The words of this song were shameful, and such as ought not to have been given to the public if those who wrote it had had any sense of shame left in them; for it was sung not only by men, but by women who surpassed men in their licence. But, in devoting itself to such unseemly frivolities, this people only revealed its true character; and it was clearly seen what its real disposition was, for we know streams are turbid or clear in accordance with the nature of their source.

After this scurrilous composition had been disseminated over the army, the king, being greatly annoyed, deemed it advisable to take vengeance in a similar way. So, he strung together himself a few lines about (his detractors), a work which involved no great strain on his powers of invention because he had such copious material; nor could any objection be taken to his answering so many trumped-up scandals with a few plain truths.

Now there can be no doubt as to the illustrious deeds of King

Richard, whom his rivals so enviously attacked when they despaired of detracting from his prowess. For the pilgrims of those days were not such as those in the expedition when our people took Antioch by force of arms—a period we still hear sung of in the *Gestes* about the famous victory of Boemund, of Tancred, Godfrey de Bouillon and other noble chiefs of highest renown. (This poem was written by Richard the pilgrim who himself took a part in the first Crusade.) They indeed won glorious victories; their deeds now flow as food from the mouth of the story-tellers; God gave them the reward for which they had toiled because they served Him out of no faint heart; and He glorified their splendid achievements with immortal memory.

After the taking of the caravan the army stayed for a few days at Betenopolis (Beit-Nûba), much saddened because the advance towards Jerusalem was given up, and they might not visit the Lord's Sepulchre though only four miles off....Afterwards setting forth they reached a spot between St. George, (Lydda), and Ramula where they rested for the night—the French fixing their tents on the left, the king and his people on the right. On the morrow they also journeyed in two divisions, and at night, on the 6th July, they camped at Casel Medium, where some left the army on account of their poverty and departed to Joppa.

Now when Saladin learnt that we had determined to retreat his hopes revived, and he sent his swiftest messengers without delay bearing letters signed with his ring, for all the *emirs* and chiefs that owned his sway. Moreover, he called upon all who were willing to receive his pay to come to him at Jerusalem at once. Nor was there any delay; there promptly assembled 20,000 armed Turkish horsemen, without reckoning an immense host of foot soldiers, such as could not easily be numbered....Thus the army returned to Acre, unspeakably saddened and amazed at its immeasurable misfortune in that God did not yet deem it worthy of a fuller favour....

1192, July 26.—Saladin besieges Joppa, which is relieved by King Richard, August 1.

Itin. Ric.,

(Richard asks Saladin to meet him in Ramleh plains. Saladin refuses unless Ascalon is dismantled. Richard then destroys Darum, as he cannot spare a garrison to keep it. Then he goes back to Joppa and from Joppa to Acre.)

On the Sunday, (26 July), before the day of St. Peter ad Vincula, when Richard and his army reached Acre Saladin came with his army to siege Joppa, and began the attack on Monday.

(*On Monday, Tuesday, and Wednesday the attack continues without success.*)

On the Thursday the fierceness of the Turks, stung at seeing themselves repelled by so small a host, grew greater, and the siege was conducted more vigorously At Saladin's command four strong stone-casters were erected against the town and two *mangonels*. What complaints might one then hear from the besieged, more than 5000 in number including the sick: "Lord God of power, what chance of safety is now left us? Alas, O King of England our leader and guardian, why hast thou gone to Acre?" . . . At last, on the Friday, (*i.e.,* July 31st), owing to the incessant efforts of the Turks and the frequent blows of the *petrariae* the Jerusalem gate was broken in. Then the wall on the right was battered down for a space of two perches. . .

The host of Turks kept on increasing till the Christians were driven back into the castle tower. Alas, how miserable then was the slaughter of the sick, whom the Turks, as they lay everywhere ailing in the houses, put to death in the most terrible ways. Such men cut off in such numbers are surely deemed martyrs. Some of our men fled before the fierce attack of the Turks down to the very beach. Meanwhile the Turks went routing out all the houses, plundering the grain, and pouring out the wine after staving in the vessels that contained it.

Part stormed the chief tower of the castle; others pursued the fugitives as they fled for safety to the ships. On this occasion many of the rear were cut off. There Alberic of Rheims, whose business it was to guard the castle had fled, in the hope of sailing off in a ship. Shame upon him! Excessive fear shewed him to be a craven; and his own comrades who had held out, reproving his cowardice and trying to rekindle his courage, recalled him and drove him by violence into the tower. Then, when he saw nothing but danger around him, he said: "Here then we must die for God since we can do nothing else." . . .

The besieged would certainly have been overpowered by the violent onset of the Turks had there not, by God's grace, chanced to be present in the town the lately created *patriarch*. He, having his wits sharpened by necessity, sent a message to Saladin and begged Saphadin to procure a truce for the tower on the understanding that, if aid did not come before the ninth hour next day each survivor should pay Saladin 10 *besants* of gold. The women were to pay five, and the children three.

As a pledge for the faithful observance of those conditions the *pa-*

triarch offered himself and other noblemen as hostages. Saladin agreed and there were handed over together with the other hostages Alberic of Rheims, Theobald of Treies, Augustin of London, Osbert Waldin, Henry de St. John, and certain others whose names we do not recollect. All these were afterwards led captive to Damascus (as might have been expected, when they gave themselves up as hostages); for the besieged had already conceived some hope of being relieved by the king, to whom they had sent when Saladin first came up.

Meanwhile, as King Richard was at Acre hastening his preparations for returning home—he had already received leave of departure from the Templars and the Hospitallers, together with their blessing; and had also sent forward seven of his galleys with an armed band to Beyrout, from which town he was to set sail—when he was on the point of embarking and was consulting with his men in his tent about these very preparations for his departure, intending to start on the morrow, lo! there appeared before him in great haste the envoys from those who were being sieged in Joppa. These now stood before the king with rent garments, telling how the Saracens had seized Joppa and all that was in it.

They recounted also how the few people who yet survived were being sieged in the tower and would certainly be lost according to the terms of the treaty unless they had immediate aid. The king, on hearing of the perilous state of things, pitied their distress and broke short the words of the envoys in the middle of their pleading, "God (yet) lives and with his guidance I will set out to do what I can."

He then made the herald immediately proclaim that the army should rouse itself for a fresh expedition. The French, however, did not think fit to honour the king with a reply, but continued asserting proudly that they would not go with him any further—ay, and they spake true, for to them there soon happened a miserable death, so that, neither with him nor with anyone else, did they march on another expedition. But those of every land, whose hearts God had touched and whom tribulation had made pious, hastened to go with the knights—to wit, the Templars, the Hospitallers, and many other stalwart knights. These all set out for Caesarea by land.

But the noble king, taking his life in his hands, advanced by sea; and with him there went the Earl of Leicester, Andrew de Chavigni, Roger de Sathya, Jordan de Humeth, ...; also, the knights of Préaux and many other famous warriors, besides the Genoese and Pisans. Those who started for Caesarea stayed there some time, as if they were besieged by Saladin; for they learnt that Saladin had set ambushes. By reason of this they had no clear path, since the son of Assasise (*sic*) kept a strict watch along the roads from Caesarea to Arsuf.

Moreover, a contrary wind bore down against the king's ships and kept them stationary at Cayphas—whither they had put in—for three days. The king, hardly brooking such delay, called out with a deep sigh, "Lord God, why dost thou detain us? Consider, we pray thee, our necessity and devotion." Nor was there any further stoppage; but, with God's good will, a favourable wind blew up from behind and brought the fleet smoothly and safely to the port of Joppa in the deep gloom of Friday night. The term fixed for the payment of the redemption money was the ninth hour of the Saturday following, and according to the terms of the agreement the whole people was to be delivered up if no succour came Now mark the faithless faith and perfidy of these perfidious men; from the very dawn of the Saturday—that is, the Feast of St. Peter ad Vincula, (*i.e.,* August 1)—the Turks began pestering the besieged to make the payment.

And notwithstanding the fact that they had been compelled to commence the payment from very early in the morning and continue it right up to the ninth hour, yet for all this the Turks, more savage than the beasts and lacking in all humanity, began cutting off the heads of those who were bringing in the money. They had already cut off seven men's heads and flung them pell-mell into a certain ditch, when those who still survived in the tower, hearing of what had occurred and utterly cowed by terror began to lament with tears and wails of grief. . . . But, pleased to behold such steadfast victims, the Divine Kindness had already sent a champion to free the survivors; for lo! already was the king's fleet seen in the harbour and already were the king's knights arming themselves for the fray.

Meanwhile, when the Turks learnt that the king's galleys and ships were putting in to shore, they rushed down to the beach in bands. . . The seaside swarmed with their hosts so that there was no spot left empty. The Turks did not wait for the newcomers to reach land but flung their missiles into the sea against the ships; while their horsemen advanced as far as they could into the water for the purpose of shooting their arrows with greater effect. Then the king, massing his ships together, took counsel, saying: "My fellow comrades, what are we to do? Shall we not push on against this cowardly crowd that holds the shore? Shall we deem our lives of more value than the lives of those who are now perishing because of our absence? What think you?" In reply, some said that the attempt would be vain with so many thousand enemies on the beach.

Meanwhile the king, who had been scanning all things with a curious eye, caught sight of a certain priest who was throwing himself from the land into the sea in order that he might swim up. This man, when taken on board the galley, with panting breath and beating heart, spake as follows: "O noble king, those who still survive are longing for thy arrival. They are oppressed by the brandished swords of yonder butchers and stand with outstretched necks like sheep for the slaughter. Assuredly they will perish at once unless, by thy means, divine aid reaches them."

To him the king answered, "Is there then anyone left alive? And where?"

To this the priest replied, "Yes, my lord, in front of yonder tower are they hemmed in and like to perish." On hearing this the king said, "Then, even though it please God, on whose service and under whose guidance we have come to this land, that we should die here with our brethren, let him perish who will not go forward." Then the king's galleys were thrust on towards the shore and the king himself, though his legs were unarmed, plunged up to his middle into the sea and so, by vigorous efforts, gained the dry land. Next to the king landed Geoffrey du Bois and Peter des Préaux; and all the others followed, leaping into the sea with the intention of proceeding afoot. They boldly set upon the Turks who were lining the beach.

The king laid the enemy low everywhere with a crossbow he had in his hands, . . . and carried on the pursuit till the whole shore was cleared. . . The king was the first to enter the town by a certain stairway which he had chanced to see in the houses of the Templars. He entered alone and found three thousand Turks plundering all the houses and carrying off the spoil. Consider the courage of this invincible king! For immediately on entering the city he had his banners displayed on the highest parts of the walls so that the besieged Christians in the tower might see them.

They, on seeing it, took heart and snatching up their arms came down from the tower to meet their deliverer, who with unsheathed sword pressed on, slaying and maiming his foes as they fled from before his face. . . . . . Indeed, the king pursued them beyond the city, thinking it well to follow up his victory lest, perchance, anyone should say that he had spared the enemies of Christ's cross when God had delivered them into his hands. Truly never did any man hold half-heartedness in greater hatred.

Now at this time the king and his followers had only three horses. And what were these among so many? Moreover out of all the *Gestes* of the ancients, and out of all the tradition of those who tell stories or write books from the most remote times, there never was a warrior of any creed who bore himself so nobly as King Richard did that day. . . . . Saladin hearing of his arrival . . . . fled like a hunted hare or other timid animal; tearing up his tents in haste, he put spurs to his horse and hurried away lest King Richard should catch sight of him. But the king and his comrades pressed on the pursuit, slaying and laying low. The king's cross-bowmen too wrought such carnage among the steeds of the fugitives that for more than two miles the Turks fled away in the deadliest terror. Then the fearless king gave orders to pitch his tents in the very place whence Saladin had a little before torn up his.

(*Next day, Sunday, Aug. 2, Monday and Tuesday are spent in repairing the walls of Joppa. Count Henry came up in a galley, having left the main body of his troops at Caesarea.*)

Thus, when, with God's aid, the Turkish Army was driven back by our little host, Saladin called up his noblest *emirs* and complained to them thus: "Who is it, pray, that works us this disturbance? Has the whole army of the Christians returned from Acre to conquer and destroy our people thus." . . . To him certain men of perverse mind who had knowledge of our condition made answer.

O Lord, it is not as you imagine. They have no horses nor beasts of any kind saving only three horses which that marvellous king of theirs found in Joppa. And he in person can, I think, be easily captured, because worn out with fatigue, he is now lying down in his tent almost unattended. Could he be seized the end of all our labours would be attained.

Then there went forth among the Turkish Army this speech—that it was an eternal disgrace for so great an army and so many thousand warriors to have been routed by so small a band.

26 July–Aug. 1.—The Saracen account of the siege of Jaffa.

Bohâdin.

(*Meanwhile Al Malec Ad-Daher, Saladin's favourite son, the lord of Aleppo, had come up to help his father, July 17; Al Adil returned from beyond the Euphrates six days later.*)

The *Sultan*, learning that the Franks were moving on Beyrout, left Jerusalem on 10th *Rajab* for Gibeon (Al Jib about 5 miles N.W. of Jerusalem).

On Sunday, 25 July, (13 *Rajab, i.e.,* 25 July, which, however, was really a Saturday), the *Sultan* set out for Ramlah and halted on the hills between this town and Lydda a little before noon. . . . On the morrow, very early, he mounted his horse and set out for Yazûr (it lies about 3½ miles S. E. of Jaffa), and Beit-Jibrin (*sic*) with a light escort. After examining the town of Jaffa, from this height he returned to the place where he had halted (near Ramleh). Then at a conference with his counsellors he decided, with their unanimous consent, to lay siege to Jaffa.

On Tuesday morning, 15 *Rajab,* (*i.e.,* 27 July, which was a Monday), a little before noon, the *Sultan* camped before the walls of this town. His army was arranged in three divisions. Of these the right and left wings rested on the sea. . . . The *Sultan* was in the centre. Al Malec ad Daher commanded the right; Al Malec al Adil the left. The remaining troops were placed between the two wings. On the 16th the attack commenced. . . . The *Sultan* drew up his troops and had his *mangonels* set up before the weakest part of the ramparts near the Eastern gate; then he sent forward his miners to begin their work upon the wall. . . Their excavations were to extend from the part north of the Eastern gate as far as the flanked angle that covered the curtain. (In fortification a curtain is the stretch of wall between two bastions.) This part of the wall had been already destroyed by the Musulmans at the first siege, but the Franks had restored it. . . .

On *Rajab* 16 the Musulmans, seeing envoys coming and going, lost the ardour that had animated them, and began to fight faintly, giving themselves up to laziness as their way is. But then the miners, who had just finished their excavations, began to fill them up (with combustible matter) by order of the *Sultan*. Then the mines were set on fire and so half the curtain fell. The enemy, however, knowing beforehand what place would be fired, had piled up behind this point a great heap of wood, to which, on the fall of the curtain, they set fire, thus making it impossible to enter by the breach.

(*On Friday the 18th the curtain was attacked vigorously, Saladin himself taking part in the onset.*)

Scarcely had the second hour of the day come when the curtain fell with such a crash that everyone thought the end of the world had come. There was only one cry heard, "The curtain has fallen." . . . Then a cloud of dust and smoke rose from the ramparts that had just fallen. The sky was overcast. The sun lost its light, and none of the besiegers dared enter the breach and breast the fire. But when the cloud, as it cleared away, let us see the rampart of halberds and lances that now took the place of what had fallen, closing up the breach so well that not even the eye could pierce it—then indeed it was a terrible sight to note the courage, the fearless aspect, and the cool precise movements of the enemy... I myself saw two men standing on the ruins and repelling all who attempted to clear the breach. One of them a stone from a *mangonel* hurled back within the enclosure, whereupon his comrade at once took his place, thus exposing himself to the same fate which overtook him in the twinkling of an eye.

(*The besieged then sent to Saladin offering terms: they would exchange knight against knight, Turcople against Turcople, &c.*)

The envoys perceiving the ardour of the fight, which raged more hotly than a strong flame, prayed the *Sultan* to stay the combat while they returned to their place. To this he made answer, "I cannot prevent the Mussulmans from continuing; go, find your own folk as best you can and bid them withdraw into the citadel, leaving the town to the Mussulmans; for nothing will now prevent them forcing their way in."
... Our men, entering the town .. found a great booty: cloths and grain in abundance ... and even the remains of the spoils taken from the Egyptian caravan. The treaty of peace was accepted on the *Sultan's* terms.

On the afternoon of Friday, ever a day of good omen, the *Sultan* received a letter ... from Acre ... announcing that the news of the siege of Jaffa had made the King of England abandon his design of going against Beyrut, and determined him to bring succour to the besieged town. On hearing this the *Sultan* determined to bring the business to a conclusion as soon as possible by making the enemy, who had now no hope, deliver up the citadel, whose fall appeared imminent...

Now I was one of those who insisted on the necessity of making the enemy come out of the citadel so that we might occupy it before the garrison received reinforcements. Such also was the *Sultan's* desire, but his troops, overpowered by wounds, heat, and fatigue, ... were incapable of stirring and little inclined to obey him. He did not cease to urge them on till a late hour of the night, when, recognising that they were quite worn out, he mounted his horse and went off to his own tent near the baggage. His attendants rejoined him, and I went off to rest in my own tent; but I could not sleep because of my apprehensions.

At daybreak (Saturday) we heard trumpets sounding from the side of the Franks, and learnt that their succours were coming up. The *Sultan* then sent for me and said:

> Beyond a doubt reinforcements have arrived by sea, but there are enough Mussulman troops along the bank to stop their disembarking. Go and find Al Malec Ad Daher, (Saladin's son from Aleppo), and bid him post himself outside the south gate; you will have to enter the citadel and make the Franks come out; you will take possession of all the wealth and arms you find there, and make an inventory with your own hand. . .

Accordingly, I set out and reached Ad Daher's quarters; he was with the advanced guard on a hill near the sea, and was sleeping in his coat of mail and his *cazaghand*, (long-sleeved tunic, see note D),—all ready for the combat. May God recompense these warriors who toil for Islam! Wakened by me, he got up, though still half asleep, mounted his horse and, while going to the place the *Sultan* bade him, heard me explain my mission.

I then went with my followers into Jaffa and, on reaching the citadel, ordered the Franks to come out. They answered they were going to obey, and began their preparations for leaving.

SATURDAY, AUG. 1, 1192.—RICHARD RELIEVES JAFFA.
Bohâdin

(*It was necessary however for Bohâdin to expel the Mussulman soldiers from the town if he would prevent the Franks from being massacred as they came out of the citadel. This process occupied time, and Bohâdin began to fear the reinforcements would come up. So:*)

Coming to the citadel gate, near where Ad-Daher was, we made forty more men issue with their horses and women. These we sent off; but those who were still inside the fortress . . . conceived the notion of resisting us. Those who were already outside had been under the impression that the ships, just come up, were very few and would be unable to help them; they did not know that the King of England was there with all his people. . . But, when the fleet drew nearer and they could count thirty-five vessels, those who were still in the citadel took courage and gave evident tokens of intending to recommence hostilities.

Seeing things take this turn I descended from the elevation I stood on and went off to warn Jordic, who was with his troops below, that the besieged had changed their mind. A few moments later I was outside the town and with Al Malec Ad Daher; the besieged had just got on their horses, made a sally from the citadel and, charging our men in a body, had driven them from the town. . .

The *Sultan*, to whom his son Al Malec Ad-Daher sent me off with the news, bade his herald call to arms. . . Our soldiers, running up from all parts, entered the town, driving the enemy back into the citadel. These last, finding the disembarkation of their allies delayed, and deeming death inevitable, were in such fear that they charged their metropolitan and their chaplain—a man of enormous stature— to carry their excuses to the *Sultan* and beg for peace on the same conditions as before. . . This delay in disembarking was due to the look of the town; for (the new comers) saw the Mussulman banners flying everywhere, and feared that the citadel was already taken. The noise of the waves, the shoutings of the combatants, and the cries of "There is no God but one, God is great," prevented those in the fleet from hearing the calls of their co-religionists. . . This fleet was composed of over fifty vessels, fifteen of them being swift galleys, including the king's. . .

Then one of the besieged, recommending himself to the Messiah, leapt from the height of the fortress into the harbour. He reached ground without harm, as there was sand beneath. Then running towards the edge of the sea he got into a galley that came up to take him in. He was then carried to the king's galley and explained to him how things really stood. Thereupon the king, on hearing that the citadel still held out, made quickly for the shore, and his galley, which was painted red . . and had a red bridge, from which there floated a red banner, was the first to disembark. In less than an hour the other galleys had all done the same—everything taking place under my eyes. The enemy then charged the Mussulmans, scattered them, and drove them out of the harbour.

Now, as I was on horseback, I galloped off to carry the news to the *Sultan*, whom I found with the two envoys before him. He actually had in his hand the pen with which to write the letter of grace (they were asking for). I whispered in his ear what had happened, while he, without writing, began talking to them, so as to distract their attention. Some moments after, seeing his Musulmans arrive, fleeing before the enemy, he called his troops to horse, had the envoys seized, and gave orders to carry off the baggage and the merchant booths to Yazûr.

The King of England came up to the place occupied by the *Sultan* during the siege . . . (where) some of our Mamelooks came to visit him and had several talks with him. The Chamberlain Abu Bekr then received an invitation to the king's quarters, where he found .... several Mamelooks of high rank, whom the king treated with extreme affability and who often gathered round him.... All these people were collected in his presence and were listening to him as he chatted with them in tones sometimes serious and sometimes jesting.

He said, among other things:

This *Sultan* is truly a wonderful man. Islam has never had on this earth a sovereign greater or more powerful than he. How then is it that my mere arrival has frightened him away. By God! I am not come here with my armour on and with the intention of fighting; see I am wearing only ship-shoes instead of proper boots. Why then have you gone off?

Then he went on:

By the great God, I thought he would fail to take Jaffa in two months, and there he has taken it in two days!

Then, turning to Abu Bekr, he said:

Salute the *Sultan* on my part and tell him that I beg him in God's name to grant me the peace I ask for. It is absolutely necessary to put an end to all this; my country beyond the sea is in a very bad state. It advantages neither myself nor you that things should continue in this state.

Then the envoys left him and Abu Bekr presented himself before the *Sultan* to tell him what the king had said. This took place on Saturday evening, 19 *Rajab*. (Bohâdin 's days of the month or of the week are wrong throughout this narrative of the siege of Jaffa. Saturday was Aug. 1.)

The *Sultan*, with the advice of his council, replied as follows:

You began by demanding peace on certain conditions, and then the negotiations hinged on Jaffa and Ascalon. Now, seeing that Jaffa is in ruins, be content with all that lies between Tyre and Caesarea.

Abu Bekr carried this letter to the king and returned with a Frank envoy:

The king replied as follows. It is the rule among the Franks that when a man gives a town to another the latter becomes the supporter and servant of the giver. Now, if you give me these two towns, Jaffa and Ascalon, whatever troops I shall place there will be always at your disposition, and if you have need of me, I will hasten to your side and put myself under your orders. And you know with what exactitude I fulfil my duties.

(*Saladin then proposed to give Richard Jaffa and to keep Ascalon for himself. Envoys still passed to and fro, and on Sunday, Aug. 2, a Frank ambassador came with the king's thanks for the cession of Jaffa, but with renewed petitions for Ascalon.*)

This envoy was by the *Sultan's* order received with great honour. . . He added that if peace was concluded in six days the king, having no reason for spending the winter in Syria, would return to his own land. The *Sultan* answered on the spot as follows:

It is absolutely impossible for us to give up Ascalon, and the king will in any case have to pass the winter here. He has got possession of all these towns, and he knows well that, if he goes away, they cannot help falling into our power—a thing that, please God, will happen even if he should stay here, as stay he must. If it seems an easy thing to him to pass a winter here—away from his family and a two months' journey from his own land—an easy thing, I say, to him at a time when he is still in the vigour of youth, (Saladin at this time being about fifty-two, Richard about thirty-five), at an age when men delight in pleasures; how much easier will it be for me to pass not only the winter but the summer here. I am in the centre of my own country.

I have my family and my children round me, and I can get all I wish. Moreover, I am now an old man and have lost taste for the pleasures of this world. I have had my fill of them in times past; now I have renounced them. The troops that I have by me in winter are replaced by others in summer. Lastly, I believe myself to be accomplishing the highest act of devotion in acting as I do. I shall not cease to pursue the same line of conduct till God grants a decisive victory to whom he wills.

5 AUGUST, 1192.—KING RICHARD ATTACKED BY THE TURKS.

Itin., Ric. vi.

On the morrow, which was a Sunday, (*i.e.*, Aug. 2), the king anxiously saw to the reparation of the walls; so too on the Monday and Tuesday till the inhabitants had some kind of a fortification, and the breaches were mended, though without cement or lime. But there was still an innumerable host of Turks threatening in the neighbourhood. Meanwhile a certain evil race of Saracens, called the Menelones (Memlooks), of Aleppo and the Cordini, (Curds?) met in conference. (The Mamlooks, or regular troops, belonging to the *Sultan*, and trained up to war from childhood.)

They deemed it a deep reproach to have deserted Joppa before so small a band—and one that had no horses too; wherefore they felt convicted of cowardice and sloth, and bound themselves arrogantly with an oath to seize Richard in his tent and deliver him to Saladin, from whom they would receive a large reward. Meanwhile Count Henry came in a galley from Caesarea, where the rest of our army was unwillingly detained by reason of the Turkish ambushes. Out of his whole host the king, in that moment of emergency, was not able to muster more that fifty-five knights and a stout body of foot soldiers, *balistarii*, sergeants, Genoese, Pisans and others—some two thousand all told. Of horses, though he gathered them in from all sides, he had but 15, good and bad.

Meanwhile the enemies were making preparations for seizing the king while unarmed and off his guard. At midnight the aforesaid Menelones and Cordini set out by bright moonlight, taking counsel on the way as regards the best mode of action. O hateful march of perfidious men! Enemies are deliberately plotting the seizure of Christ's duteous knight while he lies sleeping. Many armed men are rushing down to seize one unarmed man as he lies suspecting no evil.

They were already not very far from the king's tent—when lo, God, who neglects not those who stay their hopes on him, sent a spirit of contention among these Cordini and Menelones. The Cordini said, "You Menelones will have to go on foot to seize the king and his people, while we keep watch on horseback to cut off their flight towards the camp." But the Menelones made answer, "It is rather your business to go on foot, for we are nobler than you. We are content with that kind of warfare that rightly belongs to us. This foot service is your concern."

Whilst they were thus obstinately contending which should be the greater, there was a delay in their march, and, when at last they had agreed to accomplish this piece of treachery together, as they were rushing forward headlong the first glimmer of dawn appeared, that is of the morning of Wednesday, (*i.e.,* Aug. 5th), after the feast of St. Peter ad Vincula.

But God, taking care lest the unbelieving should surprise His own champion while asleep, inclined the mind of a certain Genoese to go forth into the neighbouring plains at dawn. As he was returning, he heard with astonishment the neighing of horses and the tramp of men, and saw the gleam of helmets against the distant sky. Thereupon, hastening back to the camp, he called out with a loud voice time after time, that the whole host should take up arms at once. The king, on hearing this hubbub, leapt up from his bed in alarm, put on his impenetrable mail-coat, and bade wake his comrades.

Lord God of strength! who is there that so sudden a clamour would not have affected to some degree at least: while enemies are rushing on men who are unprepared, armed men on those unarmed, innumerable warriors on very few, and these few unable to put on their clothes or armour owing to lack of time? For these reasons the king and many others went forth to fight with unprotected eyes; some even without breeches, and, lightly armed with whatever they could snatch up, hurried forth—ready, if need were, to continue fighting, maybe with unprotected thighs, the whole day long.

And, while our men were thus anxiously preparing, the Turks came up. The king mounted his horse, and when on the point of setting forth had only ten horsemen with him, whose names follow: Count Henry, the Earl of Leicester, Bartholomew de Mortimer, Ralph de Malo-Leone, Andrew de Chavigny, Gerard de Furnival, Roger de Sacy, William de Stagno, Hugh de Neuville, a most valiant sergeant, and Henry the German, who was the king's standard bearer. These alone had horses; and even of these, some were mean, weak, and unused to arms.

Now was the battle warily drawn up in lines and squadrons, over each of which was set a prefect to preserve discipline. The knights were set nearest the sea on the left not far from St. Nicholas' church, since in that direction the Turks were coming up in the greatest numbers. . . . To receive their fierce charge our men posted themselves as best they could, placing the right knee on the ground so as to get a firmer hold, and keeping the left knee bent. Their left hands held their shields before them; their right hands grasped a lance whose head was fastened in the ground, whilst its iron point was presented towards the enemy as he rushed on with deadly vigour.

The king, like the skilful tactician he was, put a crossbow-man between every two of these shield men; another crossbow-man was set close by the first so as to keep the bow in quick work—it being the duty of one man to stretch the bow and of the other to keep discharging it. This arrangement was of no small advantage to our men, and did not a little harm to the enemy. . . . The king, running hither and thither, encouraged his men to be brave, and reproached those whose courage was failing through fear.

> There is no chance of flight, and, since the enemy have already seized on every place, to attempt it would be to court death. Hold out then stubbornly, for it is the duty of men to triumph bravely or to die gloriously. Even if martyrdom threatens, we ought to receive it with a thankful mind. But, before we die, while life remains, let us take vengeance yielding God thanks for granting us the martyr's death we have longed for. This is the true reward of our toils—the end at once of life and battles.

Scarcely had he finished his speech, when lo! the hostile army rushed upon us headlong in seven divisions, of a thousand horsemen each

Lo! the king, looking back afar, saw that the noble Earl of Leicester had been unhorsed. Whereupon the unconquered king rescued him, as he was fighting manfully, from the hands of his assailants and helped him to remount his horse. Oh! how fiercely did the battle now rage! while the Turks rush on towards the royal banner with its blazoned lion, more eager to slay the king than a thousand other warriors. Then in the stress of this conflict the king saw Ralph de Malo-Leone being carried off captive by the Turks: upon which, flying at full speed to his rescue, he. . . .compelled the Turks to let him go

On that day might you have seen the king slaying innumerable Turks with his gleaming sword: here cleaving a man from the crown of his head to his teeth, there cutting off a head, an arm, or some other member. Indeed, so energetically did he exercise himself that the skin of his right hand was broken owing to the vigour with which he wielded his sword.

And lo! while the king was toiling with such incredible valour there came swiftly up to him a certain Turk upon a foaming steed. He had been sent by Saphadin de Archadia, Saladin's brother, a man of a most generous character and worthy to be compared with the very best of our men, were it not that he was an unbeliever.

★★★★★★★★

Ernoul tells this story somewhat differently. According to him, Saladin heard that Richard was within the tower of Jaffa and had no horse. Thinking this a disgrace to such a king, he sent one of his sergeants, with a charger for Richard's service. Richard, mistrusting the gift, thanked the messenger, but would not mount before assuring himself that there was no guile in the matter. Accordingly, he made one of his own sergeants mount. This was done, and the spirited steed, refusing to obey the bit, carried its rider off to the Saracen camp "And right shamefast was Saladin when the horse returned. And he bade get ready another and sent it."

****

Now this Saphadin sent two splendid Arabian steeds to the king as a token of his admiration for his valour. These steeds he earnestly prayed the king to accept and mount; for at that time, he seemed to need them sorely. If (ran Saphadin's message) by divine grace the king should issue from this awful peril in safety he might bear this service in mind and recompense it as seemed best. These horses the king accepted and afterwards made a most splendid return for them. O virtue rare and praiseworthy though in an enemy! Thus, a Turk and an enemy thought fit to honour the king because of his valour; and the king, not refusing the gift, declared that in so urgent a moment he would accept many such horses even from a fiercer foe.

Then the battle was renewed with vigour; innumerable warriors poured down upon our little band . . . . till it could no longer sustain the weight of battle; our galley-men fled away shamefully in the galleys by which they had come; and, being the only ones who secured their own safety by running away, they were also the only ones who lost the praise due to firm valour. Meanwhile there rose a great cry from where the Turks were now seizing the town. For they had begun to enter from every side in the hopes of cutting off any of our party whom they might find there.

On hearing this the king hurried up at the head of his crossbowmen, but with only two knights. In a certain street he met three Turkish horsemen most splendidly attired and, rushing on like a king, he slew them and thus became master of two horses. The other Turks whom he found offering resistance in the town he drove off with his sword till they were so frightened that they scattered, seeking for an exit in vain. Then the king ordered the breaches in the walls to be filled up and set guards to keep the city from attack.

Having settled matters in Ascalon, the king hurriedly rode down to the galleys near the shore, and by the force of his arguments heartened the trembling fugitives for battle. At his words they all returned to the combat, ready to receive with thankfulness whatever fate God should assign them. So, leaving five men to protect each galley, the king returned to the field, bringing no slight assistance to his struggling little army In the meanwhile our men, not beholding the king anywhere, conjectured with trembling hearts that he, whom they could not see, had perished

But what can we think of the king—one man hedged in by many thousand foes: to record his deeds would cramp the writer's finger joints and stun the hearer's mind. What need for many words? The strength of Antaeus in the story was renewed by contact with the earth; and yet Antaeus perished in the long run. The flesh of Achilles, who had been dipt in the Stygian waves, is said to have been impenetrable to weapons; but he too died, being smitten in his only vulnerable part. Alexander of Macedon, whose ambition prompted him to subdue the whole world, achieved great wars it is true, but it was by an innumerable band of chosen soldiers. That most valiant of men, Judas Macchabeus, of whose doings all people tell, after many wonderful exploits, fell when deserted by his own followers, fighting with his scanty host against many thousand aliens.

But King Richard, hardened to war from his youngest years—Richard to whom Roland himself cannot be compared—abode unconquerable and unwounded in accordance with the divine decree . . . In the fury of his wrath his valour rejoiced at having found material on which to expend itself. Wherever he turned, the sword in his mighty right hand devoured flesh, and if he found himself alone the more eagerly did he press on to the battle

Amongst many other illustrious deeds, with one blow of wonderful force, he slew a certain *emir*, who surpassed his fellows in height and in the splendour of his apparel. This *emir*, vaunting much and reproaching his comrades with their cowardice and want of energy, had put spurs to his horse and galloped up to overthrow the king, who, receiving him with his sword, cut off his head, his shoulder, and his right arm. . . . The king's body was everywhere set thick with javelins, as a hedgehog with bristles; so too his horse was covered with innumerable arrows that stuck to its harness. . . . Moreover, the number of Turkish horses that lay dead all over the plain is said to have exceeded 1,500; while of the Turks themselves more than 700 perished, and that too without their carrying the king off as a present to Saladin, according to their boast.

Now, while the Turkish Army had drawn off from our men, whom the divine mercy had thus preserved from harm, Saladin is said to have taunted the arrogance of his men by enquiring:

Where are those who are bringing me *Melek* Richard as my prisoner? Who was the first man to seize him? Where is he, I say, and why is he not brought before me?

To which a certain Turk, who came from the very extremities of his empire made answer:

Know, O king, for a surety that this *Melek* of whom you enquire is not like other men. In all time no such soldier has been seen or heard of: no warrior so stout, so valiant, and so skilled. In every engagement he is first to attack and last in retreat. Truly we tried hard to capture him but all in vain; for no one can bear the brunt of his sword unharmed; his onset is terrible; it is death to encounter him; his deeds are more than human.

Now from the fatigue of this day and the stench of the bodies which made the air corrupt King Richard and our army were much distressed, and fell ill to such an extent that they almost all died.

1192. Aug.—K. Richard's negotiations with Saladin.

I   *tin.* vi.

Meanwhile Saladin sent word to the king that he was coming to seize him if he dared await his approach. To this the king made answer that he would certainly wait for him. . . . But the king, considering his own illness and the stress of circumstances, sent Count Henry to Caesarea with a request that the French there would come to him and help to guard the land. He sent word also about his illness and Saladin's message. But the French were unwilling to give him even a little help. . . . and he would have perished unless he had secured a truce, which some of these very French were the first to blame him for making. What else could he do? Was his position safe with so few men and those few sick, among such swarming hordes of Turks?

It was more prudent, at that time, to have dismantled Ascalon than to run the risk of an engagement. For, if the enemy had captured the king as he lay sick on his couch, Ascalon would have been easily seized, nor would Tyre and Acre have long remained in safety.

Then the king, anxious as to his health, ordered his kinsman Henry, the Templars, and the Hospitallers into his presence. To them he made known his illness, and declared that he must leave Joppa on account of its weakness and insalubrity. Some of these he enjoined to keep a watch over Ascalon; others he bade remain and guard Joppa; he himself would return to Acre that he might be cured by medicine, for no other plan was feasible. Then, with one heart and one voice, they all gainsaid his proposals, declaring that they could not keep guard if he were away. So, they rejected his proposals and walked with him no more.

Now the king's mind was worried by this reply, and the estrangement of his own followers caused him the bitterest grief. Then after long hesitation.... seeing that all were deserting him and that no one had the slightest care for the common weal he issued a proclamation to collect all who were willing to take his pay. Thereupon, without any delay, 2,000 foot soldiers and 50 knights came in. But now the king's sickness grew worse, and he began to despair of all recovery.... So, he thought it better to ask for a truce than to go away leaving the whole land to be laid waste as all the others had done when they went off by crowds in their ships.

The king then in his perplexity sent a message to Saladin's brother Saphadin, begging him to secure the best terms he could. Saphadin, a man of signal generosity, deeming the king worthy of honour, procured a truce on the following conditions. (1). Ascalon, which had always been a standing menace to Saladin's power, was to be dismantled, nor was it to be refortified till three years had elapsed from Easter next. After three years Ascalon should go to the most powerful party, *i.e.*, whoever could get it. (2). Saladin granted the Christians free and peaceable possession of Joppa and its whole neighbourhood, shore and heights. (3). There was to be inviolable peace between Christians and Saracens, and each side was to have free passage everywhere, and right of access to the Holy Sepulchre without any payment and with full liberty to carry on commerce over the whole land....

The king now sent word to Saladin and told him, in the hearing of his *satraps*, that he only asked a truce for three years with the intention of going back home where he would collect money and troops with which to rescue Jerusalem from Saladin's sway. To Richard's envoys Saladin made answer that his regard for King Richard's valour and nobleness of character was so great that he would rather lose the land to such a man, if lose it he must, than to any other prince he had ever seen..... Then when the truce had been reduced to writing and confirmed by oaths, the king departed to Caiphas, (Haifa at the foot of Carmel), as best he could, in order that he might there be healed of his illness by medicine.

Meanwhile the French had been enjoying their ease at Acre, and getting ready for returning home. Yet, for all the bitter fault they found with the truce just concluded, they agreed among themselves that they ought to complete their pilgrimage by a visit to the Holy Sepulchre before seeking their own land. Now the king remembering their slackness (in not helping to recover Joppa) and his former difficulties, sent word to Saladin and his brother Saphadin asking them to allow no one to visit the Holy Sepulchre without letters from himself and the Count Henry.

The French were much put about at this, and seeing that they would profit little by a longer stay, set out for their own land not long after, carrying nothing back with them except the memory of the quarrel due to their ingratitude. The king on hearing of their departure had a proclamation made by herald that all who wished it might now visit the Lord's Sepulchre and bring back their offerings to help in completing the walls of Joppa, instead of leaving them there.

THE GLUTTONY OF THE ENGLISH CRUSADERS.

Rich, of Devizes.

The King of England had now completed his second year in getting possession of the region round Jerusalem, and yet from none of his own lands had he received any help. (*This of course is an over-statement; as Richard had only been in the Holy Land one year and four months when he departed. The reckoning in the text is perhaps made from the time of his leaving England in the spring of 1190.*) Nor had his one brother, John Count of Mortain, nor his justices, nor his remaining magnates seemed even to think about sending him his dues nor about his return. Yet did the Church make prayers to God on his behalf without intermission. (All this time) in the Land of Promise the king's army was daily diminishing... And, since it seemed that all must die, each one had to choose whether he would die in peace or in war.

On the other hand, the strength of the pagans grew greatly and their boldness waxed with the misfortunes of the Christians, while their army was reinforced at regular intervals. Moreover, to them the air was that of their native land, the place their fatherland, their labour was health, and scanty provision was as medicine. To the Neustrians (Normans) however all that was an advantage to the enemy was mischievous. If our men were to live too sparingly just once in a week, they would feel the effects of this for the next seven.

A mixed crowd of French and English used to banquet (together); and, no matter what the price of things, so long as the money lasted, they banqueted daily with splendour and, saving the respect due to the Frenchmen, I may add, nausea. But, for all this, they kept up the memorable English custom and with due devotion drained their goblets dry, even though the trumpets were sounding to horse and the drums beating.

The country merchants who brought food into the camp wondered, even when they had got accustomed to it, and could scarcely believe that they saw truly when one people, and that few in numbers, consumed three times as much bread and a hundred times as much wine as what supported many Gentile peoples each innumerable. . . Such want followed this great gluttony that men's teeth could scarcely spare their fingers when their hands offered their jaws less to swallow than usual.

KING RICHARD'S ILLNESS. SAFFADIN'S LOVE FOR HIM.
Rich, of Devizes

The king lay very sick on his couch; the typhus continued, and the leeches were whispering about the greater semi-tertian fever. They began to despair, and from the king's house the (same) wild despair spread over the camp. There were few amongst many thousands who did not meditate flight, and the utmost confusion of dispersion or surrender would have followed, had not Hubert Walter, the Bishop of Salisbury, quickly called a council. Strong arguments were brought forward to prevent the army from melting away till a truce has been got from Saladin. All the armed men (said Hubert) must stand in array more closely than their wont, and a threatening countenance must cover their inward fear with a lying pretence of valour. No one was to speak of the king's illness lest the enemy should learn the secret of their great sorrow. . . .

Meanwhile there came down to see the king, as was his wont, a certain gentle Saffadin, Saladin's brother, an old soldier, very courteous and wise, and one whom the king's magnanimity and munificence had won over to his side. When the king's servants received him with less glee than usual, and would not admit him to speech with their master, he said: "By the interpreter I perceive ye are in great sorrow, nor am I ignorant of the cause. My friend your king is sick, and it is for this reason ye close the door against me."

Then, bursting into tears, "O God of the Christians," he said, "if thou indeed be God, thou canst not suffer such a man and one so needful to die so early. . . ." More things he wished to say, but his tongue, failing him for grief, would not suffer him to speak more, but resting his head upon his hands he wept bitterly.

The Duke of Burgundy dies. The treasure of the French and Germans.

Rich, of Devizes

While Richard lay sick at Jaffa it was announced to him that the Duke of Burgundy was grievously ill at Acre. That was the critical day of the king's (illness), and his fever was driven off through his delight at this news. Then straightway raising his hands the king prayed, saying: "May God destroy him because he was unwilling to help me to destroy the enemies of our faith, although he had long been fighting at my expense." On the third day the duke died; and, when this was known, the Bishop of Beauvais with all his men left the king and hastened to Acre... When he had returned to France my Lord of Beauvais secretly whispered in the ear of his king that the King of England had despatched two assassins into France to slay him.

Troubled at this news the king, contrary to the custom of the land, set choice guards to keep his body safe; moreover, he sent envoys with gifts to the emperor of Almain (Germany), and anxiously inclined the imperial mind against the King of England. Accordingly, it was enjoined by imperial edict that all cities and all chiefs of the empire should receive the King of England with arms if he should come to their lands on his return from Judea and present him (to the emperor) live or dead... All obeyed the emperor's bidding; and most carefully of all that Duke of Austria whom the King of England had put to shame at Acre.

5 Aug.–2 Sept. 1192.—The Sultan's move upon Richard's camp at Jaffa failing, peace is made at last.

Bohâdin.

At the beginning of the night he (Saladin) set out, preceded by some Arabs who served as guides, and, journeying till morning, arrived in the neighbourhood of (Richard's) camp. On learning that it consisted of only about a dozen tents he conceived the idea of seizing it, and made a vigorous charge against the enemy. But the Franks displayed such resolution in the presence of death that our troops . . had to retreat... I was not present in this business, thanks to God! But I have heard from a man who was that the enemy had only seventeen horsemen according to the largest calculation and only nine according to the smallest. Their foot soldiers did not reach a thousand; others say only three hundred, while others again give a higher figure.

(*Between Aug. 7 and Aug. 22 troops come up from Mosul, from Egypt, and finally Taki-ad-din's son, El Mansur, so lately a rebel. On Saturday, Aug. 7, Richard's envoy went back to Jaffa; for the negotiations were still continuing at this last date. Then about Tuesday, Aug. 25.)*

The *Sultan,* seeing all his troops assembled, and calling his counsellors together, spoke as follows: "The King of England is very ill, and it is certain that the Franks are on the point of embarking for their own country... Here we have the enemy overpowered by God's might. My opinion is that we should surprise Jaffa if possible; or else we might make a night march and fling ourselves against Ascalon."..

During (all) this time the king did not cease to send messengers to the *Sultan* to procure fruit and snow, for during the whole course of his illness he had a great longing for pears and peaches. The *Sultan* never failed to supply them; for he hoped, thanks to these frequent messengers, to get the information he needed. And indeed, he thus learnt that there were at the most only three hundred knights in the town, or according to another reckoning only two hundred; he also learnt that Count Henry was busily engaged in trying to persuade the French to remain with the king; while they, with one mind, were resolved to cross the sea. He was also told that the enemy was neglecting to repair the walls of the town and spending its energy solely on putting those of the citadel in good order....

Having had his information confirmed in this manner, on Thursday morning (*i.e.,* Aug. 27) the *Sultan* advanced towards Ramleh, where he pitched his camp towards noon. The body of troops that had been charged to make incursions (into the enemy's territory) then sent him the following message:

> We have advanced towards Jaffa. The enemy only sent about a hundred knights against us, and of these the greater part were only mounted on mules....

Soon after the chamberlain Abu Bekr arrived (from Richard, who had just sent for him). A messenger accompanied him, bearing the king's thanks to the *Sultan* for the snow and fruit.

(Richard now begs Al Malec Al Adil to get the Sultan to leave him Ascalon, which he only wants to keep up his reputation before the Franks. Or at least let the Sultan pay for the expenses incurred in fortifying Ascalon. Saladin tells his brother he is wearied of the war, and will conclude peace if only Ascalon is renounced, 28 Aug. There were still, however, disputes as to how far Richard had disowned his previous claims, and late on Sunday, 31 Aug. (sic), he sent word to say that he had never specifically abandoned his demand for

compensation.)

"But," said the king, "if I have I will not revoke my word. Tell the *Sultan* on my part that it is well; I accept the treaty, throwing myself on his generosity and acknowledging that if he does anything further in my favour it will be sheer kindness on his part."

(Saladin's) ambassador returned after the last prayer of Monday, and a convention was drawn up according to which peace was made for three years from the date of the document, that is from Wednesday, 2 Sept., 1192. Ramleh and Lydda were to be left to the Franks. . . . The *Sultan* judged it best to make peace because his troops had suffered so much, and because their means were exhausted. He knew also how eager they were to return home, and he did not forget the ill-will they had shewn before Jaffa in refusing to obey his order for an attack. . . . One of the articles of the treaty provided for the destruction of Ascalon, in the overthrow of which city the enemy's troops were to assist ours. For they feared that if we received the city in a good state we should not destroy it. . . . (But) we feared that this conference, like preceding ones, was but another of the king's ordinary stratagems to gain time. . . .

When Al Adil (Saladin's envoy) reached Jaffa, they made him enter a tent outside the town. The king was informed of his arrival, and, ill as he was, had him brought in along with the other members of the embassy, and on receiving the leaf on which the treaty was written said: "I haven't strength to apprehend its meaning; but I declare that I make peace and confirm it by giving you, my hand." The envoys then met Count Henry, the son of Barezan, and the other members of the council, and explained to them the substance of the treaty. When all its terms had been accepted, even to the division of Ramleh and Lydda, it was determined to confirm it by oath on Wednesday morning, (*i.e.,* Sept. 2.) The Franks said they could not do this at once because they had eaten, and it was their custom to take oaths fasting.

Accordingly on Wednesday, Sept. 2, the members of the embassy were called into the king's presence. He gave them his hand, whilst they, on their side, bound themselves to him. He excused himself from swearing on the plea that sovereigns never did so—an excuse which satisfied the *Sultan*. The bystanders then took their oaths between the hands of Count Henry . . . . assisted by Balean, the son of Barezan and the Lord of Tiberias. (Balian and Barezan; *i.e.,* Barisan or Balisan, are really the same words.) The Hospitallers, the Templars, and all the Frankish leaders gave in their adhesion. . . . On the following morning,

Sept. 3, the king's ambassador was presented to the *Sultan*, and, taking his noble hand, declared that he accepted the terms of peace. He and his colleagues then demanded that Al Adil, Al Afdal, Ad Daher, &c, and all the other chiefs whose territory bordered on that of the Franks should take an oath to observe this peace; (and) the *Sultan* promised to send a commissary to these districts to receive the oath.

It was truly a day of rejoicing when the peace was proclaimed; and God only knows the boundless joy to which the two people gave themselves up. Yet it is well known that the *Sultan* had not made peace entirely of his own accord. As regards this, in one of our talks he said to me:

> I fear to make this peace, because I know not what will happen to me. Should I die, the enemy would renew their strength, and they would be quite capable of issuing from the territory we have left them to repossess themselves of what we have taken from them. You will yet see each one of these princes on the height of his own stronghold. May I not die so long as the Musulmans are exposed to perish.

Such were his very words; but he saw that peace was advantageous for the moment. . . . God saw that the peace could not but be favourable to us; for the *Sultan* died soon after its ratification. Had he died during actual warfare Islam would have been in great danger.

Thus, it was, by God's special grace and in accordance with Saladin's general good fortune, that he was able to conclude the peace himself.

THE DREAD OF KING RICHARD.

Erodes, xxvi.

Whilst the King of England dwelt at Ascalon and Jaffa he ever held himself ready for battle, and was so dreaded that the fear of him was in the heart and mouths of the Saracens. Insomuch that when their children wept they would say to them "Be quiet—the King of England is coming!" And if their horses started, they would jestingly say "Is the King of England in front of us then?"

1192, SEPT.—UNDER THE TRUCE THREE BODIES OF PILGRIMS VISIT JERUSALEM SAFELY.

Itin. Ric. v.

Before setting out the people was divided into three bodies; and to each body there was given a leader: Andrew de Chavigny leading the first and Ralph Taissun the second and Hubert Bishop of Salisbury the third. The first body set out under Andrew with the king's letters, but owing to their sins they only just missed experiencing the gravest disasters on the way. For in their journey, they came to Ramleh plain whence they sent messengers to Saladin signifying how they had arrived with King Richard's letters and begging a safe passage and return. The men appointed to this mission were noble and capable; but their character was well-nigh ruined by their sloth. Their names were William de Rupibus, Gerard de Furnival, and Peter de Pratellis. When they reached Toron of the Knights they stayed there so that Saphadin might protect their further progress.

Now, whilst tarrying there, they all slumbered and slept till, as sunset drew on, the rest of their company, on whose behalf they had been sent forward, passed them by.

Then the main body, proceeding along the road in due order, had already crossed the plain and was nearing the hill district when lo, as Andrew de Chavigny and his fellows looked back, they saw the envoys hastening after them. On learning this the host halted in the greatest terror and some called out: "Lord God be our aid or we perish and are as sheep for the slaughter... Evening is at hand; we are unarmed and nigh unto death." Then, having sharply rebuked the envoys because of their sloth, they once more sent them forward with orders to hasten. The envoys now reached Jerusalem and found 2,000 Turks or more dwelling in tents outside the city.

Having discovered Saphadin they laid their case before him and he sharply rebuked their leaders' folly, saying that they did not value their life at a straw if they thus pressed on among their enemies, at nightfall, without anyone to lead or protect them. While Saphadin and our envoys were thus talking together, just at sunset the main body of the pilgrims came up unarmed and in disarray. The Turks watched them passing by with fierce eyes and countenances that witnessed to the anger of their thoughts; and, by reason of this, even the bolder men among us would then have preferred to be at Tyre or Acre, whence they had started. That night the pilgrims spent in the utmost fear near a certain mountain not far from Jerusalem.

On the morrow the Turks came before Saladin, praying him on their knees for leave to avenge on these Christians the death of all their fathers, brothers, sons, and other relatives, who had been slain at Acre and elsewhere. To consult on this matter Saladin called a council of his chiefs. Mestoc, Saphadin, Bedreddin, (probably Bedr-ad-Dîn,

Governor of Damascus), and Dordernus, (Bedr-ad-Dîn Dolderim, Lord of Tell-Bacher, *i.e.,* Turbessel) were present and decided unanimously to give the Christians free passage and return. They said to Saladin:

> It would be highly detrimental to our honour if, by our duplicity, the treaty between thee and the King of England should be broken. For thus would the word of the Turks, which should be kept with nations of every creed, be reckoned worthless—and rightly so.

Accordingly, Saladin ordered his followers to see to the safety of the Christians both as they entered and as they left the city. At his own request Saphadin was appointed to ensure the full observance of this injunction; and so, thanks to his care, in freedom and peace did the pilgrims visit the Lord's Sepulchre—which they had so long desired to see. Whereupon, having met with the most generous treatment and finished their pilgrimage, they returned gladly to Acre.

On their return, between Castle Arnald and Ramlah, they met the second division of the pilgrims under Ralph Teissun. Now Saladin, as we have said, had set his people to guard the roads when the pilgrims began their journey towards Jerusalem; and so, thanks to this, we passed along without let or hindrance, and after crossing the mountains came to the Hill of Joy unharmed. (The Mons Gaudii of mediaeval literature, whence pilgrims got their first view of Jerusalem, generally identified with Neby Samwil, from 4-5 miles N.W. of Jerusalem.) From this spot we could see the city of Jerusalem afar off; wherefore, as is the wont of pilgrims, in great delight we fell down upon our knees and rendered humble thanks to God.

From the same place we also saw the Mount of Olives. Then the whole body set forth eagerly; but those who had horses hurriedly forestalled the others in their eagerness to kiss the Lord's Tomb. Moreover, according to the account of three knights, who thus rode ahead of the main body, Saladin allowed them to kiss and worship the true Lord's Cross which formerly used to go to the war. But we footmen in the rear saw what we could, *viz.*, the Lord's Tomb, at which we made our offerings. And, finding that the Saracens were in the habit of carrying away our gifts, we placed little there, but divided our presents among the French and Syrian captives whom we saw there in chains, toiling at the tasks assigned them.

Thence, turning to the right, we came to Mount Calvary where our Lord was crucified and where the stone was on which His cross was fixed in Golgotha. After having kissed this place, we came to the church that lies on Mount Zion, towards the left of which is the spot whence Mary the blessed Mother of God left this world for the Father. After gazing our fill here with tear-filled eyes, we hastily ran on to see the holy table where Christ condescended to eat bread and, after just kissing it, we departed all together without any delay. For it was not safe to walk about except in bands because of the snares set by that profane race.

Indeed, if the pilgrims wandered about by threes or fours the Turks drew them off secretly to the entrances of the crypts and there strangled them. Next, we hastened to the Sepulchre of the blessed Mother of God in the middle of the valley of Jehosaphat, near Siloe, and kissed it with devotion and a contrite heart. Then, in some peril, we entered the very chamber in which our Lord and Redeemer is said to have been kept on the night preceding his crucifixion. After gazing here with tearful eyes, we departed in haste, grieving no little at the way in which the Turks, who drove us off, had profaned those sacred sites by stabling their horses there. Then we left Jerusalem and came to Acre.

The third body, led by the Bishop of Salisbury, was not far off Jerusalem when Saladin sent out a company to meet the bishop and conduct him with due honour to the Holy Places. To this bishop, on account of his uprightness, his reputation for wisdom and his wide renown, Saladin sent, offering him a house free of cost. But the bishop refused on the ground that he and his company were pilgrims. Then Saladin bade his servants shew all kinds of courtesy to the bishop and his men. Saladin also sent him many gifts of price and even invited him to a conference in order to see what kind of a man he was in appearance. He had the Holy Cross shown him and they sat together a long time in familiar conversation.

On this occasion Saladin made enquiries as to the character and habits of the King of England. He also asked what the Christians said about his Saracens. To him the bishop made answer, "As regards my lord the king, I may say that there is no knight in the world who can be considered his peer in military matters, or his equal in valour and generosity. He is distinguished by the full possession of every good quality. But why waste words? In my opinion—putting aside your sins—if anyone could give your noble qualities to King Richard and his to you so that each of you might be endowed with the faculties of the other then the whole world could not furnish two such princes."

At last Saladin, having heard the bishop, patiently broke in: "I know the great valour and the bravery of your king well enough; but, not to speak too severely, he often incurs unnecessary danger and is too prodigal of his life. Now I, for my part, however great a king I might be, would much rather be gifted with wealth (so long as it is alongside of wisdom and modesty) than with boldness and immodesty." Then, after a long interview by means of an interpreter, Saladin bade the bishop to request any gift he liked and it should be granted him. For this offer the bishop gave many thanks, begging to have a space of time—till the morrow—granted him for deliberation.

Then, on the next day, he begged that two Latin priests and two Latin deacons might be permitted to celebrate divine service with the Syrians at the Lord's Sepulchre. These priests were to be maintained out of the offerings of the pilgrims. For, in visiting the Lord's Sepulchre, the bishop had found only the services half celebrated after the barbarous fashion of the Syrians. He made a similar request for Bethlehem and Nazareth. This was a great petition to make, and, as is believed, one very pleasing to God. When the *Soldan* consented, the bishop, in accordance with his request, established priests and deacons in each place, thus inaugurating a fitting service to God, where there had been none before. Then having received leave to depart from Jerusalem the party returned to Acre.

1192, OCT. 9.—RICHARD LEAVES THE HOLY LAND AND SETS SAIL FROM ACRE.

I   *tin. Ric,* v.

Now some people in their foolish talk were wont to say that the pilgrims had done very little good in the land of Jerusalem because they had not freed the city. Such speech, however, was only ignorant babble of men without knowledge. But we deem ourselves worthy of credence, for we saw and experienced all the sufferings and trials of these pilgrims. . . . And we know for certainty that at the siege of Acre and afterwards in the city itself there perished more than 300,000 pilgrims owing to illness and famine. Now who can doubt as to the salvation of such good and noble men who heard service daily from their own chaplains?

Meanwhile King Richard's fleet was being got ready; all things necessary, both arms and stores, were being prepared and put in order for the passage home. Then the king, out of pure generosity and regard for his noble character, set free ten of his noblest captive Turks in exchange for William des Préaux, who had formerly been taken prisoner in mistake for him. Now the Turks would gladly have paid a large sum of money might they only have been allowed to keep William; but the magnanimity of the king disdained to be tarnished by any such bargain.

All things being now ready, the king, when on the point of embarking, thought fit to take heed that not the slightest matter should be left unattended to, lest his fair fame could be impeached. And so, by herald's voice, he had all his creditors called up and paid in full.

On St. Michael's day, *(i.e.,* Sept. 29), the two queens, Berengaria Queen of England, King Richard's wife, and Joan, formerly Queen of Sicily, King Richard's sister, went aboard at Acre. On St. Denis's day, *(i.e.,* Friday, Oct. 9), Richard went aboard ready to return to England. When the royal fleet set sail how many sighs broke out from pious hearts, how freely flowed the tears from people's eyes? . . . With what bitter lamentations and sobs were the voices of the mourners heard crying, "O Jerusalem, thou art indeed helpless, now that thou art reft of such a champion. If by any chance the truce is broken, who will protect thee from thy assailants in King Richard's absence?"

Whilst all men were reiterating such sad prognostications the king, whose health was not yet fully restored, set sail with the prayers of everyone. And all night long the vessel went on its course by starlight, till, as the morning broke, the king, looking back with pious eyes upon the land behind him, after long meditation broke out into prayer: "O Holy Land, to God do I entrust thee. May He, of his mercy, only grant me such space of life that, by his good will, I may bring thee aid. For it is my hope and intention to aid thee at some future time." And, with this prayer, he urged his sailors to display full sail so that they might make a speedier course.

THE CAUSES OF THE DUKE OF AUSTRIA'S ENMITY AGAINST RICHARD.

Ansbert, ed. Dobrowsky

Now as (King Richard) was tarrying on foot near Vienna with only two followers, the duke's spies found him in a vile plight. And the illustrious Duke of Austria, seeing that he had many and grievous charges against the king, deemed that he had been delivered into his hands by Divine judgment. Nevertheless, he treated him honourably, beyond his deserts, and ordered him to be kept in his castle of Tyernstein, near the Danube. One strong reason for the duke's conduct was that the king had treated him with scorn at the siege of Acre; another that he held captive Isaac, Prince of Cyprus, and his wife, both of whom were akin to (Leopold); another that he suspected (Richard) of having slain Conrad, his aunt's son.

Matt. Paris, ii.

About this time (c. June 1192) came the Duke of Austria to Acre. . . And when his marshals, going ahead, had made choice of a resting-place and prepared the things that were necessary for him, there came up precipitately a certain knight belonging to King Richard's train, a Norman by race. Now this man, who, after the manner of his tribe, was over-brimming with pride, declared that he had a better right to this abode than anyone else. For to him and his comrades he declared it had been assigned on their first arrival. And there was much quarrelling, till the din of it reached the king's ears. Now he, being over-well-disposed to the cause of the Norman, waxed wroth with the duke's train and forgetting the God-like moderation of "I will go down (allusion to the destruction of Sodom and Gomorrah) and see," gave a headstrong, unseemly order for the duke's banner to be cast into a cesspool.

And when the duke knew of this and how that he had been deprived of his abode and basely insulted by Norman jesters, he brought his grievance before the king, from whom however he could get no justice. Whereupon, being scorned by an earthly king, he turned him to the King of Kings and invoked the Lord God to whom vengeance belongs. And soon after he hastened home being shamed and in confusion; and there was no little shame to King Richard by reason of this thing later on.

KING RICHARD'S SHIPWRECK AND CAPTURE.

Ralph of Coggeshall

Whilst the King Richard, after this incredible victory, was staying for six weeks at Joppa, a certain baleful disease born of the air's corruption settled upon him and almost all his men to their great damage; for, with the exception of the king, to whom the Lord granted a safe recovery, as many as were stricken with the illness died off quickly.

Then King Richard, seeing that his treasure which he had been distributing to his knights with too liberal a hand was beginning to fail; seeing, too, that the army of the French and other strangers whom he had hired and kept with him for a year at his own expense wished to go home; seeing that his own army was gradually growing less, owing partly to engagements with the enemy and partly to the baleful sickness, whilst the number of his foes increased every day, took counsel of the brethren of the Temple and the Hospital, as well as of the leaders who were with him. He was minded to go home at once with the intention of returning with greater store of knights and treasure. To this he pledged himself with an oath, giving security also. And there was an additional reason in the news as to how his brother, Earl John, whom he had left in England, was plotting to subdue that country, and had already deposed his chancellor on the pretext of tyranny.

So, in the autumn, when his ships were ready and his affairs all duly arranged, King Richard, the lady, Queen Berengaria, his sister Joan, Queen of Sicily, and his nobles, together with the army, crossed the Mediterranean. As they were setting off by the just judgment of God there sprung up unusual tempests. Some suffered shipwreck, and barely got to shore with the loss of all their wealth after their ships had been battered to pieces; but a few reached their intended harbour in safety. Those who escaped the perils of the sea found hostile ranks rise up against them everywhere on shore. They were pitilessly taken prisoner, robbed, and soon burdened with a heavy ransom.

They had no place of safety left, just as if land and sea had banded together against the fugitives of God. Whence it was sufficiently clear that God was wrath at their return before completing their pilgrimage. For he had intended to magnify them greatly in that land, after a short season (of trial), by subduing all their enemies and handing over to them the land on whose behalf they had undertaken so toilsome a pilgrimage. For in the very Lent after their departure the enemy of the Christian faith, the invader of the land in question, to wit Saladin, ended his life by a miserable death. Now had they been present at that time they might easily have seized the whole land, seeing that the sons and kinsmen of Saladin began to quarrel among themselves.

But King Richard, after being tempest tossed with some of his comrades for six weeks (during which time sailing towards Barbary, he had come within three days of Marseilles), learnt by frequent reports that the Count of St. Giles, (Raymond V., Count of Toulouse from 1148-1194), and all the princes through whose lands he was about to pass had banded together against him, and were laying snares for him everywhere. Accordingly, he made up his mind to go home secretly by way of Dutchland (Germany) and, turning his sails, at last reached the island of Corfu. There he hired two beaked pirate-vessels. For you must know the pirates had dared to attack the king's ship but, on being recognised by one of the sailors, had entered into a league with (Richard). The king, knowing their bravery and boldness, went on board with these pirates, taking with him also Baldwin de Betun, master Philip, the king's clerk, and Anselm, the chaplain, who brought us word of all these things as he saw and heard them.

Certain brothers of the Temple also went with him, and they all landed on the coast of Sclavonia near a certain town called Gazara, (Zara, on the coast of Dalmatia), from which place they at once sent a messenger to the nearest castle begging a safe conduct from its lord, who chanced to be the marquis's nephew. Now, on his return, the king had brought three precious stones, to wit three rubies, from a certain Pisan, to whom he paid 900 *besants* for them. One of these while on board he had set in a gold ring, and this ring he sent to the lord of the castle by the aforesaid messenger. This messenger, when asked by the castle-lord for whom he was seeking a safe conduct, made answer that it was for pilgrims returning from Jerusalem.

Thereupon the lord asked for their names, to which the messenger replied: "One of them is called Baldwin de Betun; but the other, who has sent you this ring, is called Hugh the merchant."

Then that lord, having regarded the ring for a long while, rejoined: "Nay, he is not called Hugh but King Richard," adding, "though I have sworn to take prisoner all the pilgrims coming from those parts, and to receive no gift at their hands, yet by reason of the noble gift and the lord who sends it as a gift of honour to me whom he does not know, I will return him his gift and give him free leave to depart."

So, the messenger, returning, brought back this news to the king, who, with his comrades, trembling greatly, got their horses ready in the mid of night, stealthily quitted the town and, in this fashion, set out through the land. For some time, they proceeded without molestation. But the lord we have spoken of before sent out a spy to his brother, bidding him seize the king when he reached his territory. When the king had entered the city where this lord's brother dwelt, the latter called in a very faithful follower, Roger de Argenton, a Norman by birth.

Now, to this man, who had dwelt with him for twenty years and married his niece, he gave orders to take special note of the houses where pilgrims were in the habit of lodging and to see, if by any chance, he could discover the king through his speech or any other sign. This lord made his follower promise of half his city if he could intercept the king. So, this Roger, routing and enquiring at every inn, at last found the king, who, after long attempts at hiding his personality, in the end yielded to the earnest prayers and tears of his dutiful questioner and confessed what rank he held.

Upon this Roger, anxious for his safety, gave him a very goodly steed, begging him take to flight secretly and without any delay. After this, returning to his own lord, Roger said that the talk about the king's coming was an idle rumour. (The strangers, he added,) were Baldwin de Betun and his comrades, who were on their way back from their pilgrimage; upon which the lord, mad with rage, gave orders for all to be arrested.

Meanwhile, the king, leaving the city stealthily, in the company of William de Stagno and a certain lad, who could speak German, journeyed three days and nights without food. Then, being hard pressed by hunger, he turned aside to a certain town called Ginana (? Vienna), near the Danube in Austria, a place where—to put the finishing stroke to all his woes—the Duke of Austria was then staying. Thither the king's boy came to make a purchase; and, as he offered more *besants* than he should have done and comported himself with overmuch state and pomp, he was seized upon by the citizens. On being asked who he was he made answer that he was the servant of a very rich merchant, who would reach that city in three days.

Then, being set free, he returned secretly to the king's retreat, telling the king all that had happened and urging him to flee at once. But the king, after his great hardships at sea, was eager to rest a few days in this city. Now when this lad went (more often than was safe) to the public market, he chanced once on the day of St. Thomas the Apostle, (*i.e.*, Dec. 21st, 1192), imprudently to carry his lord the king's gloves under his belt. The magistrates of the city, learning this, seized the boy a second time and, after many and fearful tortures, threatened to cut out his tongue unless he confessed the truth quickly; till he, constrained by torments he could not bear, told them how things really stood. Whereupon the magistrates, after carrying the news to the duke, surrounded the king's retreat and demanded that he should yield of his own accord.

How King Richard was taken Captive (French Account).

Chron. d'Ernoul.

When (King Richard) had made truce with the Saracens he had his ships and his galleys fitted out and laden with provisions and people. Then he put on board his wife and his sister and the Emperor of

Cyprus' wife (the emperor himself had died in prison) the emperor's daughter, his knights, and his sergeants. Then came he to the Master of the Temple (Robert de Sabloil, probably an Englishman) and said:

Sir, I know well that all folks do not love me, and I know well that, if I cross the sea in such a manner as to be recognised, I shall reach no place where I shall not be liable to death or captivity. Now I pray you, for the love of God, that you give me certain of your knights and your serving-brothers to accompany me in a galley, and after we have reached land to conduct me in peace to my own country as though I were a Templar.

The master said that he would willingly do so. Then secretly he got knights and sergeants ready and made them go on board a galley; after which the king, taking leave of Count Henry, the Templars, and the men of the land, at even entered the galley where the Templars were. He also bade farewell to his wife and his own train; the one party going one way and the other another. But the King of England could not do things so secretly as to escape detection; or as to prevent (an enemy) entering the galley with him to secure his apprehension. And (this enemy) went with him till he landed and further yet. . . .

When the Templars and the King of England had arrived (at Aquilea) they purchased sufficient conveyances, and mounting them proceeded by way of Germany. And he who had got abroad to secure the king's apprehension was with them still. And he accompanied them till they rested in one of the Duke of Austria's castles in Germany. And it chanced that the Duke of Austria was then at the castle.

Now, when he who was pursuing the king knew that the duke was in the castle, he came to him and said: "Sir, now is the chance of doing yourself a good turn. The King of England is lodged in this town: take heed that he does not escape."

The duke was greatly delighted at hearing this news, for some folk say that the king had done him shame in the army before Acre. Accordingly, he bade his people close the castle gates; and putting on his own arms made his men don theirs and went to the inn where (the king) was resting, taking with him the man who had brought the news that he might identify the king.

Now it was told the King of England how they were coming to the house to seize him; and in his surprise he knew not what to do. Wherefore he took a mean jacket and threw it over his back to disguise himself and so entered the kitchen, and sat down to turn the capons at the fire.

Then the duke's men entered the house and made search here and there, but only found the Temple folk and those who were attending to the food in the kitchen. Then he who had betrayed the king entered the kitchen and saw the king turning the capons as we have said. Then he went up to him and said to him "Master, get up; too long hast thou tarried there already." Then he said to the duke's knights, "Sirs, behold him here and take him." And they laid hands on him and took him and put him in prison.

4 MARCH, 1193.—THE DEATH OF SALADIN.

Bohâdin.

(*On Wednesday, 4 Nov., 1192, Saladin returned to Damascus. On Nov. 24 Al-Adil came up from Crac and for some days the two brothers hunted together, Saladin's two sons, Al Afdal and Ad Daher joining in the sport. Bohâdin came up from Jerusalem on Tuesday, Feb. 16, 1193, and next day went to pay his respects to the Sultan, whom he found surrounded by a crowd of officials.*)

Now, when he learned that I was there, he had me in before the others and rose up to meet me. Never before had his features expressed such joy at seeing me; and, as he pressed me in his arms, his eyes filled with tears. May God have mercy on him! . . . .

On Thursday he sent for me once more, and I found him seated on a bench in the garden with his little children round him. He asked if anyone was waiting an audience, and, on hearing that there were some envoys from the Franks, . . he gave orders for them to be brought in. One of his little children, (afterwards) the *emir* Abu Bekr, for whom he had a great affection and whom he used to pet and play with, was there also. Now when the child caught sight of these folks, with their clean-shaven chins, their close-cut hair, and their strange apparel, he was afraid and began to cry.

On this, the *Sultan* excused himself to the envoys and dismissed them without hearing what they had to say; then, speaking to me in his usual kindly way, he said: "Have you had anything to eat today?" adding: "Help yourself to what is by you."

The attendants then brought him milk-rice and other light food, of which he partook, but, as it seemed to me, without much relish. During the last days he had given up receiving people on the plea that it caused him pain to move; and, of a truth, he was suffering from fulness and some other ailment, not to mention his extreme lassitude.

When we had done eating, he asked me if I had brought any news of the caravan, and I told him how I had passed a part of it on the road. "If the roads had not been so muddy," I added, "they would have been here today; but they are sure to come tomorrow." He then said that he would go out to meet them. . . . On this I withdrew, though not without noticing that he no longer possessed his old elasticity of spirit.

On Friday morning (Feb. 19) he set out on horseback and I, leaving the baggage, made haste to join him just at the time he met the caravan. In the caravan there were Sabek-ed-din and Karaja'l-Yaruki whom, with his customary respect for old men, he received kindly. Al Afdal, who now came up, drew me aside to say a few words. I noticed that the *Sultan* was not wearing his *cazaghand* or wadded coat, without which he never rode out. It was a splendid sight this day, for the townsfolk had crowded out to meet the caravan and to see the *Sultan*. Then I was unable to restrain myself any longer, and made haste to rejoin him and tell him how he had forgotten his *cazaghand*. He seemed like a man waking from a dream and asked for this garment; but the master of his wardrobe could not be found.

Now this seemed to me a serious thing, and I augured ill of it, saying to myself "The *Sultan* asks for a thing he has been in the constant habit of wearing, and lo! they cannot find it." Then, turning towards him, I asked if there was no other less crowded way into the city. He answered that there was, and took a path leading between the gardens leading towards Al Moneibe. . . . This was the last time he went out on horseback.

In the evening he felt extremely weak, and a little before midnight was seized with a bilious fever. . . On Saturday morning . . . I entered his room along with the Cadi Al Fadel, (Rahim Ali Abd ar Rahmun), and his son Al Malec al Afdal. We had a long interview with him, and though at first, he began to complain of the bad night he had passed, he afterwards found a certain amount of pleasure in talking to us. . . At noon we withdrew, leaving our hearts behind us. He bade us go and share the repast at which his son Al Afdal was going to preside. . . I made my way into the great south hall, where I found the table laid out and Al Afdal in his father's place. Unable to bear the sight I went off without even taking my seat; and several people seeing Al Afdal in his father's place shed tears and augured ill.

(*Saladin's physician in chief was absent.*)

On the fourth day of his illness the doctors bled him, . . . and from that moment his ailment grew worse. . . . On the sixth day we set him

205

on a seat and put a pillow behind his back. Then we gave him a cup of warm water to drink. . . . This he tasted and found too hot; upon which they gave him another. But this was too cold. Howbeit he showed no anger against the slave, merely saying, "Great God, is there no one here that can warm water properly?"

As for the Cadi Al Fadel and myself, we went out shedding many tears; and he said to me, "See what a noble soul the Musulmans are going to lose. By God! any other man would have flung the cup at his servant's head."

On the ninth day he became extremely weak and unable to take his medicine. The whole town was in a stir and the trembling merchants had already begun to pack up their goods in the bazaars. It is impossible to give an idea of the grief that ever) one felt. Each evening Al Fadel and myself passed the first third of the night together ((?) in prayer) and then went to the palace gate. If we could enter the sick man's room, we would look at him for a moment and then withdraw. If the door was shut, we could only gather news. On our return we used to find a crowd of folk waiting for us, eager to form some idea of the state of the *Sultan's* health from the expression of our features.

On the tenth day (at night) we went to the gate of the palace and found Jemal Ad Daula Ikbal there. At our request he entered the sick man's room to see how he was. Afterwards he sent us word that there was still some sign of life in the two legs. For this news we thanked God and prayed the prince to pass his hands over the other parts of the body and see if they too presented signs of transpiration. He returned to tell us that they were covered with perspiration, on which we went off with somewhat lightened hearts.

Next morning, the 26 of *Safar*. . . . we were told that the perspiration had been so copious as to pass over the mattrass and the mats even to the ground. The dryness of the body, however, had increased so much . . . that the physicians had lost all hope.

(*Next evening Al Afdal begged Bohâdin and his friend to spend the evening by the Sultan's bedside. They, however, refused to do so, and a certain sheikh, Abu Jiafer, watched there "in case God should that night call the sick man into his presence. This holy man stationed himself between the Sultan and the women folk who surrounded the bed, and began to repeat the profession of faith and bid him think on God." Bohâdin and Al Fadel then went off "ready to give their lives to save the Sultan's," and Abu Jiafer was left reciting passages from the Koran all night at the sick man's bedside.*)

From the ninth day of the fever the *Sultan* had lost his wits, and they only returned at intervals. The *sheikh* told us what follows: As I was reciting the *Koran* I came to this passage: "He is a God besides whom there is no God; he knows both what is visible and what is invisible"; and I heard him utter these words, "It is truth." Thus, he had a moment's wakefulness at the most opportune moment—a token of God's great favour towards him.

The *Sultan's* death took place after the hour of morning prayer Wednesday 27 *Safar*, 589 A.H. With dawn the Cadi Al Fadel hastened to the *Sultan's* house where I too had arrived; but the *Sultan's* soul had already appeared before the kindly justice of God. I have been told that at the moment when the *sheikh* Abu Jiafer had finished saying the words: "There is no other God than He; in Him have I set my confidence" the sick man smiled; his features lit up and he surrendered his soul to God.

Never since the death of the four first *caliphs*—never since that time have religion and the faithful received such a blow as that which lighted on them the day the *Sultan* died.

A WESTERN LEGEND CONCERNING SALADIN'S FUNERAL.

Vincent of Beauvais, Spec. Hist. xxix and *Franc Pippinus ap. Muratori,* vii.

Thus did Saladin die in the 1193rd year from that in which the Word left his royal abode (for earth). And, as he lay dying, he called his standard-bearer to him and charged him, saying: Do thou, who art wont to bear my banner in the wars, carry also the banner of my death. And let it be a vile rag—which thou must bear through all Damascus set upon a lance, crying:

Lo, at his death the King of the East could take nothing with him save this cloth only.

And thus, he died.

Appendix Notes

Note A.—Mediaeval Coinage

The *solidus, besant* or *numisma*, was originally a gold piece of which, according to Constantine's orders, 72 went to the Roman pound. Thus, each *solidus* would weigh about 72 grains. From the days of the Merovingians, who struck gold *trientes*, till the middle of the thirteenth century there was, practically speaking, no gold coinage in Western Europe; such gold coins as passed current being the *besants* of the Greek Empire. If we overlook the unimportant issues of Roger II. of Sicily (ob. 1154) and that of Frederick II., gold coinage begins in West Europe with florins of Florence (weighing about 54 grains each) struck in 1252.

Five years later Henry III. issued a gold penny weighing about 45 grains, and equal to 20 silver pennies; but the city of London petitioned against the innovation, and the gold coin was soon withdrawn. Ninety years later (1343) Edward III. coined the first English florin weighing 108 grains, or double the Florence florin. Half florins and quarter florins were struck at the same time. The florin was to exchange against 6 shillings. Next year the new florins were supplanted by the noble, weighing about 138 grains and equivalent to 6s. 8d. of the current silver money. Louis IX. began the new French gold coinage with a golden *denarius*; worth 10½ *solidi* (Tournois).

From the days of Charlemagne to the thirteenth century the silver *denarius* of c. 24 grains was the coin currently used for the payment of all debts. But the *solidus* or shilling continued to be used as a money of account. Sums were thus reckoned in *solidi* but actually paid in *denarii*. Twelve *denarii* went to the *solidus* and twenty *solidi* to the pound. But large sums were settled by weight, the fineness of the silver being always liable to be tested by fire.

The Dialogus de Scaccario (c. 1177) gives an interesting account of the methods of receiving and making payments at the English Exchequer in the latter half of the twelfth century. When the sheriff brought in the chest or bag containing his debt to the treasury, it was emptied on the table and thoroughly mixed so that the *denarii*, good and bad alike, might be equally distributed throughout the heap. From this heap 44 *solidi* (*i.e.*, 528 *denarii*) were counted out, put into a separate receptacle which was sealed with the sheriff's seal, as a precaution against its being tampered with.

Later on, these forty-four *solidi* were handed to the fusor or refiner, who proceeded to perform his duty in the presence of representatives of the sheriff and the crown. Twenty *solidi* (*i.e.*, 240 out of the 528 *denarii*) were melted till the silver was separated from the dross. The silver was then weighed against the standard treasury pound. Normally this Standard Pound should exactly balance the resulting silver after the assay just made; but, if the silver did not weigh as much as it should, enough *denarii* were added to the assayed metal to turn the scale. *The fineness of the whole payment made by the sheriff was reckoned according to the result of this test.*

Thus, if the fusor had added ten *denarii* before the pure silver balanced the Standard Pound, every 240 *denarii* paid by the sheriff was counted as only 230. It seems however that, at all events in paying away money, the treasury might allow itself a margin of six *denarii*; and, so long as no more than 246 *denarii* went to the Standard Pound, discharged its dues at the rate of 240 to the £. After the money had been counted in the treasury every hundred *solidi* (*i.e.*, 1,200 *denarii* or £5) were put up by themselves in a wooden case (*vasum ligneum*); while twenty of these *vasa lignea* (*i.e.* £100 or 2,000 *solidi* =ing 24,000 actual *denarii*) were packed up in a larger case called a *forulus* or 'pouch.' These *foruli* strapt and sealed with the royal seal were deposited in the treasure vaults or in boxes (*archae*), to which there could be access but by duplicate or triple keys.

Of Arabic coins the chief were the gold *dinar*, weighing about 65 grains; and the silver *dirhem*, weighing about 43 grains. For purposes of comparison, it may be well to note that the modern sovereign weighs a little over 123 grains.

The twelfth century *mark* was not a coin, but a money of account, like the *solidus*. It was 2 thirds of the pound whether gold or silver.

The white money in the text would seem to represent newly stamped coin that had been made of assayed silver and so was of true weight and quality; but, as no coinage of Richard I. is known to numismatists, it is perhaps only the ordinary coin with the Treasury addition of 6d. in the £; for in the XIIth century the Treasury used to pay money in two ways (1) with the ordinary coin then current, and (2) in the same manner but with an additional 6 *denarii* for every £. The latter payments in the Rolls are entered as so many '*li. bl.*' (*libra blancae* or *livres blanches*).

The pound of Paris and the pound of Tours, though both divided into *solidi* and *denarii,* stood to one another in the proportion of 25: 20.

Note B.—On the Esnecca Regis

The *Esnecca* in the text is probably the special vessel reserved for royal use. Under Henry II. the treasury had standing orders to pay 12d. a day to the 'captain of the royal ship which we call *Esnecca*': '*liberatio naucleri, custodis scilicet navis regiae quam esneccam dicimus.*' (*Dialogus de Scaccario,* c. 6). See also Pipe Rolls of this reign. The name of Richard's *esnecca* was probably *Trenchemer,* or '*The Sea Cleaver*'; and its captain was Alan Trenchemer; for in Peter Langtoft (as Englished by Robert of Brunne), more than a hundred years later, we read, in the incident of the capture of the great Saracen vessel:

> The Kinges owen Galeie, he called it Trencthemere
> That was first in weie, and com the ship fulle nere.

When Richard was released from prison, he went to Antwerp, and there found a number of ships waiting to meet him. Rejecting all other service, however, he entered the 'galley of Alan Trenchemer, that therein he might with greater east make his way between the islands. But, as each night came on, he left this galley and went aboard a great and very fair ship, which had come from the island of Re, and lay there for the night. With the day, howbeit, he returned to the galley.' From this passage it is evident that Richard had a special liking for Alan Trenchemer's vessel. Not a few payments are ordered to Alan Trenchemer, in connection with the *Esnecca* (*regis*), in the *Rotuli Curiae* during the course of Richard's reign; and there is at least one similar entry under John. (Rot. Norm. Ed. Hardy, sub. aim. 1203). Southampton seems to have been the English port where the *Esnecca Regis* usually put up.

Note C—Topography of Acre

Acre lies partly on a tongue of land jutting out into the sea towards the south-east. It is placed on the western coast of Palestine on the edge of a large plain some 20 miles long by from one to four broad, which extends from Ras-en-Nakureh on the north, to Mount Carmel on the south. Owing to its position the great walls lay towards the east on the land side. About a mile to the east of the old city walls rises the hill Tel El-Fokhkhâr, the Mons Turo of the Crusading Chroniclers, some 100 feet above the level of the sea. Here at the beginning of the siege King Guy fixed his tents. The *Turris Maledicta* stood in the middle eastern wall at the N.E. corner just where the fortifications turned west for a space before once more bending round north to the sea. The tower of Flies, against which Philip Augustus directed his efforts, lay out in the harbour towards the S.W. parts of the town.

Saladin's headquarters were at the hill of Ayâdîyeh, which rises (to a height of some 65 feet above the level of the sea) about 5 miles E. of the city. His troops were spread N.W. to the sea and S.W. as far as the Kishon.

A mile south of the city the River Belus (Nahr-en-N'amein) joins the sea after a northerly course of a few miles. The River Kishon (Nahr El-Mukutta) reaches the sea from the S.E. about a mile E. of Cayphas.

Shefa Amr lies 9 or 10 miles E. of Haifa and about the same distance S.E. of Acre.

Note D.—On Mediaeval Warfare, &c.

The Frankish fortifications of Syria, in the twelfth and thirteenth century, are among the most remarkable series of buildings ever constructed.

Generally speaking, the town itself was surrounded by single or double walls. Of these the outer wall? and works went by the name of *antemuralia* or *barbican*. In front of these lay the moat (*vallum, fossatum*). Not unfrequently, as in the case of Darum and perhaps Tiberias too— the walls surrounding the towns were somewhat weak; but, where there was a *citadel or castrum* perched upon some natural or artificial height, it was strengthened with all the engineering science of the age. Other towns, such as Acre, had no special *castrum*, and in these cases it may be that the town itself was fortified with extra care.

Acre, at all events some twenty years after the great siege, was surrounded by two walls of almost equal strength, separated from one another by a space of some 120 feet. This space between the two walls was, like the primitive *pomoerium* of ancient Rome, in some cases laid out in gardens. The Foss of Acre lay beyond the outer wall, and was, as far as can be gathered from the present lay of the land, something under 150 feet wide. In the great mountain castles this foss was often dug out of the solid rock, in which case, as at Sahyoun, in North Syria, its width may have been 50 feet. In other instances, as at Darum, the moat was wholly (or partly) faced with stone. At regular intervals along the town walls there were great and strong towers. Along the walls of Darum there were 17, at Ascalon 53, at Antioch, so the First Crusaders reckoned, no less than 450

The walls themselves were in many cases of greater thickness and height than would at first be imagined. Dr. Tristram found the walls of Reginald of Chatillon's castle, at Kerak, 27 feet thick in one place at least; at Athlit they are 16, and at Belvoir near Beisan 9. The towers of Antioch are 80 feet high; so are the ruins of Montfort; while, in some places, the walls of Kerak rise over a hundred.

Armour.

The knight of this period wore a coat of ring-mail, generally known by the name of the *brunie*, *broigne*, or *hawberk*. Underneath this he wore a long-sleeved tunic, or *bliaud* (in later times called the *gamboisin*), of leather or wadded stuff, which was the sole protection of the unmounted soldier. This *gamboisin* doubtless corresponds to the *cazaghand* of our text. In the eleventh century and early twelfth the *brunea*, or *broigne*, consisted of small plates of mail, sewn or nailed upon a leathern ground. It was loose fitting, descended below the knees, and covered the back of the head and the neck also. It was sometimes furnished with sleeves; but was not worn with a belt.

The *hawberk* was a close-fitting robe of interlacing ring-work, which continued to develop itself till the end of the twelfth century, by which time it was the "*grand hawberk*" that appears on the later seal of Richard I. This *grand hawberk* was not sewn upon any ground, but simply formed of interlocking rings. It comprised more than one robe; for, while the lower half covered the legs and reached up as far as the waist, the upper part protected the neck, the arms, the hands, and the body, descending below the thighs in somewhat looser fashion to the knees. The *hawberk* was cloven behind so as facilitate horsemanship. Over the *hawberk* the knight in the east wore a coat of arms, a long, sleeveless tunic of linen or silk, often broidered or painted with his bearings.

The shield was, generally speaking, heater or kite shaped, and was suspended round the neck by a strap. It had a boss on the outside, and was made of wood, covered on the exterior with leather, strengthened with metal bands. In the thirteenth century a helmet of iron or steel-plate protected the head; and this helmet, more or less supplanting the earlier ring-mail hood of the *hawberk*, was topt with a small cone-shaped cap, from which there depended a narrow iron-plate (the nasal) to protect the nose.

WEAPONS.

The knight bore a horseman's lance, some twelve feet long, and a broad sword, short sword tapering to a point. The chief weapon of the foot soldier was the crossbow—which Anna Comnena describes as a "real devilish" weapon. Richard did not disdain to use this arm himself. The Saracen bows were often made of horn or bone, as Albert of Aix notes. Among weapons peculiar to the *infidels* were the reed spears and, to some extent, the mace, studded with (iron) teeth.

MILITARY ENGINES.

These have been noticed in the text. Perhaps the most graphic description of the moveable *castrum* is to be found in Anna Comnena's account of the siege of Dyrrachium. The ropes with which the *castrum* is represented as being girdled were used like net-work, to deaden the shock of the great stones hurled from *mangonels* or stone bows.

Note E.—The Mohammedan Calendar

The Mohammedan system of chronology starts from 15 July 622 *A.D.*, the year of the Hegira or Mahomet's flight from Mecca. The Mohammedan year consists of 354 days, and is divided into twelve months, of alternately 29 and 30 days. Out of every cycle of 30 years eleven add an extra day to their last month, thus making the number of days for these years 355. The following is a calendar for the years of the Hegira 587-89, intended to illustrate the dates in Bohâdin and other Arabic chroniclers quoted.

	No. of days.	Begins in A.H. 587 on		Begins in A.H. 588 on		Begins in A.H. 589 on	
Muharrem	30	29 Jan.	1191	18 Jan.	1192	7 Jan.	1193
Saphar	29	28 Feb.	,,	17 Feb.	,,	6 Feb.	,,
Rabia I.	30	29 March	,,	17 March	,,	7 March	,,
Rabia II.	29	28 April	,,	16 April	,,	6 April	,,
Jomada I.	30	27 May	,,	15 May	,,		
Jomada II.	29	26 June	,,	14 June	,,		
Rajab	30	25 July	,,	13 July	,,		
Shaaban	29	24 Aug.	,,	12 Aug.	,,		
Ramadân	30	22 Sept.	,,	10 Sept.	,,		
Shawall	29	22 Oct.	,,	10 Oct.	,,		
Dulkaada	30	20 Nov.	,,	8 Nov.	,,		
Dulheggia	29	20 Dec.	,,	8 Dec.	,,		
[And in intercalary years 30 days.]							

Note F.—On Certain Disputed Sites in Richard's March from Acre to Jaffa; and Beit-Nûba to Khuweilfeh.

Of the other places mentioned in Richard's march the Casal of the Narrow Ways is probably the Athlit, 8½miles S.W. of Haifa. Captain Condor, however, for reasons which I can hardly comprehend, would identify both the Casal and Capharnaum with Tantûra, 6½ miles S. of Athlit and 7-8 miles N. of Casarea. Merla, according to Capt. Condor, is perhaps the modern El Mezra'a, where a strong crusading tower still remains in ruins beside the main road here traversed. The Bombrac the same traveller would identify with the modern Ibn Ibrak. The Yazûr is 3½ miles S.E. of Jaffa and 7 miles N.W. of Ludd.

Dr. Stubbs' identification of Galatia with Keratîyeh, 23 miles S.W. of Beit-Nûba, is on the whole to be preferred to that given in the foot note. In favour of Jeledîyeh may be urged its comparative proximity to Ascalon, whence the army was expecting its provisions; but, on the other hand, it is very much out of the direct line of march from Ramleh to Tell Khuweilfeh, where as we learn from Bohâdin Richard plundered the caravan. Bohâdin makes Richard spend the first night of the expedition at Tell-es-Safi, 10 miles E. of Ascalon and 15 miles S.W. of Beit-Nûba, from which place he started.

From Tell-es-Sâfi he passed on to El Hesy, a distance of 6½ miles, if in this we may recognise Tell-el-Hesy. From Tell-el-Hesy he made his second night march to Tell Khuweilfeh, which lies 14 miles to the S.E. As the crow flies Tell Khuweilfeh is about 34 miles S.W. of Beit-Nûba and about 31 S.E. of Ascalon. At Keratîyeh there are remains of walls and a square tower from twenty to thirty feet high; there are also ruins of an old fortress and church on the slopes and top of Tell Khuweilfeh.

Keratîyeh lies to the W. of the direct route from Tell-es-Safi to Tell-el-Hesy, 8 miles S.W. of the former, 6½ miles N. of the latter, and 20 miles N.W. of Tell Khuweilfeh. Dr. Stubbs strives to harmonise the two accounts by supposing that Richard came to Keratîyeh (where he spent the first night, *i.e.,* that of Saturday, June 20) by way of Tell-es-Safi. At the latter place he may have left his foot while he pushed forward to Keratîyeh with the horse.

At Keratîyeh he spent the next day (Sunday, June 21) "received the first report of the spies and sent them out again." On Monday he moved to Tell-el-Hesy, where the spies brought him their second report, after which a night march brought him to the caravan on the Tuesday morning.

Note G.—Assassins.

The Mohammedans are divided into two great sections, the Sunnites, *followers of tradition*, who recognise the *Caliphs* of Damascus and Bagdad, and now the Sultan of Turkey, as the legitimate successors of Mahomet and the Shiites who, rejecting their authority, hold for Mahomet's true successor his nephew and son-in-law, Ali and the Imams his successors. The Shiites or followers of Ali soon split up into minute sections. Of these none was more famous than that of the Ismailites, who drew their name from Ismail, a descendant of Ali in the latter half of the ninth century.

About the same time a certain Persian, Abdallah, conceived the idea of turning the new doctrines to a political end. Under the assumption that all religions were true and all false he established a secret society divided into various grades. Each grade, in ascending order, was taught the comparative worthlessness of preceding knowledge till the neophytes reached the final one, which, according to some authorities, inculcated the indifference of all actions and a creed whose practical results could be hardly distinguished from blank Atheism.

A descendant of Abdallah established himself in Africa about the year 909 *A.D.* He pretended to be a descendant of Ali, and his third successor Moizz li din Allah founded the dynasty of the Fatimites, who ruled Egypt from about 960 *A.D.* to 1199. In the latter half of the eleventh century another Persian, Hasan ben Sabeh, after a life of unprincipled adventure, became an Ismailite and for a time settled in Egypt, whence he was before long banished for his share in a political intrigue.

Returning home, he soon settled himself (1090) in the impregnable Castle of Alamut, (the Vulture's Nest), south of the Caspian Sea, where the descendants of his immediate successor ruled for a century and a half, till they were overthrown by the Mongol Prince Hulagu (1256 *A.D.*). It is to this section of the Ismailites founded by Hasan that the name Assassin or Hashashin, *hemp-eaters*, was applied, because a drug prepared from this plant, which is the great Frenchman's *pantagruelion*, was used during the initiation of members or to nerve them for any extraordinary effort.

Hasan's influence was political rather than religious; his teaching enforced a blind obedience to the grand master's commands; and, for nearly two hundred years, the Ismailites became the terror of East and West. His devoted sectaries, assured that death itself was but the gateway to Paradise, never hesitated to execute their leader's mandate. Neither private friendship nor public greatness interfered with his plans; and Hasan ordered the murder of his old schoolfellow Nizam-al-Mulk, the great *vizier* of Malik Shah, just as lightly as his followers in a later generation murdered *caliphs* in their tents or hurled themselves in succession against Saladin in his camp.

Early in the twelfth century the Assassins began to multiply in Syria. By purchase or conquest, they became masters of a ring of fortresses east of Tortosa among the mountains of Lebanon. Their first prior in Syria died about 1169, and was succeeded by the famous Sinan, Saladin's enemy, who, as it seems, sent the celebrated embassy to Amalric I. of Jerusalem, offering to become a Christian if released from his tribute to the Templars. Sinan seems to have introduced fresh tenets into his creed; he threw off the authority of his nominal lord at Alamut, and in later days is said to have declared himself an incarnation of the Deity. He died in September, 1192.

Eighty years later the great Syrian fortresses fell before the Mamlook Sultan of Egypt. Massiaf was taken 1270; Kadmous and Katif had fallen by July, 1273. In Persia Hulagu had already done his best to exterminate the Assassins; but in Syria Beibars contented himself with their political subjection. Fifty years later (1326) an Eastern traveller, Ibn Batatah, found the Ismailites inhabiting their old castles in the Lebanon. He tells us the Egyptian *calif* of that time did not scruple to use the Ismailites against his enemies, and, to this day, (1900), a few thousands of the sect hang round the ruins of their old fortresses.

More than twenty-five years ago it was discovered that a group of sectaries in Bombay—the Khodjas—were Ismailites, and paid a tribute of £50,000 a year to their religious chief Aga Khan. He was the son of Khalîloullah, who in the latter half of the eighteenth century was chief of the Ismailites of Persia; and his pedigree goes back to Hasan 'Ala Dhikrihissalâm, the grand master of the Assassins in the middle of the twelfth century. In 1875, when the Prince of Wales was meditating his tour in India, Aga Khan wrote him an English letter with his own hand begging to be honoured with a visit; and the possible successor of Richard Coeur de Lion accepted the hospitality of the descendant of the grand master of the Assassins, then living as a private gentleman in India and passionately addicted to racing and field sports. Aga

Khan's son has several times ridden as a gentleman jockey in Bombay. (See M. St. Guyard's "*Un Grand Maitre des Assassins au temps de Saladin*," *Revue Asiatique*, Apr.-June 1877, VII. Series, vol. ix.)

Note H.—On the Legend of the Old Man of the Mountains

A curious parallel to this story of devotion to a man's leader may be read in Ibn Batuta, a Mohammedan who travelled in the East c. 1326 *A.D.*:

I one day saw in the assembly of this prince (*i.e.,* the King of Mul Java, in S.E. Asia) a man with a knife in his hand, which he placed upon his own neck; he then made a long speech, not a word of which I could understand. He then firmly grasped the knife, and its sharpness and the force with which he urged it were such that he severed his head from his body, and it fell on the ground. I was wondering much at the circumstance, when the king said to me: "Does any among you do such a thing as this?" I answered, "I never saw one do so."

He smiled and said: "These our servants do so out of their love to us". . . One who had been present at the assembly told me that the speech the man made was a declaration of his love to the *Sultan*, and that on that account he had killed himself, *just as his father had done for the father of the present king, and his grandfather for the king's grandfather.*

The account of the Assassins given in the text mainly coincides with that which was current in Europe during the XIIIth and XIVth centuries. Marco Polo's description (cf. 1300 *A.D.*) is as follows. I borrow Colonel Yule's translation of this writer, and incorporate passages from his version of Friar Odoric, who travelled in the East c. 1322 A.D.

("The Old Man was called in their language Aloadin. He had caused a certain valley between two mountains to be enclosed and had turned it into a garden—the largest and most beautiful that ever was seen, filled with every variety of fruit. In it there were erected pavilions and palaces. . . all covered with gilding and exquisite painting. And there were runnels, too, flowing freely with wine and milk and honey and water; and numbers of ladies and of the most beautiful damsels in the world who could play on all manner of instruments and sung most sweetly and danced in a manner that it was charming to behold. For the Old Man. . . . had fashioned (the garden) after the description that Mahomet gave of his Paradise. . . And surely enough the Saracens of those parts believed that it was Paradise.")

("And when the Old Man found any youth of promise he caused him to be admitted to his Paradise.")

("And he would introduce them into his garden some four or six or ten at a time, having first made them drink a certain potion which cast them into a deep sleep, and then causing them to be lifted and carried in. So, when they awoke, they found themselves in the garden. When therefore they awoke and found themselves in a place so charming, they deemed that it was Paradise in very truth.")

("And when the Old Man desired to cause any king or baron to be *assassinated* . . . he called on the officer who was set over that Paradise to select someone who was most fitted for the business and who most delighted in the life led in that Paradise of his. To this young man a certain potion was given which immediately set him fast asleep; and so, in his sleep he was carried forth from that Paradise. And when he awoke again and found himself no longer in Paradise, he went into such a madness of grief that he knew not what he did. And, when he importuned that Old One of the Mountain to let him back into Paradise, the reply was: 'Thou canst not return until thou shalt have slain such a king or baron. And then, whether thou live or die, I will bring thee back into Paradise again.'

"And so, through the youth's great lust to get back into his Paradise he got murdered by his hand whomsoever he list. And thus, the fear of the Old One was upon all the kings of the East, and they paid him heavy tribute.")

With these accounts compare the interesting Chinese narrative given by Chang Te—a Chinese envoy sent by the Great Khan Mangu to his brother Hulagu in 1259. Though much shorter, this account hardly differs from that quoted above. Chang Te, however, adds a curious touch. "The *Mulahi* (*i.e.,* Assassins) sent their emissaries secretly to the countries which had not yet submitted, with orders to stab the rulers. It was the same also with the women." According to Chang Te the Assassins had 360 mountain fortresses when Hulagu reduced them in 1256. For Chang Te's travels see Bretschneider's *Chinese Mediaeval Travellers, I.*

Note I.—On the Knowledge of Arabic Among the Crusaders

Henfrid of Toron, who figures as Richard's ambassador to Saladin, was probably well acquainted with Arabic. His mother's father was Lord of Kerak and Syria Sobal—a district where Arabic must have been practically the only tongue spoken. His father-in-law, Reginald of Châtillon, had spent years in a Saracen prison; and his grandfather Henfrid II. of Toron, who was bound by intimate ties of brotherhood to one of Nuradin's great *emirs*, seems to have understood this language (William of Tyre xvi. c. 17). The Saracens themselves speak with admiration of this Henfrid's valour. His name, says Ibn Alathîr, passed among the Mohammedans as a proverb to signify bravery and military skill, and Saladin himself received knighthood at his hand (*Itin. Ric.* I.; W. of T. xxi.)

It is plain that the office of interpreter or *"drogoman,"* known to the Egyptians 2,000 years before, was recognised by the Franks. William Drogomanus owned a house at Jerusalem under Fulk of Anjou (*A.D.* 1135), and signed a charter in 1144 (Cart of Holy Sepulchre, Nos. 80 and 82). Another document shews us the *dragomanship* as a kind of feudal fief. Caesar of Heisterbach seems to imply that, before the fall of Jerusalem in 1187, it was customary for Saracen chiefs to be brought up among Christian Franks and noble Franks among Saracen chiefs for the sake of learning the two languages.

In Baldwin III.'s retreat to Gadara a Christian knight negotiated with the enemy "because he could speak Saracen well" (W. of T. xvi.). William of Tyre undoubtedly knew Arabic well, as his works were to a large extent based upon Arabic MSS., which King Amalric had collected for him. Even so early as the first Crusade one chronicler tells us that Tancred understood this language; and, when it was necessary to make terms with Kerbogha before Antioch, the besieged Christians made use of one *"Arluinus Drogamundus,"* a knight, to bear their final challenge (*Tudebode* L. iv.).

If they had not picked up a tongue commonly spoken on their own estates, many great Frankish lords must have learned it during long years of captivity. For example, Reginald of Sidon, who figures in this book, could speak and perhaps read Arabic. Bohâdin tells us that he was so fond of history that he employed an Arabic reader to explain the passages he did not understand. It is probably, on this account, that we find him acting as Conrad's envoy to Saladin.

Note K.—On the Decapitation of the Dead

This common Eastern practice appears lasted till the very end of the Crusades, even among the most cultivated of Mohammedan princes. At the final siege of Acre in 1291, Abulfeda's cousin, El-Modaffer, the prince of Hamah, after defeating a body of Franks, cut off the heads of the dead, slung them round their horses' necks, and sent horses and heads as a present to the Sultan of Egypt.

Note L.—On Beards.

The mediaeval knight of the 12th century did not, as a rule, wear a beard, though the '*barba prolixa*' was one of the distinguishing features of Templars. Orderic Vitalis has a curious story, shewing how in his day it was regarded as a sure sign of extreme effeminacy, and almost of heresy, in a man if he did not shave.

This chronicler tells how the sight of the long-haired and bearded courtiers of Henry I. moved the indignation of Serlo Bishop of Seez, who preached an eloquent sermon against this new fashion before the king and his nobles in the church of Charenton. "Their long beards," he told his audience, "made them look like goats and bristly Saracens rather than Christians; and St. John had foretold these effeminacies in his Revelation." After finishing his discourse the good bishop whipped out a pair of scissors and called upon the king to show an example of decency. Henry, in a fit of sudden penitence, sacrificed his royal beard; the Earl of Mellent and all the other nobles followed suit, "treading their dearly-loved locks under foot."

The view taken by Christians of the Eastern custom of wearing a long beard comes out very characteristically in William of Tyre's story of Baldwin of Edessa (afterwards Baldwin II. of Jerusalem) and his father-in-law, Gabriel of Melitene. Baldwin, wanting money to pay his stipendiary knights with, led them down to this town on a visit. After some days had elapsed, his followers appeared before Gabriel, saying they must have their money or some ample security for its speedy payment; and as the son-in-law was impecunious, the father-in-law must pledge his credit.

He asked, by an interpreter, what security they would require, and was told his beard. "On hearing this he was struck all of a heap; for it is the fashion with Eastern folks—Greeks and other nations alike—to tend their beards with all care. And they hold it for the greatest shame and ignominy that a man can offer them to lose a single hair of their beards." It was to no purpose that Gabriel appealed to his son-in-law and finally he redeemed his beard by a payment of 30,000 *Micheliatae*. Strangely enough, however, Baldwin I., Baldwin II., and Fulk, the first three kings of Jerusalem, all wore beards.

The Saracen point of view comes out well in Bohâdin's description of Henfrid de Toron: "I saw this young man on the day when the peace was concluded. He was indeed beautiful to look at, *but he had his beard shaved* in accordance with the fashion of his nation." See too, in the last extract from Bohâdin, where Saladin's little child begins to cry at seeing the strange Franks with their foreign dresses and shaven faces.

In the earlier 11th century Chansons de Geste, not only Charles the Great wears his beard long but his knights also. Thus, in the Chanson de Roland, in the Baligant Episode, 1. 3084-3095, and 1. 3315-3319

Behold the pride of France that all men praise!
Right proudly rides the Emperor to war,
He cometh last with that good bearded folk,
Over their mail coats they have cast their beards,
That are as white as snow that lies on ice.

So, in 1. 1823 Guenes, the traitor earl, who is always described as exceedingly handsome and careful of his personal appearance and dress, is shown with beard and moustaches, and in 1. 209 the emperor speaking to Naimes swears—

By this my beard and this moustache of mine.

Roland himself wears a beard, 1. 2283. But in the Bayeux tapestry of c. 1100 the Normans are mostly clean shaven, while the English wear moustaches but no beards save the Holy King

Edward, who wears hair and beard long. The curious in this matter may consult Rodolph Glaber (Book III. *sub finem*) as to the introduction of the habit of wearing short hair and of shaving 'like actors' into northern France about the year 1000 *A.D.*; the difficult passage at the end of Geoffrey of Vigeois (c. 1185 *A.D.*); and, above all else, James de Vitry's invectives against the Latins of the Holy Land for adopting the Eastern custom. Guibert of Nugent tells us that, at the night capture of Antioch (1098 *A.D.*), the Latin Christians hoped to distinguish their fellows from the Turks by the absence of beards; but the long siege had not afforded opportunities of shaving to the Frank knights and hence in the darkness not a few perished.

Note M.—On the Battle of Arsuf

It is almost impossible to get a clear idea of the details of this battle from the account given in the *Itinerarium*. If, however, we turn to Bohâdin we can make out a fairly vivid picture of the engagement as a whole, though perhaps one that is not, in some minute points, quite in harmony with that of the Frankish writer. The following is Bohâdin's account of the line of march adopted by the Crusaders "as I saw it myself and learnt it from some French prisoners and the merchants who used to visit their camp."

The infantry was divided into two great sections, of which one marched along the sea shore and relieved the other when it grew too tired to support the attacks of the Saracens. This second section was stationed near the hills that fringed the coast and no very great distance from the water. Between these two sections marched the mounted warriors who never left this middle position except to charge.

The infantry, drawn up in front of the cavalry, held itself firm as a wall—each man being clad in a jerkin of thick felt and a coat of mail. I saw some of them with ten arrows fixed in their back and yet marching along at their ordinary pace without quitting the ranks.

The cavalry was divided into three bodies: in the van went the King of Jerusalem (Guy) accompanied by the troops of his own realm; in the centre went the King of England and the King of France, (a mistake for the Duke of Burgundy); the rear was formed of another troop of horse under "the sons of the lady of Tiberias," *i.e.,* Hugh of Tiberias and his brothers. In the centre of the army was "a car surmounted by a tower as high as a minaret "from which the standard floated.

Such, according to Bohâdin, was the disposition of the Christian troops on the march towards Joppa. The words of the author of the *Itinerarium* would, however, seem to imply that Richard modified his arrangement on the day of the great battle; against which, however, must be set the fact that Bohâdin 's account of the engagement itself is consistent with his own arrangement rather than with that of the *Itinerarium.*

When the battle commenced Bohâdin was with the centre, and the combat evidently opened by an attack on the Mohammedan right wing; in other words, with a charge from the Christian rear-guard, where the foot opened their lines to let the cavalry pass through. Again, it seems evident that, after the battle had opened with the engagement of the two rear-guards, as Bohâdin clearly saw, the two vans were the next to come into the contest.

Such appears to be the plain inference from the Christian account as well as a fair deduction from Bohâdin's statement that when the centre was routed, he thought it best to flee to the left wing, which was nearest him. But, by the time he got there, it was already more utterly defeated than the right. All this agrees very well with the *Itinerarium*, from which it would appear that the English and Norman troops (*i.e.,* Bohâdin's centre) were the last to join battle.

Note N.—On the Causes of the Failure of the Third Crusade

Though the failure of the Third Crusade may at first seem strange, its causes are perhaps not difficult to understand. The defection of Philip, the quarrel for the crown, the national rivalries that had gone far to wreck the two previous Crusades, all precluded vigorous action. Had Richard been able to advance on Ascalon some weeks earlier, as he doubtless intended to have done, the whole coast south of Acre would probably have fallen into his hands without a blow; so disheartened were the Saracens at the fall of this city.

Probably a second tactical mistake was also made in not pushing on for Ascalon at every hazard after the battle of Arsuf. Such at all events seems to have been the opinion of so capable a general as Conrad of Montferrat who, according to Ibn Alathîr, reproached the king keenly for this neglect: at the very rumour of its projected destruction, he urged, Richard ought to have hurried up and saved a town which the *Sultan* could not defend, and which, if once destroyed, Richard must well have known he would have to rebuild. 'By Christ's truth,' concluded Conrad, 'had I been near thee, Ascalon would be in our hands this day and that without the loss of a single tower.'

Again, there seems to be little doubt that had Richard marched Boldly on Jerusalem in the early part of June, 1192 it would have fallen. But it is more doubtful whether he would have been able to retain it. The great crowd of warriors, having fulfilled their vows and worshipped at our Lord's Tomb, would have hurried home, taking no thought for the defenceless land. Nor could the Holy City have itself held out long after their departure. The feudal polity which, five years before, had proved too weak to defend the state could not have been reorganised in a few weeks or months.

It was a sound instinct which taught the Crusaders that the true way to the reconquest of Palestine was across the Delta of the Nile. Their ancestors had acquired the Holy Land and held it at a time when Damascus and Cairo were at variance; directly the valleys of the Orontes and the Nile acknowledged one lord the Latin kingdom of Jerusalem fell. Whether any Crusading force could have been mustered strong enough not only to conquer but to garrison Egypt while its fellows pushed on against Jerusalem is uncertain; but so long as the wealth, the fertility and the fleet of the Lower Nile were at the disposal of the *Sultan* of Damascus, Aleppo and the further East, no Christian power could hope for the permanent possession of Jerusalem.

Note O

The following account of the capture of the caravan from the lips of an eye-witness is worth preserving.

Ibn Alathîr, II.

One of our friends whom we had sent to Egypt and who was with this caravan told me as follows: "When the Franks fell on us, we had just put up our packages to resume our march. They flung themselves upon us and attacked us fiercely. I flung away my packages—for I had a number of packages belonging to someone else—and began to climb the hill. A troop of Franks came up with us and seized the packages that I had been in charge of. For my own part I was about a bowshot ahead and they did not reach me. So, I escaped with what I had by me and continued my way not knowing in what direction I was going; when, all of a sudden there rose before me a huge building set on a mountain. I asked its name and they told me 'Karak.' And there I went and, later, returned safe and sound to Jerusalem."

This same man left Jerusalem in perfect safety; but, on reaching Bozaa not far from Aleppo, he was seized by brigands. He had only escaped one death to perish at the moment when his danger seemed over.

Note P.—On the Count of St. Pol, &c.

Hugh IV., Count of St. Pol, is said to have succeeded his father Anselm in 1174. Villehardouin tells us how he took part in the fourth crusade, was one of the envoys to the Venetians, and shared in the Conquest of Constantinople, where he died of gout almost immediately after the taking of the city (1205 *A.D.*).

Stephen of Turnham, or Marzai, seems to have been Henry II.'s *seneschal* or treasurer in Anjou. On Richard's accession he was flung into prison at Winchester till he would deliver the royal treasure (£45,000) and castles. According to Dr. Stubbs he was Sheriff of Wilts, and justice in eyre in 10 Richard I. (1198-9). Richard of Devizes calls him a man "*magnus et potens, singulariter ferus et dominus domini.*" He had led

Berengaria back to England by way of Rome (1192-4).

Baldwin, advocate of Bethun, was one of the hostages for King Richard's release in 1194. Next year he was created Earl of Albemarle after marrying Hawisa, the widow of William de Forts. He is said to have died 13 Oct. 1213.

The Third Crusade

THE GATHERING OF THE HOST

The news of the fall of Jerusalem reached Europe about the end of October, 1187. It is hard at this distance of time to realise the measure of the disaster in the eyes of the Western world. It was not merely that the Holy City had fallen; that all the scenes of that Bible history which constituted emphatically the literature of mediaeval Christendom, had passed into the hand of the *infidel*. It was all this and something more; the little kingdom of Jerusalem was the one outpost of the Latin Church and Latin culture in the East; it was the creation of those heroes of the First Crusade whose exploits had already become the theme of more than one romance; it lay on the verge of that mysterious East with all its wealth of gold and precious stones and merchandise, towards which the sword of the twelfth-century knight turned as instinctively as the prow of the English or Spanish adventurer four centuries later turned towards the West.

If the sword had won much, much yet remained for it to win; Aleppo the chief town of Northern Syria, Damascus the garden of the world, Alexandria the storehouse of the East—all these and other prizes fired from time to time the ambitions of those who aspired to rival the successes of the two Baldwins, of Raymond and Reginald, or of Fulk and Guy; while for those who fell in battle and lost the prize of temporal power, there was secured an eternity of happiness in heaven. Thus, Palestine inspired alike the imagination, the enterprise, and faith of Western Christendom.

No wonder that both religious enthusiast and knightly adventurer were stirred to the very utmost at the tidings of Saladin's victory. Pope Urban III. was alleged to have died of grief for the loss of the Holy City. Unfounded though that report was, we know with what profound emotion the news was received in the papal court, where the cardinals laid aside their luxury, and pledged themselves to take the cross and beg, if need be, their way to Palestine. (Urban died on October 20, 1187, before the fall of Jerusalem could have been known in Europe.) Nor was the feeling less profound in the lands beyond the Alps; it was not, we may be sure, any peculiar grief which made Abbot Samson of Bury St. Edmund's (familiar to all readers of Carlyle's *Past and Present*) wear sackcloth next his skin, and leave off animal food from the time when he heard that the Holy City was in the hands of the *infidel*.

One of the first acts of the new Pope, Gregory VIII., was to bid the princes of Europe lay aside their private quarrels and unite for the service of Christ in a new Crusade. First to take the Cross in November, 1187, was our own Richard, then Count of Poitou; two months later, on January 21, 1188, the kings of France and England were reconciled by the Archbishop of Tyre, and both received the cross at his hands; their example was quickly followed by the Count of Flanders. The three princes agreed that white, red, and green crosses should be the badges of their respective followers.

Nor was the enthusiasm confined to words; the famous Saladin-tax in England, and perhaps in France also, bound every man, on pain of excommunication, to contribute a tithe of his means for the contemplated expedition; to all who would pledge themselves to personal service, special privileges were offered. In England the Crusade was preached by Baldwin of Canterbury himself; in his journey through Wales the archbishop was accompanied by the famous Giraldus Cambrensis, who made this the occasion of his *Itinerary*. The foremost preacher in France was Berter of Orleans, the echo of whose eloquence has come down to us in the song which bears his name.

Many nobles in both countries followed the example of their kings, but before long the feud between Henry and Philip broke out again. Time after time the expedition was postponed, and it was nearly three years after the fall of Jerusalem, when Henry himself was dead, that the chivalry of France and England were led over sea by their feudal lords to share in the siege of Acre.

The kings of the Spanish peninsula were too busy with the *infidel* at their own gates to go and fight for the Faith at the other extremity of the Mediterranean. In Italy, however, William of Sicily was first of the great princes to act; when the Archbishop of Tyre, in his black-sailed galley, brought the news of Hattin, William had forthwith diverted to the relief of the Holy Land the fleet which he had collected for an attack on Constantinople. This armament, under its great admiral, Margaritus, saved Antioch from Saladin, helped to preserve Tripoli, strengthened Conrad at Tyre, and recovered Jaffa. William was preparing for a fresh expedition when his death, and the troubles which ensued put an end to the design.

A yet more potent sovereign had already pledged himself for the second time to the service of the cross. Forty years had passed since Frederick Barbarossa had borne his part in the Second Crusade, and now as a man of nearly seventy he renewed the promise of his youth. The troubles of the great emperor's reign had come to an end, and it had seemed that he might now close his life in peace; but all thoughts of rest were banished by the news of the fall of Jerusalem, and Frederick, though last to take the cross, was first to take the field.

Whilst Richard and Philip were banded together in treason to their father and fellow-Crusader, the aged emperor was already toiling through Hungary and Bulgaria on his way to the East. In the previous year his envoys had obtained from Isaac Comnenus the promise of ample provisions, but the promise of the Greek proved as worthless as ever. Not, indeed, but what Isaac may well have looked on this new enterprise with alarm. Bright, though perhaps misty, visions of a Latin Empire in the East long floated before the eyes of Western Europe. William of Sicily had actually been preparing for such an attempt, and later legend tells how Richard of England hoped to crown the glory of his life by the conquest of so rich a prize. In 1188, the world was full with whispers of a coming change; strange prophecies were told to ready ears, and many hoped that in Frederick they might find the yellow-haired king of the West before whom the golden gate of Constantinople was to open; might he not also be destined to fulfil that other prophecy, and drive back the last remnant of the unconverted Turks beyond the withered tree.

On May 11, 1189, Frederick's great army started from Ratisbon. In Hungary he was received hospitably, but on entering Bulgaria in July he began to experience the nature of Greek promises. Markets were ill provided, and the natives dogged the line of march to cut off stragglers or in the hope of plunder. At Philippopolis on the 24th of August there came the news that Isaac had made a league with Saladin, and contrary to all right and custom thrust the German ambassadors into prison. Isaac's promises were clearly valueless, and Frederick accordingly sent word to his son Henry at home to hire all the ships he could in Italy, and send them to Constantinople in readiness for its siege in the following March.

STATUE OF FREDERICK I.

This represents the contemporary (1170-1190) statue of the
Emperor in the cloisters at the church of S. Zeno, near
Reichenhall, in Bavaria.

Isaac presently took alarm, released the envoys and came to terms.

The German Army then went into winter quarters at Adriano-
ple; in February, 1190, they started once more, and soon after Easter,
which fell this year on the 25th of March, crossed the Bosphorus and
entered Asia. At Laodicea they reached the dominions of Kilij Arslan,
who, by his envoys had promised Frederick good guidance and stores
of food. It was, however, soon evident that Kilij Arslan was no more
to be trusted than Isaac; no food was brought for sale, and as the
army toiled along the rocky ways that led to Iconium their steps were
dogged by the hostile Turks. When at length, on the 18th of May, the
Crusaders appeared before his city, Kilij Arslan, declaring that it was
not he but his son who was to blame for the past, came to terms and
opened to the Crusaders an abundant market

From Iconium Frederick passed on towards Cilicia. Leo, the Prince of Armenia, sent him envoys with promises of all support and good-will. But on the 10th of June while the army was struggling over the rocky hills that separated Cilicia from Lycaonia they were startled by the news of the emperor's death. Desirous to avoid the labours of the recognised path which wound up the rocks above the River Saleph, Frederick had determined to make a short cut; with his attendants he came down to the river side; the day was hot, and willing to shorten his journey, and at the same time cool his heated limbs: the emperor attempted to swim the rapid stream; the swirl of the waters sucked him down, and so "he, who had oftentimes escaped from greater dangers, came to a pitiful end." His followers sadly carried his body to Tarsus, where they buried the intestines with great reverence; his bones were taken to Antioch and interred in the Church of St. Peter.

Thus, perished the noblest type of German kingship—the Kaiser Redbeard, of whom history and legend have so much to tell. Tradition was soon busy with his death. Men could not believe that he was gone away for ever from his own land: like Arthur, he was but in hiding for a time, and would return in some hour of supreme necessity to save the empire which he had ruled. The spot which witnessed his destruction was fabled to have been marked out by fate from remote antiquity, and a rock near the river's fount was alleged to bear the ominous words—"*Hic hominum maximus peribit*" ("Here shall perish the greatest of men").

After Frederick's death the German host divided into two. One body went to Tripoli; the rest, under the Duke of Swabia, made their way to Antioch, where they stayed for some time, recruiting themselves after their labours, and assisting the prince of that city in his warfare.

It was not till June, 1190, that Richard and Philip Augustus were ready to commence their journey. The two kings met at Vézelay, and proceeded in company to Marseilles, whence Philip sailed in a Geno-ese fleet for Sicily, and landed at Messina on the 16th of September. Richard had ordered his fleet to meet him at Marseilles, but the Eng-lish Crusaders, mindful of the exploit of their forefathers nearly half a century before, stopped on the way to help Sancho, of Portugal, in his warfare with the Moors. It was the 14th of September before they reached Marseilles.

Meanwhile Richard, impatient of delay, had started in a single gal-ley. Slowly he sailed from port to port along the western shores of Ita-ly, varying his journey from time to time by a ride on shore. At last, on the 23rd of September, he joined his main fleet, and entered Messina in state and pomp amidst the blare of trumpets, whilst the Frenchmen and Sicilians on the beach marvelled at the splendour of his coming.

The two kings stayed on in Sicily for six months. The winter was passed in unseemly wrangling; Tancred, the new ruler of the island, was an illegitimate grandson of Roger I.; he had seized the person and property of his predecessor's widow, Joanna, and she, as Richard's sister, naturally turned to her brother for protection. An ill-advised quarrel soon gave Richard a pretext for an attack on Messina; the old chronicler says:

Quicker than priest could chant *matins*, did King Richard take the city.

Such prompt action brought Tancred to his senses and though Richard did not get the golden table and chair, which he claimed as part of his sister's dower, he received what was perhaps more useful, namely, forty thousand ounces of gold.

If the taking of Messina proved Richard's military prowess, his castle of Matte Griffin, or Check Greek, showed him as the skilful engineer; and the great Christmas feast, when he gave his guests the golden goblets which they used, displayed his generosity. Now also, though late, he recognised his sin against his father, and showed the sincerity of his sorrow by submitting to public penance. In the presence of all his prelates he confessed his sin, and "from that hour once more became a God-fearing man."

On the 30th of March, 1191, Richard's mother, Eleanor, brought to Messina her son's destined bride, Berengaria of Navarre. That same day Philip had sailed for Palestine, but Richard did not start till eleven days later. The English fleet, which numbered more than one hundred and eighty vessels, was scattered by a great storm two days after it set sail. Richard himself put in at Crete; but some of his ships were wrecked on the coast of Cyprus, and the crews thrown into prison by order of Isaac Comnenus, the ruler of the island. A little later the ship which carried Berengaria and her future sister-in-law, Joanna, reached Limasol. Somewhat doubtfully they accepted Isaac's invitation to land next day, Monday, the 6th of May; but that same afternoon the sails of the main fleet appeared on the horizon, and on the following morning the king himself arrived. Richard was not the man to suffer tamely the wrongs which had been done to his followers; when Isaac refused redress, the English king determined to use force; a short campaign of three weeks sufficed for the conquest of Cyprus, and Isaac was imprisoned in chains of silver.

At Cyprus Richard married Berengaria, and after a month's stay in the island sailed, on the 5th of June, for Palestine, in the company of Guy de Lusignan, who had come to meet him with many of the great Syrian nobles. On his way Richard encountered and sank a great Saracen vessel laden with provisions for Acre, and after two days entered the harbour of that city in triumph. Baha-ed-din says:

> For joy at his coming, the Franks broke forth into public rejoicing, and lit mighty fires in their camps all night long. And seeing that the King of England was old in war and wise in council, the hearts of the Mussulmans were filled with fear and dread.

THE SIEGE OF ACRE

We must now turn back to record the fortunes of the Christians in Palestine during the interval between the fall of Jerusalem and the arrival of the main host of the Crusaders under the kings of France and England.

Guy de Lusignan had been set free towards the beginning of July, 1188, but not until he had promised to abandon his claim on the kingdom. From this engagement he was soon released by the clergy, who assured him that there was no binding force in such an oath. Near Tortosa he met his wife, and with her proceeded to Antioch at the invitation of Bohemond. The year passed in anxious expectation of succour from Europe. But by the following spring Guy had assembled a little army, and feeling sufficiently strong to take the initiative, marched southwards to Tyre.

Conrad refused him admission to the city, declaring that God had entrusted it to his care, and he would keep it; if the king sought a resting-place let him find it elsewhere. After four months' vain delay near Tyre, Guy marched on to Acre with an army which now numbered seven hundred knights and nine thousand foot, gathered from every nation in Christendom. With this little force he set down to besiege that great and strong city on the 28th of August, 1189.

Acre lies on an inlet of the Mediterranean which bears its name; a tongue of land running southwards into the sea serves as a partial protection for the harbour; at its extremity rose the famous "Tower of Flies," which, together with a chain, helped to guard the harbour; to the east the city overlooked a fertile plain. (So called, if we may trust the chroniclers, because it marked the spot where heathen sacrifices

COIN OF GUY DE LUSIGNAN.

COIN OF GUY DE LUSIGNAN AS KING OF CYPRUS
This is a denier. Legend REX GUIDO DE CIPRO.

had of old attracted swarms of flies.)

The harbour of Acre was the best in the kingdom properly so called, if not along the whole coast of Syria, and the town itself was the chief emporium of Frankish trade. In recent years it had been gradually supplanting Jerusalem as the royal residence, and had become the recognised landing-place for pilgrims from the West. An Arab writer, who visited it some five years before this time, says:

> Acre is the column on which the Frankish towns in Syria rest Thither put in the tall ships which float like mountains over the sea. It is the meeting-place of crafts and caravans: the place whither Mussulman and Christian merchants muster from all sides.

At a little distance from the walls a small hill rises above the level of the plain; here Guy pitched his tent, whence he could look forward over the city for the sails of his expected friends. But to the east a less pleasant sight soon met his gaze, as one after another the Saracen contingents hastened up to hem in the Christian Army between the River Kishon and the sea; before long the Christians were themselves besieged, and their numbers were so few that they could not prevent the Saracens from passing almost at their will to and from the town.

The siege had hardly commenced when the first ships of the autumn passage began to arrive. First came the Frisians, closely followed by a contingent from Flanders and England. Then came the hero of the siege, James of Avesnes, a warrior proud and turbulent in his own land, but in the eyes of his fellow Crusaders the model of all chivalric virtues—in counsel as Nestor, in arms as Achilles, in faith as Regulus. Other arrivals were Robert of Dreux, grandson of Louis VI., and his brother Philip of Beauvais, the warrior prelate of the expedition; the Counts of Brienne and Bar, and the Landgrave, Louis of Thuringia, whose influence induced Conrad of Montferrat to lend his aid to an enterprise, from which he had as yet held sullenly aloof.

By mid-September the Christians perhaps numbered nine thousand horse and thirty thousand foot, and were able to establish an effectual blockade. Saladin therefore determined on an attempt to break through their lines, and in the early dawn of September 14th, a sudden onset from both the city and the camp proved successful; despite their valour, the Christians could not prevent the passage of the loaded camels into Acre, nor the escape of one of Saladin's sons from the beleaguered town.

Three weeks later Guy retaliated by an attack on the *Sultan's* camp; the Saracens gave way before the charge of the Franks, who were already plundering Saladin's tent, when a sally from the town cut off the Christians in the rear, and called Geoffrey de Lusignan to his brother's aid, from the camp which he had undertaken to guard. In vain did the Templars offer a stout resistance to the new attack; twenty of their knights were slain, and among them Gerard de Rideford, the grand master. Gerard died a hero's death; his comrades urged him to seek safety in retreat; "God forbid," was his reply, "that men should say of me to the shame of our order, that to save my own life I fled away leaving my fellows dead behind me."

Nor was Gerard alone in his gallantry; Guy himself, in the true spirit of chivalry, rescued his enemy Conrad from the imminent danger of death, whilst James d'Avesnes owed his safety to the self-sacrifice of one of his knights. In the end the Christians lost the day, but they gained, nevertheless, a substantial advantage, for the Saracens were so exhausted, that Saladin gave orders to fall back on El Kharruba, about twelve miles southeast of Acre.

★★★★★★★★

This probably refers only to part of Saladin's army. Previously the main host had been encamped on the hill of A'iadiya, about four and a half miles south-east of Acre. This retreat was occasioned chiefly by Saladin's ill-health; but none the less does the Arabic contemporary historian—wise after the event—blame the hero of Islam.

★★★★★★★★

The Christians turned this respite to the best use; in order at once to secure their own position, and to complete the blockade, they dug a deep trench outside their camp from sea to sea, and strengthened it with a wall of earth. Night and day, they toiled at the task till all was finished. Young and old, men and women, all joined in the labour, and the Christian historian records with enthusiasm, how when one woman was mortally wounded in the midst of her labour, she adjured her

235

husband to let her dead body be flung into the mound, that thus she might further in death the work for which she had sacrificed her life.

The winter passed away without any important result, though the Egyptian fleet succeeded in revictualling the town on October 31st, and two months later drove the Christian vessels to seek shelter at Tyre. Saladin occupied himself with preparations for mustering a large army; Baha-ed-din was sent on an embassy to summon the lords beyond the Euphrates, and to beg aid of the *caliph*; both missions proved successful, and in April, 1190, the various contingents began to arrive.

Meantime Conrad had brought back the fleet from Tyre, and, in return for a compact, by which he was to have Tyre, Sidon, and Beyrout, lent his hearty aid. But though the Christians could now confine the Saracen fleet at Acre, they still could not prevent the entry of provisions from time to time. The siege was nevertheless prosecuted with vigour from the land side; three great towers of wood were constructed, and fitted with engines; when manned by five hundred men a-piece, they were brought to bear on the walls. Perhaps the town would have fallen save for the energy of a young charcoal-burner of Damascus; but by his direction certain ingredients were mixed together in pots, which on being hurled against the towers set them ablaze; thus they were all destroyed, and the confusion of the Christians was increased by an attack from the Saracen camp, which was maintained during eight days.

After this many of Saladin's best troops were called away to oppose the Germans near Antioch. This circumstances perhaps encouraged the Christian common folk, contrary to the will of their leaders, to sally out on July 25th against the foes surrounding them. The wrath of the chiefs was powerless against the lust for spoil, which stirred the crowd to madness; for a moment the suddenness of the attack made it successful, and the rude host was soon rifling the tents of El-Adel. But the Saracen soldiery quickly mustered to arms, and the Franks, who had no thought except for the plunder, woke up to find their retreat entirely cut off. Hardly one would have escaped but for the valour and self-devotion of an English clerk, Ralph of Hautrey, Archdeacon of Colchester. The Christians themselves admitted a loss of over five thousand men, and Baha-ed-din, who rode over the plain after the battle, declares that he had to cross "waves of blood," and that he could not count the number of the dead.

The next few months were passed in comparative quiet, but were marked by the coming of the first large contingents of the French and

English hosts; the former under Henry of Champagne and Theobald of Blois, the latter under Ranulf Glanville, Archbishop Baldwin of Canterbury, and his destined successor, Hubert Walter, then Bishop of Salisbury. About the same time the Germans arrived from Tripoli, under Frederick of Swabia; but of the vast host which started from Ratisbon, scarcely five thousand were now left

Count Henry brought with him ten thousand men, and he was at once appointed to command the army in place of James d'Avesnes and the Landgrave, who had so far held the office by turns. The attack from the land side still met with but indifferent success, but at sea the blockade was so strictly maintained, that famine began to press hard on the besieged. Saladin, however, maintained his communications with the town, through the agency of a messenger named Eissa. This man would creep down to the shore at dark, carrying in his belt letters and money for the payment of the troops; thence plunging into the waters he would strike out for the harbour, often diving beneath the very keels of the Crusaders' ships. At last one of his journeys proved fatal, and a few days later the citizens of Acre found his dead body on the sand with his belt still untouched. The Arab historian, quaintly says:

Never before, had we seen a man pay a debt after his death.

Provisions grew scarce within the town, but the state of the Christian camp was scarcely less doleful. Archbishop Baldwin, writing home, says:

The Lord is not in the camp; there is none that doeth good. The leaders strive one with another, while the lesser folk starve, and have none to help. The Turks are persistent in attack, while our knights skulk within their tents. The strength of Saladin increases daily, but daily does our army wither away.

Saladin, however, on October 20th, went into winter quarters at Shefr 'Amr close to El Kharruba; for the unhealthiness of the place was proving fatal to himself and to his troops. His troops began to murmur at the long campaign, and one by one many of his chief followers withdrew, till in March, 1191, the *Sultan* was left with only a small force. On the other hand, the stress of winter had prevented the Franks from watching the harbour with the usual closeness, and Saladin had contrived to throw a fresh garrison into the town (Feb. 13th).

Moreover famine was rife in the Christian camp, and during the enforced idleness of winter the soldiery gave way to dicing, drinking, and even worse. Baldwin took the evil that he saw around him so much to heart, that he fell sick, and after a short illness died, thankful for his speedy delivery from his sojourn in so godless an army. Conrad had withdrawn to Tyre, and promised to send provisions thence; but he either could not or would not fulfil his engagement, and at length the famine grew so severe that the knights slew their chargers to save themselves from death. When it was known that an animal had been slaughtered, men flocked together from all parts of the camp to beg or steal a portion for themselves. Men of noble birth might be seen going out into the plain and eating grass like cattle, others ran about the camp like dogs on the scent for old bones.

At last, one Saturday early in March, a ship arrived with a cargo of grain, and by the following day the price of a measure of corn had fallen from a hundred pieces of gold to four. After this there was an end of the famine, and only those grieved who, like a certain Pisan, had hoarded their grain in the hope of an even higher price:

> But his wickedness did God show by a plain token; for it chanced that his house suddenly took fire and was consumed with all that was in it.

About the end of March, 1191, Saladin renewed his leaguer of the Christian camp; but the besieged within the city were now hard pressed, and the *Sultan* could do no more to help them than to order an attack on the Christian camp whenever the Christians made a special effort against the town. Philip Augustus arrived on April 20th, and Richard on June 8th; it seemed for the moment that Acre must fall at once. The machines which the King of England had constructed in Sicily, including the huge wooden tower Matte Griffin, were brought to bear on the walls.

But before anything had been effected, the old feuds broke out afresh; Guy and Conrad renewed their quarrel, and the latter departed in wrath to Tyre. Next Richard and then Philip fell sick, and during the illness of the two kings the Mohammedans were enheartened by the coming of fresh forces. Philip soon recovered, and on July 3rd a great effort to carry the town was made; though the assault fell short of complete success, the defenders were reduced to despair.

Richard, though still unwell, was eager to emulate the deeds of his rival; so a few days later he had himself carried to a shed whence he could direct the efforts of his engineers; in his ardour he himself aimed the shots from the *balista*, while his miners worked with such vigour

SEAL OF RICHARD I. (1195.)

The date of this seal is 1195. It shows the grand hauberk complete; but as yet there is no "barding" for the horse and no surcoat or coat-of-arms flowing over the armour. The "bliaud," worn underneath the mail, may be seen flowing behind the left leg. Notice the extreme length of the sword as compared with that of Louis VII.

that at length a piece of the wall fell down with a crash. At last—so the story was told, a little later in England—on July 8th, as the Christians were keeping watch, there shone round them a sudden light, "for fear of which the guards became as dead men;" in the midst of the light appeared the Virgin, bidding those to whom she spoke bear her message to the kings; let them abandon their efforts against the walls, the city should be theirs on the fourth day.

Next morning the rulers of the city begged for a truce, and promised to capitulate if Saladin did not send immediate help. The *Sultan* was forced somewhat unwillingly to consent to terms; Acre was to be given up together with two hundred knights and fifteen hundred other Christian captives; the Holy Cross was to be restored, and the sum of two hundred thousand *besants* paid to the Crusaders. So, after a siege of nearly two years, on Friday, July 12, 1191, the Christians once more obtained possession of Acre. The city and the captives were divided between the two kings; Richard took possession of the royal palace, whilst Philip hung his banner over the house of the Templars. But even in the hour of victory the princes quarrelled one with another as to their respective shares therein.

Leopold of Austria—so the story goes—had set up his banner side by side with that of the King of England as though arrogating to himself an equal share in the triumph; with Richard's connivance, if not by his command, the duke's banner was torn down and cast into the ditch. Leopold, feeling himself unable to revenge this indignity, departed for his own land, bearing in his breast the seeds of a direful hatred for the English king.

THE CAMPAIGNS OF RICHARD, (1191–1192)

Hardly was Acre taken; hardly had the two kings established themselves in their quarters in the city; hardly had the papal legate, the Cardinal Adelard of Verona, and his brother bishops, reconsecrated the churches which for four years had been polluted with Mohammedan rites; hardly had the Pisan merchants begun to exercise their former privileges and renew former trade, when the slumbering jealousy of the two kings once more brought peril on the common enterprise.

Philip Augustus owed no ordinary gratitude to the late King of England and his sons; it was the young Henry who had stood by Philip's side at his coronation and helped to raise the crown that bore too heavily on the boy-king's head; it was the elder Henry who by his wise statesmanship had preserved the first years of Philip's reign from rebellion and civil war; later, when Richard was at feud with his father, it was to his alliance that Philip owed the grand success of 1189. But the friendliness of the young princes could not survive Richard's elevation to the crown; and with his father's and his mother's lands Richard inherited the traditional hostility of the king at Paris.

Other special grounds of quarrel there were between Richard and Philip which had not existed between Henry and Louis. After long dallying, Richard had repudiated his engagement to Philip's half-sister Alice; and though the French king could stoop to accept compensation in money, he can hardly have put out of mind the insulting reason which Richard gave for his refusal. Cupidity also had its share in the quarrel; the two kings had sworn to divide all the spoils of their conquests; but both had with more or less of reason found occasion to recede from this engagement.

Moreover, while yet in Sicily they had quarrelled openly; for Tancred had shown to Richard certain letters which he professed to have received from Philip, and which invited his assistance in a treacherous attack on the English. Philip denied all knowledge of the letters, but it was only with great difficulty that the Count of Flanders contrived to effect a seeming reconciliation.

Nor were personal dissensions the only troubles with which the two kings had to contend. National rivalry, which had nearly wrecked the First Crusade, was destined to be the ruin of the Third. Richard's coming to Acre had been hailed as the "coming of the desired of all nations;" but the joy was of short duration, for soon the old jealousies broke out, and it was found necessary to forbid the two nations even to fight side by side, the English chronicler says:

> The two kings and peoples did less together than they would have done separately, and each set but light store by the other.

So, it was agreed that when the knights of one nation advanced against the city, the others should remain to keep ward in the trenches.

But a yet more serious rock of offence lay in the struggle for the kingship of Jerusalem. Sibylla and her infant children had died in the latter part of 1190. Their death encouraged some of the native nobles to dispute Guy's title once more. According to the normal rules of the land Henfrid IV. of Toron should have governed in the name of his wife Isabella, Sibylla's younger sister. But the great nobles had never forgiven Henfrid for his refusal to join in their rebellion four years before; they therefore sought another candidate in Conrad of Mont-ferrat, whose vigour had saved Tyre for the Christians, and whose brother William had been Sibylla's first husband and the father of their last accepted king.

Conrad was a man of resource and action, who, both for his birth and his personal merit, ought to satisfy even the proud barons of Syria. The one obstacle was Isabella's previous marriage; but with the lady's consent a divorce was procured on the plea that she had been married to Henfrid against her wish. The attitude of Philip and Richard was foreshadowed in the action of their followers, for Baldwin of Canterbury was foremost in opposing the divorce, whilst the new marriage was celebrated by Philip of Beauvais, cousin to the king of France.

Guy could not be expected to acquiesce in the loss of his title and power; naturally enough he had sought in Cyprus the aid of his former overlord, King Richard, who had there promised him his support. Before the siege of Acre was over the quarrel had culminated in open violence; Guy's brother Geoffrey bluntly accused Conrad of treachery, and Conrad rather than maintain his innocence by gage of battle withdrew to Tyre; nevertheless, Philip Augustus took that noble under his protection, and openly declared his opposition to the wishes of the King of England. However, at the end of July, after a formal trial, a compromise was arranged, under which Guy retained the title of king, but shared the royal revenues with Conrad, who was to be hereditary lord of Tyre, Sidon, and Beyrout; at Guy's death the crown was to pass to Conrad and his children by Isabella.

By this time Philip had already wearied of the Crusade, and a little later he rejected Richard's proposal that they should both bind themselves to stay in the land for three years. Soon he went even further, and begged Richard's sanction for his return, pleading that his health was bad and that he had sufficiently performed his oath. The remonstrances of Richard and of his own followers had no weight with Philip, who on July 31st set out for Tyre. Before his departure the French king swore neither actively nor passively to do any wrong to the King of England's men or lands in Europe.

> How faithfully he kept his oath the whole world knows. For directly he reached home he stirred up the whole land, and threw Normandy into confusion. What need for further words! Amid the curses of all he departed, leaving his army at Acre.

Richard waited for Saladin to pay the agreed ransom; but August 14th arrived and the Mohammedans had not completed their engagement. So, on the Eve of the *Assumption* Richard left Acre and pitched his tents beyond the eastern trenches; here he waited again six days more, till, on the afternoon of August 20th, the king and his knights advanced into the plain. Then the captives were brought out and massacred in full view of their countrymen; it was in vain that the Saracens threw themselves upon the murderers of their kinsfolk, and in all five thousand prisoners are said to have been thus slain, the more notable only being preserved for ransom.

The massacre was not, perhaps, so gratuitous and unwarrantable as would at first sight appear; Roger Howden asserts distinctly that Saladin had slain his Christian captives two days before, an assertion which the words of Baha-ed-din seem to countenance; Richard may also have felt the danger and difficulty of keeping so many prisoners, and have honestly doubted the good faith of Saladin as to the stipulated ransom.

On August 23rd Richard started for Ascalon; the army marched along the shore, whilst the fleet accompanied them at a little distance from the land. Every evening, when the tents were pitched, the herald took his stand in the midst of the host, and thrice cried aloud: "Aid us, Holy Sepulchre!" As he cried the whole army took up the shout with tears.

Who would not have wept, seeing that the mere recital moves all that hear to sorrow?

Inland on the low hills to the left Saladin's host followed and harassed the Crusaders. Despite the enemy, and the terrible heat, which caused many to fall dead by the way, the Christians marched on past Haifa and Caesarea, till on September 1st they reached the Dead River, where the coast became so bad for marching that Richard struck inland by the mountain road. On September 3rd a fierce attack was made on the Templars in the rear; the arrows flew so fast that there was not a yard of the army's march where they did not lie; Richard himself was among the wounded.

But still the host pressed on, till on the 6th they rested by the Nahr Falaik, or River of the Cleft, some sixteen miles from Caesarea. Here they learnt that Saladin was awaiting their approach with an army of three hundred thousand men, three times the estimated number of the Crusading host. With the early dawn of the 7th of September, the Christians resumed their march in five divisions. First went the Templars; then the Bretons and men of Anjou; next the Poitevins under Guy; fourth came the Normans and English with the royal banner; in the rear were the Hospitallers. The Christian Army, marshalled in close array, filled the whole space between the hills and the sea Richard and the Duke of Burgundy with a band of chosen knights rode up and down the lines keeping a wary eye on the order of their troops.

About nine o'clock the battle began with an attack by Saladin's negro troops and Bedouins—pestilent footmen with bows and round *targes*; in their rear the heavier Turkish troops kept up an incessant din with their drums and cymbals. Again, and again the Turks rushed down on the rear of the Christians; at last the Hospitallers could bear up no longer, and begged Richard to let them make but one charge. Richard, however, would permit no deviation from his plans. The heavy horses of his cavalry with their armoured riders were no match for the swift-footed Arab steeds of the lightly-clad Saracens; it would be worse than useless to charge till the enemy was well within their grasp. When the decisive moment arrived six trumpets were to give the signal; then the footmen were to open wide their ranks, and let the knights pass through to the attack.

So, the Hospitallers endeavoured to still endure the renewed onset of the foe; one knight in despair invoked the great warrior-saint of

KNIGHTS FIGHTING.

KNIGHTS FIGHTING.

These illustrations are taken from a late thirteenth-century manuscript, "Histoire de la commencement du monde jusques a la naissance de Jesu Crist." They show the full development of surcoat, barding and closed helmet; notice also the large crests. The manuscript (Reg. 16. G. vi.) from which these illustrations are taken is now lettered on on the back, "Les Chroniques de S. Denys"; it is most lavishly adorned with beautifully coloured illustrations of scenes from military and domestic life. These illustrations are to be found at the foot of most pages, and in many cases are crowded with figures. Unfortunately bad colours were used, and in many places the paint has now peeled off or worn away. They may have been in better condition when Shaw made his drawings; otherwise he has certainly given his copies a finish which the original barely justifies. On many pages towards the end of the volume only the outline of the picture has been sketched; in other places their outlines are only partly filled in with colours.

the Crusaders, who perhaps from this period tended to become the patron saint of England:

Oh, St. George! Why dost thou leave us to be destroyed? Christendom perisheth, because we strive not against this accursed race.

Then the grand master petitioned the king in person, but Richard still replied:

It must be borne.

Most of the Hospitallers murmured but obeyed; two knights, however—the marshal of the order, and Baldwin de Carew, "a right good warrior, bold as a lion"—burst from the ranks and overthrew each his man; the remaining Hospitallers could be no longer restrained and out they charged to their comrades' aid. The battle soon became general and for a time threatened to go ill for the Crusaders; but when Richard himself came up on his Cyprian bay, the Turks fell back before him as he clove his way into their ranks with his sword. The Christians then resumed their march, and were already encamping outside the walls of Arsûf when the enemy attacked once more; but again the Turks turned in headlong flight as Richard galloped up to the rescue thundering out his war-cry: "God and the Holy Sepulchre aid us!"

The Christians counted two-and-thirty *emirs* dead upon the field of battle, besides seven thousand corpses of meaner folk. They boasted that their own loss was not as many hundred. But one death in particular they had to mourn; the heroic James of Avesnes was surrounded and slain by the Turks. On the morrow his corpse was found with fifteen of the enemy lying dead around him.

On Monday, September 9th, the march was renewed, and next day, just three weeks after leaving Acre, the Crusaders encamped in pleasant quarters amid the orchards outside Jaffa. At the same time the fleet arrived bringing an abundance of food.

Past experience had taught the Crusaders that until they held Ascalon and Jaffa they could not hope to maintain themselves in the Holy City, even if they should succeed in capturing it at once. Worse still would be their position if they had to conduct a prolonged siege with all the seaboard, from Caesarea to Damietta, in the hands of the foe. To all this Saladin was not less alive than Richard himself; but he was too weak to hold Ascalon, and so ordered it to be dismantled in haste, before the Crusaders could come up. The Christians, however, were as busy with the restoration of Jaffa as the Saracens were with the destruction of Ascalon. Not that Richard was blind to the importance of the latter city, which he would have attacked before but for the supineness of Philip; but now as then French opposition compelled him to postpone the advance, and this delay perhaps ruined the expedition.

Six weeks of precious time were lost at Jaffa, and it was only in the end of October that Richard renewed his march towards Jerusalem. Even then he had to stay at the Casal of the Plains and Casal Maen, between Ramleh and Lydda, for two months. At the end of the year he advanced to Beit-Nuba, some ten miles nearer the Holy City, but was there once more detained by the violence of the winter storms. The wind tore up the tents, and the wet rotted the store of provisions, whilst sickness played havoc both with the men and their horses. Yet in the midst of their misfortunes the Crusaders were glad in heart with the hope of reaching the Lord's Sepulchre, and the thought that nothing should now prevent the accomplishment of their pilgrimage. But the military orders and the Syrian Franks knew the Angers of a winter campaign, and feared that ever success would have no other result than to shut up the host in a city which they could not defend.

In a council held on January 13th their opinion prevailed, and the order was given for a retreat to Ramleh. Many of the French then withdrew to Jaffa, or elsewhere; but Richard, full of wrath at the turn affairs had taken, determined to lead his diminished army to Ascalon. Two days of weary marching through snow and rain brought them at last to the ruined town on January 20th.

After a little the French were induced to rejoin the host, and pledged themselves to obey Richard's orders till Easter. All then set about the task of restoring Ascalon; nobles, knights, squires, and men-at-arms working together with their own hands, and with one will. But the main glory of the work belonged to the king; he was everywhere directing, exhorting, and even working. His eloquence heartened the great lords to fresh efforts and larger liberality. Where means were lacking, he supplied them, till when at last Ascalon was restored, it was said that Richard had paid for three-quarters of the work.

The previous autumn had witnessed some lengthy, if not perhaps very genuine negotiations between Richard and Saladin. Richard at first demanded the restoration of the whole kingdom as it existed under Baldwin IV. When this was refused, he suggested a marriage between El-Adel or Saphadin, the *Sultan's* brother, and his own sister Joanna, who might then rule together in a new kingdom of Palestine.

(This probably gave Sir W. Scott the hint for the proposed marriage of Saladin himself to Edith Plantagenet, a purely fictitious character, in *The Talisman*.)

The proposal flattered El-Adel, who visited Richard in or near the Crusaders' camp; the king had just undergone his autumn bleeding and could not receive his visitor in person, but had him entertained at a great banquet. This was followed next day by an interview and the exchange of costly presents, from which there sprung up a warm friendship between the two princes. The negotiations, however, fell through, according to the Saracens, because Joanna refused to wed a Mohammedan. The Christian account makes no mention of the marriage, and ascribes the failure to Saladin's refusal to dismantle Kerak. Perhaps, indeed, the chief object of both parties had been to gain time—Richard that he might complete the fortification of Jaffa, Saladin that he might postpone hostilities till winter had made a serious campaign impracticable. At the same time both parties may have found good reasons to wish for peace—Richard in his suspicions of Philip Augustus, and Saladin in his fears of the descendants of Zangi.

Richard, moreover, was at this time much hampered by the behaviour of Conrad of Montferrat. The marquis had not only held aloof from the main enterprise, but had also a party among the Syrian Franks, with Balian of Ibelin and Reginald of Sidon for his chief supporters. Conrad and his party, like Richard, had opened negotiations with Saladin, but the *Sultan's* council had declared against them on the ground that there could be no sincere friendship between the Saracens and the Syrian Franks. When in February, 1192, Richard called Conrad to his aid at Ascalon, the marquis found occasion to excuse himself. The Duke of Burgundy had about the same time withdrawn from the army because Richard refused him any further loans of money. The French now went to Acre, where they took up the cause of the Genoese against the Pisans, who were partisans of Guy. The Genoese called on Conrad, whilst the Pisans sent word to Richard, on whose approach the marquis went back to Tyre, taking Burgundy with him.

Despite a personal interview the breach between Conrad and Richard grew wider, and the latter presently renewed his negotiations with Saladin. So friendly did the king and *Sultan* become that, on Palm Sunday, Richard knighted El-Adel's son at Acre in great state. However, some hostilities of the Franks near Darum inclined Saladin to turn once more to Conrad, who agreed to join in open war with his fellow Crusaders.

Richard, who by this time had returned to Ascalon, was now forced to let the French, who had thus far remained with him, depart to their compatriots at Tyre. The news of troubles in England which arrived about this time, made Richard himself anxious to go home. Some settlement of the kingdom was now imperative, and Richard rather reluctantly consented to the recognition of Conrad as king.

Hardly had the marquis thus attained the object of his ambitions, when he was cut off by a mysterious fate. On Monday, April 27th, so runs the story in the Franco-Syrian chronicles, Conrad, weary of waiting for his queen, who had stayed late at the bath, went out to dine with Philip of Beauvais. Finding that the bishop had already dined, Conrad turned home. As he came out of the bishop's house into the narrow road, two men advanced to meet him; one of the two offered him a letter, and whilst Conrad was thus off his guard, they stabbed him with their knives. Conrad fell dead on the spot; of his murderers one was instantly slain, and the other was captured soon after. When put to torture this man confessed that he and his comrade had been despatched by the Old Man of the Mountain to take vengeance for the robbery of one of his merchant vessels. (The French accused Richard of having suborned the Assassins to murder Conrad.)

Queen Isabella now declared that she would hold Tyre for Richard, but the French clamoured for the city to be surrendered to them on behalf of their king. But as it happened Richard's nephew, Henry of Champagne, had hurried to Tyre on the news of Conrad's death; the people at once hailed him as lord, and begged him to marry Isabella. Richard readily assented to the proposal, and so Palestine once more had a king, whose claim was supported not only by the French and English, but also by the Syrian Franks. With these brighter prospects before him Richard once more postponed his departure. Like a true knight-errant, he was more attracted by the hope of conquering a new kingdom from the Saracen, than by the prospect of merely preserving the one which God had given him.

Richard did not when assenting to his nephew's elevation forget the deposed king for whom he had struggled so long. Cyprus was bestowed on Guy, whose family ruled in that island for more than two centuries after the last remnants of the Christian kingdom on the mainland fell into the hands of the Moslem.

In the middle of May Richard, who was anxious to strike a blow whilst Saladin was still troubled with the threatened revolt on the Euphrates, left Ascalon with a small force to besiege Darum. That fortress was very strong, but the fleet soon arrived with the siege train, and on the 22nd of May Darum surrendered after only four days' siege. Hardly was the fortress taken when King Henry arrived with the French, and received Darum from his uncle as the first-fruits of his new realm. Very shortly afterwards fresh news of a disquieting nature from England made Richard think once more of returning home. But after some hesitation he pledged himself to stay till the following Easter, and ordered preparations to be made for an immediate advance to Jerusalem. At this news, "all began to rejoice as a bird at dawn of day," and forthwith made themselves ready for the journey, crying out:

We thank Thee, O God! because we shall now behold Thy city, where the Turks have dwelt so long.

On Sunday, June 7th, the Crusaders marched out from Ascalon, and after a few days' journey, once more pitched their tents at Beit-Nuba. Here they had to stay a month till King Henry brought reinforcements from Acre. This delay was unfortunate for the Christians, for there seems little doubt that if they had pushed on at once they could have taken the city. Whether they could have held it for long is another matter. Probably most of the Crusaders, after paying their vows at the Holy Sepulchre, would have returned home, without further care for the land they had so hardly won.

Two incidents in the desultory warfare of this tedious month deserve notice. One day in June Richard came upon a party of Turks near the fountain of Emmaus unawares, and slew twenty of them. In his pursuit of the remainder along the hills he advanced so far that as he chanced to raise his eyes, he caught a glimpse of the Holy City from afar. A little latter there came news of a great caravan on its way up from Egypt Richard with characteristic generosity invited the Duke of Burgundy and the French to share in the spoil.

Marching by moonlight, the king's force of five hundred knights and a thousand serving men came out to Keratiyeh, where during a short halt they learnt that one caravan was already marching past the "Round Cistern." The report was confirmed by Richard's own spies, who were sent out in disguise as Bedouins. Another night's march brought the Crusaders within a short distance of the caravan. At dawn the bowmen were sent out in advance, and the king with his knights followed in the rear. The caravan was surprised while resting, and its escort fled before the charge of the Crusaders like hares before the hounds. Besides a very rich spoil of spices, gold, silver, silks, robes, and arms of every kind, there were captured no less than four thousand seven hundred camels, besides mules and asses beyond number.

Baha-ed din writes:

The loss of this caravan was an event most shameful to us, not for a long time past had such a disaster befallen Islam. Never did any news so trouble the *Sultan*.

Saladin was, indeed, in no small alarm lest the Crusaders should advance forthwith on Jerusalem. But after a few days there came the welcome news that the Franks were in retreat.

The causes of this retreat are more or less of a mystery. It would seem that about a fortnight previously, before the arrival of King Henry with the reinforcements, the Franks were very eager for an immediate advance. Richard declared that the idea was impossible, and that he would not take the responsibility for an enterprise which would expose him to the censure of his enemies. If others saw fit to attack Jerusalem, he would not desert them; but in that case he would follow, and not lead. He pointed out the dangers of their present position, and urged that the Crusaders should follow the advice of the native lords as to whether it was wiser to besiege Jerusalem, or march against Cairo, Beyrout, or Damascus.

So, at Richard's suggestion the plan of campaign was referred to a committee of twenty sworn jurors. The twenty decided in favour of attacking Cairo. At this the French cried out, declaring that they would march only against Jerusalem; Richard in vain offered the assistance of his fleet which lay at Acre, and promised a liberal contribution towards their expenses; his efforts were without avail, and on the 4th of July he ordered a retreat towards Ramleh.

Richard now withdrew to Acre, and reopened negotiations with Saladin. But the *Sultan*, hearing of an intended expedition against Beyrout, determined to divert the attack, and on July 26th appeared before Jaffa. After a five days' siege the town was captured, and the remainder of the garrison in the tower promised to surrender if aid did not come by the following day. But Richard had been well informed of the danger, and though the French would lend him no assistance, had already left Acre with a few galleys. Through contrary winds he only reached Jaffa at midnight on the 31st. When day dawned, it seemed that he had arrived too late, for Saladin's banners were already flying on the walls. Richard was in doubt what to do, until a priest swam out to the ships with news of the peril to which those in the tower were exposed.

The king delayed no longer, but ordered his galleys to be rowed towards the shore, and himself led the Christians as they waded through the water to the land. The Turks fled before them, and the royal banner was soon waving from the walls. Richard himself was foremost in the fight:

Never did warrior bear himself so nobly, as did the king that day; Saladin fled before him like a hunted hare.

For more than two miles the English cross-bowmen pursued the Turks with terrible carnage, and at night Richard pitched his tent on the very spot where Saladin's had lately stood. Richard's position was still one of considerable peril. He had with him but fifty knights, and only fifteen horses good or bad. An attempt at a surprise was only frustrated by a happy accident. At dawn on the 5th of August a Genoese, who was out in search of fodder, heard the tramp of men and caught sight of their helmets gleaming in the eastern sky. Hurrying back, he roused the sleeping camp, but hardly was there time to arm or even dress before the Turks were upon them. Richard was marshalling his little army, when a messenger came up crying out that they were all lost, and that the enemy had seized the town.

Sternly ordering the man to hold his peace, Richard bade his followers be of good cheer, and to show his own confidence rode off with half-a-dozen knights to discover what had actually taken place in Jaffa. The Saracens who had gained the town fled before the king as he forced his way into the streets, and Richard could soon rejoin his army outside. There the enemy, though they continually charged close up to the Christian line, would not venture to attack. At last in the afternoon Richard advanced, and after a fierce engagement put the Saracens to flight. It was on this day that, according to the romantic tale, El-Adel, hearing Richard had no horse, sent him two Arab steeds; a generous gift, which the king accepted in a like spirit, and afterwards splendidly recompensed.

After this battle negotiations were once more resumed. The French would render no help, and sickness was playing havoc with the Christian host. Richard himself fell ill, and thought it better to ask for a truce than to go away leaving the whole land to be laid waste, as did others who departed by crowds in their ships. By the mediation of El-Adel terms were at length arranged on the 2nd of September;

Ascalon was to be left unoccupied for three years, during which time the Christians were to have peaceful possession of Jaffa, and free access to the Holy Sepulchre; commerce was to be carried on over the whole land.

LEONAUR

ALSO FROM LEONAUR
AVAILABLE IN SOFTCOVER OR HARDCOVER WITH DUST JACKET

A DIARY FROM DIXIE *by Mary Boykin Chesnut*—A Lady's Account of the Confederacy During the American Civil War

FOLLOWING THE DRUM *by Teresa Griffin Vielé*—A U. S. Infantry Officer's Wife on the Texas frontier in the Early 1850's

FOLLOWING THE GUIDON *by Elizabeth B. Custer*—The Experiences of General Custer's Wife with the U. S. 7th Cavalry.

LADIES OF LUCKNOW *by G. Harris & Adelaide Case*—The Experiences of Two British Women During the Indian Mutiny 1857. A Lady's Diary of the Siege of Lucknow by G. Harris, Day by Day at Lucknow by Adelaide Case

MARIE-LOUISE AND THE INVASION OF 1814 *by Imbert de Saint-Amand*—The Empress and the Fall of the First Empire

SAPPER DOROTHY *by Dorothy Lawrence*—The only English Woman Soldier in the Royal Engineers 51st Division, 79th Tunnelling Co. during the First World War

ARMY LETTERS FROM AN OFFICER'S WIFE 1871-1888 *by Frances M. A. Roe*—Experiences On the Western Frontier With the United States Army

NAPOLEON'S LETTERS TO JOSEPHINE *by Henry Foljambe Hall*—Correspondence of War, Politics, Family and Love 1796-1814

MEMOIRS OF SARAH DUCHESS OF MARLBOROUGH, AND OF THE COURT OF QUEEN ANNE VOLUME 1 by A. T. Thomson

MEMOIRS OF SARAH DUCHESS OF MARLBOROUGH, AND OF THE COURT OF QUEEN ANNE VOLUME 2 by A. T. Thomson

MARY PORTER GAMEWELL AND THE SIEGE OF PEKING *by A. H. Tuttle*—An American Lady's Experiences of the Boxer Uprising, China 1900

VANISHING ARIZONA *by Martha Summerhayes*—A young wife of an officer of the U.S. 8th Infantry in Apacheria during the 1870's

THE RIFLEMAN'S WIFE *by Mrs. Fitz Maurice*—*The Experiences of an Officer's Wife and Chronicles of the Old 95th During the Napoleonic Wars*

THE OATMAN GIRLS *by Royal B. Stratton*—The Capture & Captivity of Two Young American Women in the 1850's by the Apache Indians

AVAILABLE ONLINE AT **www.leonaur.com**
AND FROM ALL GOOD BOOK STORES
07/09

www.ingramcontent.com/pod-product-compliance
Lightning Source LLC
Chambersburg PA
CBHW032041080426
42733CB00006B/158